On Aboriginal Religion

W. E. H. Stanner

With Introductions by Francesca Merlan and L.R. Hiatt

SYDNEY UNIVERSITY PRESS

Originally published as a series of articles in the journal *Oceania*, between 1959 and 1963

This reprint edition published in 2014 by SYDNEY UNIVERSITY PRESS

Sydney University Press
Fisher Library F03
University of Sydney NSW 2006
AUSTRALIA
Email: sup.info@sydney.edu.au

National Library of Australia Cataloguing-in-Publication entry

Author: Stanner, W. E. H. (William Edward Hanley), 1905-1981, author.

Title: On aboriginal religion / W. E. H. Stanner ; introductions by Francesca Merlan and L.R. Hiatt.

Edition: Reprint edition.

ISBN: 9781743323885 (paperback)

Subjects: Aboriginal Australians--Religion.
Mythology, Aboriginal Australian.
Philosophy, Aboriginal Australian.

Other Authors/Contributors:
Merlan, Francesca, writer of introduction.
Hiatt, L. R. (Lester Richard), 1931-2008, writer of introduction.

Dewey Number:
299.9215

Cover image

Not very much is known about this 55 x 26cm painting on bark, which was bought from among a stack on the counter in a department store in Darwin in 1965. Of the six figures, almost certainly men, three are musicians using a didgeridoo and two sets of clapsticks, and three are dancing. It is possible that a religious ceremony is depicted. Private collection.

W.E.H. Stanner c. 1960 (Photograph by courtesy of Mrs. Patricia Stanner)

Contents

List of Figures

List of Tables

Note to the 2014 Edition

Peter White

Professor W.E.H. Stanner's account of Aboriginal religion was originally published as a series of articles in the journal *Oceania* between 1959 and 1963 and then gathered into Oceania Monograph 11 in 1963. Its continuing status as a classic led to a facsimile reproduction as Oceania Monograph 36 in 1989, with an Appreciation by Dr Francesca Merlan and an Introduction by Dr Les Hiatt, both of the University of Sydney. Continuing demand, and the usefulness of having a searchable version available online, led to this retyped reprint edition by Sydney University Press. I note that the page references to Stanner's work in both Appreciation and Introduction are to the pages of this edition. There are also some minor corrections, omission of some cross-referencing and re-orientation of the original very large fold-out tables in which, however, we have tried to retain Stanner's plan and structure.

On Aboriginal Religion: An Appreciation

Francesca Merlan

Though W.E.H. Stanner's essays 'On Aboriginal Religion' are a continuing—one may say without exaggeration, inexhaustible—source of insight to students of Australian Aboriginal society (cf. Keen 1986:26), they are not as widely known as their ethnographic and interpretive richness would seem to warrant, and regrettably, have not found a regular place in the cross-cultural study of religions. There are several reasons for this, some simple and some complex. This appreciation attempts to account for this relative neglect through a broad interpretation of Stanner's aims and methods, and greater and lesser successes, in this work.

One reason that the work is not as well known as its appreciative readers might expect has been its limited availability as a monograph, something this edition is intended to rectify. The essays which comprise 'On Aboriginal Religion' were originally published as a series of articles (spanning the years 1959–1963) in the journal *Oceania* (based at Sydney University). In 1963 they were reprinted, with the addition of a brief introduction by Stanner but otherwise unmodified, as Number 11 in the *Oceania Monographs* series, in a limited edition. A second impression appeared in 1966. This too was soon exhausted, and editorial files reveal continuing inquiries about the monograph's availability and possible reprinting. But Stanner himself, when contacted about this, was reluctant to allow its re-issue. The reason was, as his letters reveal, that he planned revisions of the work, though their intended nature and extent is not revealed in the correspondence. Some time after the possibility of a revised edition disappeared with Stanner's death in 1981, *Oceania* sought Mrs. Stanner's permission to re-issue the monograph in order to gain for it the wider distribution it deserves, permission for which we here express our sincere gratitude.

Almost certainly, Stanner's reluctance in the matter was linked to the fact that 'On Aboriginal Religion' was written as a series of articles, not conceived and written as a book. Thus while many of the ideas contained in the later articles are prefigured in the earlier ones, showing that from the first one Stanner had a conception of the linkages he wanted to make, nevertheless in refusing to allow re-issue it is likely that he had in mind a re-casting which would give a stronger unity to the whole. The work is ethnographically of a piece, in that all the material Stanner discusses comes from a single region, indeed in the main from one tribal grouping, the Murinbata, of the northwestern Northern Territory (see Barwick, Beckett and Reay 1985:4–8 [BBR] for background to Stanner's fieldwork of the 1930s in this Daly River region). It is noticeable, however, that some of his main theoretical themes, such as his objections to interpretations of Aboriginal religion as reflecting the social order, recur throughout the essays, resulting in a degree of repetitiveness that his intended revisions might have eliminated. In the final essay, which contains some of Stanner's broadest and most powerful constructions of an Aboriginal ontology, he observes (page 325) that it should perhaps have been first rather than last, and that the first article, with its interpretation of an Aboriginal rite under the guise of sacrifice, might more appropriately have come last, so that (one infers) the aptness of the analogy could be felt to follow naturally from the preceding generalisations concerning the religion (see Maddock 1985 for examination of the adequacy of the analogy, also comments on this by Keen 1986:42). To some extent, then, Stanner himself imposed limitations on the availability of the monograph because he still regarded it as a work-in-progress.

There are other, more complex reasons to explain why this work is not yet as well known as it should be. One, in my opinion, is an uncertainty or ambivalence in direction which developed over the course of writing of the essays. Thus certain themes broached in the earlier essays remain suggestive but unelaborated. Especially the first three essays moot revisions in significant anthropological concepts, specifically, the development of a notion of a system or structure of operations over then-current notions of social structure (see below, also BBR 1985:33–34, Keen 1986 for further commentary). The reader presumes that Stanner will use the rich Murinbata ethnographic material to illustrate the utility and force of the proposed revisions. The later articles, however, evince no significant development of them through the material. Instead, alongside and partly through the comparative examination of Murinbata myth and rite, conducted by methods which do not significantly rely on, and in fact seem to by-pass, the intended development of a notion of operations, Stanner develops a rich and suggestive view of Aboriginal religion as an ontological system which, indeed, he had prefigured in the earlier articles as his main **object** of study (page 98, page 113). Thus, the development of the articles eventually reveals some lack of continuity between his earlier-stated initiatives concerning anthropological theory, and the methods he actually applies in elaborating his portrayal of the ontology. Though there is a disjunction in the essays between the two emphases, they have an underlying point of contact in Stanner's rejection of reductionist, impoverishing views of Aboriginal religion, varieties of which he claims are inherent in approaches to Aboriginal society through contemporary social structural analysis, and which he clearly intends his portrait of the ontology to redress.

One may object to focussing attention on Stanner's discussion of such theoretical issues for, it may be argued, that turns out not to be the major emphasis or strength of the work. But that Stanner himself placed importance on his initiatives in this regard is shown by the fact that he devotes to them about half of the several pages he wrote in 1963 as a brief Introduction to the monograph, when all the articles had been completed.

The following sections examine main themes in the work, leading up to Stanner's conceptualisation of the Dreaming in the final article, the centrepiece of his exploration of Aboriginal ontology.

Defects of Social Structural Analysis

Stanner's studies at Sydney University, which out of necessity he combined with work as a reporter, took a decisive turn in 1929 when he enrolled for Anthropology I with A.R. Radcliffe-Brown, foundation professor at Sydney from 1926–1931 (see BBR 1985 for a detailed biography of Stanner, and a full bibliography of his work). Drawn by Radcliffe-Brown's authoritative and winning style as teacher and mentor, Stanner graduated in 1931 with first class honours in anthropology, and soon undertook a seven month period of fieldwork in the Daly River region from 1932, one aim of which was to supplement Radcliffe-Brown's survey of 'The social organisation of Australian tribes' (1930–1).

While at the Daly, Stanner became aware of the impact of European intrusion on the Mulluk Mulluk, Madngella, Marithiel and Nangiomeri people with whom he worked, then mostly employed on peanut farms established in the Depression era here and elsewhere in the upper Northern Territory. This first-hand experience of the effects of colonisation, missionisation and usurpation kindled in him a continuing concern for the contemporary conditions of Aboriginal people, and prompted his increasing involvement over the years in policy and administrative developments, not only in Aboriginal affairs, but also in Africa and the Pacific, where he subsequently gained extensive field and administrative experience. There are, however, indications that in his fieldwork in the Daly he was most strongly drawn, intellectually and temperamentally, by insights into traditional religion and social life; and some of his later Aboriginalist writings (e.g. Stanner 1958) show a related tendency to explore even radical social transformation under the rubric 'culture contact' or 'culture change', with the attendant break between culture as a continuity of transmitted 'values' (cf. BBR 1985:31), and the actualities of social life, that such labels often entail.

Following completion in 1934 of his master's thesis, 'Culture Contact on the Daly River', Stanner carried out another long stint of fieldwork in the Northern Territory, some of which formed the basis for his Doctoral thesis, 'Economic Change in North Australian Tribes', submitted at the

University of London in 1938. Early in his stay in England, Stanner briefly renewed his contact with Radcliffe-Brown, then at Oxford, and accepted his advice to write his thesis under Bronislaw Malinowski at the London School of Economics. Stanner found the intellectual environment there both taxing and stimulating (BBR 1985:9), and it certainly put him in touch with influences other than Radcliffe-Brown's structural-functionalism, which he always acknowledged as formative (BBR 1985:4), but against which he registered a strong reaction in 'On Aboriginal Religion'.[1]

Radcliffe-Brown's structural-functionalism had of course partly been developed in relation to Australianist materials, but Stanner was obviously dissatisfied with it in general, and with its specific applications to Australian Aboriginal society. His own form of analysis of the Murinbata material owes little to it, and turns out to bear greater resemblance to Lévi-Strauss' structural approach than to any form of sociological analysis (though Stanner notes that he was unaware of Lévi-Strauss' work on myth until 1960, see page 325).

What defects, in Stanner's view, inhere in the usual notions of social structure, and why are such notions inappropriate in relation to the Aboriginal material?

In a number of places Stanner makes it clear that, for him, the worst failing of social structural analysis is its aridity, its proceeding by reification and abstraction of social relations that have another nature (p. 16), resulting in models not **of** or **after** them, but **about** them. (We might now see this in light of Bourdieu's 1977 theme of the limits of objectivism). Accordingly, modern anthropology is anxious that it is not yielding 'clear pictures of human persons at the business of life' (p. 16).

Stanner repeats the image of social structural relations as enduring connections between points of force in a network (page 99 page 112, page 325, page 163), and he quotes Geddes' definition to the effect

1 See also Keen (1986:33–34) for indications of the positive influences of Firth on Stanner's concepts of transaction and operation, discussed below, and some other aspects of Radcliffe-Brown's influence.

that it is 'categories of people and the regular forms of relationship between them that anthropologists mean when they speak of social structure' (page 113). In a passage which clearly alludes to (but does not mention) Radcliffe-Brown, Stanner says that social structural principles—the equivalence of alternate generations and the like—are inappropriately separated analytically from conduct as in some sense prior to it or causal of it. Rather, such so-called principles are 'necessary and enabling conditions' of social conduct (page 89), and insofar as they can be made concrete, are only known by their content, i.e. in conduct. Such principles do not yield a picture of sociality (page 113). What anthropology has become, Stanner complains, is a 'dialogue over abstract nouns', and ought to be converted into a 'conjugation of verbs' (page 63).

Were Radcliffe-Brown to have been confronted with these complaints, he probably would have regarded them as quite beside the point of constructing a 'natural science of society' (Radcliffe-Brown 1957, based on his University of Chicago lectures of 1937). The disagreement about what it is important and plausible to study would seem to be fundamental. Using an old figure to compare the views, we may say Radcliffe-Brown had in mind a comparative science of anatomy (despite his later moves towards a different formulation, see Radcliffe-Brown 1952:4), while Stanner here argues that the prime object of study should be physiologies, the emphasis shifted more definitively from structure and function to process; and that the anatomical image is not even apt—structures may only be said to exist as functions (in a slightly different sense) of social acts, or operations, which are the only plausible object of ethnographic observation.[2]

2 Singer (1984) has argued that Radcliffe-Brown's work shows a movement from early functionalist, empiricist and naturalist tendencies to moments of 'genuine structural analysis' later on (cf. Radcliffe-Brown 1952, 1957), possibly influenced by conceptions of structure, and the philosophy of events and relations among them, of Russell and Whitehead. However this may be, it is clear that Stanner's own view of Radcliffe-Brown's principal contributions was that these lay in his efforts

Stanner says that operations are acts of sociality (page 113), and may be studied as having a distinguishable structure. Earlier (page 89), he had broached a notion of transaction to capture the sidedness of human dealings, and had distinguished transitive and intransitive types of conduct (i.e. as to whether they have or are intended to have perceptible effect), in an effort to deal with the old question of whether it is appropriate to regard many types of religious acts as evidence of an 'illusion of technical competence' (page 91), i.e. some sense of direct efficacy, on the part of those who participate in them.

How does Stanner envision the notion of operations or structure of operations contributing to an improved Australian Aboriginal anthropology? Its potential application is not made fully explicit, yet there are clear instances of his insight into the possibilities. Consider totemism, that hoary subject, which in Durkheim's *Elementary Forms*, as well as works of lesser imaginative force, had been seen as the key to the description of Aboriginal society, as a segmental organisation of totemic clans. Besides deploring the reduction of Aboriginal religion to totemism (page 301, Stanner further contends that an image of segmental clans is a fundamentally inadequate view of Aboriginal sociality/society. It falsely tends to suggest that society can be seen as a unified whole (page 112), or rather, its organisation as unidimensional. He excoriates those (page 112)—no doubt he has W.L. Warner in mind, among others—who have thought to find in kinship a unifying principle which underlies interaction. There is not a social system which exhibits a structure. Totemism is an operational relation, which may indeed be seen as providing the fundamental mode of linkage between cosmology/ontology and the social order. It provides the basis for men's (sic) acting through totemic signs towards the putative ground of dependency (the 'totemic endowment'), and in those actions reproducing types of

---

to define types and forms of structure as that which is discoverable, coherent and consistent in social systems (albeit always acknowledged by Radcliffe-Brown to be virtual in what he distinguished as social organisation), and to develop a comparative social science based on the abstraction of such general features (see Stanner 1968).

groupings and identifications 'of a totemic determination' (page 110). Thus, totemism constitutes an important ground of action, including the terms by which people act as a group, but only in relation to certain objects of activity, not all. Sociality, the 'common life of interaction' (page 111), is composed of many different types of relation and activity—marriage, trade, hunting, etc., which rest on diverse ('conjugate' page 111) principles of association. No single one can be seen to organise all activities, nor do the various principles of organisation have a 'ground of unity' (page 111). Relations of association are 'visible' (page 111) as 'conjoint acts', and it is this structure of operations, Stanner proposes, that rightly constitutes the more concrete 'matter' in relation to which one may speak of a structure of functions, or regular forms of relations among (categories of) persons which, as in rite, sometimes presuppose a segmental structure. Thus, the totemic principle is relevant to certain types of social acts (e.g. the performance of rite, and perhaps to a lesser degree, many others), and any groups organised according to this principle can only be properly construed as complex functions of the activity types, not as one-dimensional, perduring, organ-like structures constituting society (see Sansom 1980 for recent development and ethnographic application to Aboriginal material of ideas which bear some similarities to these). It is not that Aboriginal sociality/society has no form, but it is the forms and objects of action that are primary, rather than categories and groups, which are to be seen as functions of action.

It is not clear how far Stanner would have thought it appropriate to generalise this view to other societies. In any event, from this interesting beginning Stanner's use of the term 'operations' becomes scarcer, and especially in the later analyses of myth and rite it gives ways to a profusion of other terms—event (page 129), incident (page 212), parallel structures of rite and myth (page 212), sequences of conduct, process, forms of process (page 114)—to which he no doubt wants to relate it, but without ever explicitly doing so. In short, 'operation' drops out as an analytical category as the examination of myth and rite deepens, and the reader becomes aware that what Stanner wants to say about these forms here—what they reveal about the 'ontology of a type of thought and life' (page 98)—does not depend upon its clarification.[3]

Before we leave this subject we may note one peculiarity in Stanner's intended concept of operations which, I think, does owe something to Radcliffe-Brownian naturalist and empiricist influence.

Stanner writes that 'one may actually see the constituent operations' of the rite of Punj (page 99); also, that there occur 'things which I have seen and could have been seen by anyone'; further on (page 166) he refers to operations as 'manual acts'. The sum of such characterisations (see also BBR 1985:31, Keen 1986:41) leaves little doubt that Stanner was searching for a perceptually-based, empirical point of departure which could be claimed to be at least as real as in the most realist view of social structure. If the matter had been put directly to him, I do not believe Stanner ultimately would have adhered to the view that there is any simple relation between observation—'things I have seen'—and the interpretation of them as particular kinds of social acts. Nevertheless there is a distinct positivist impulse here, a tendency to want to develop theoretical concepts of the same putative order of reality as social action appears to its participants/observers to be.

But in any case, as we shall see, Stanner's analysis is not principally directed to real time social acts as these can be observed, but rather to segmentations of rite and myth, and correlations between them, that contribute to his main theme, the interpretation of Aboriginal ontology.

What *Is* Aboriginal Religion?

Stanner is duly cautious about the possibility of defining Aboriginal (or any) religion (page 63). Beyond this, however, it is of interest to consider briefly how he uses the term, for it is nowadays widely

3 See also Keen (1986:41) for a related critique, that the 'lack of an adequate theory of action' is the main defect in Stanner's approach to the analysis of religion in social life.

thought that Aboriginal life is in some way suffused with spirituality or religiosity, a generalisation with which I think Stanner would agree, and which, in considerable measure, his writing has probably helped to establish.

Above, we have already discussed Stanner's objection to reductionist/reflectionist views of Aboriginal religion as a 'dependent variable' (page 62), a mere secondary reflection of a primary social order (page 99). In his view, many discussions of totemism have been basically flawed for this reason.

Stanner also deplores views that Aborigines have nothing worthy of the name 'religion', or—to re-cast this in a way that illustrates the sort of conditions he places on such an identification—that they were a primitive people who 'could not possibly have had serious thoughts about life' (page 320). That Aborigines have something worthy of being called 'religion' would now certainly be accepted by many, not only because of a general feeling (which, as we have noted, Stanner shared) that to attempt to rigorously define it is futile, but also partly because not all would associate with its definition the high criterion of moral insight (he often softens this to 'intuition concerning men's life and condition', page 299) that Stanner does.

Stanner says he uses 'religion' indicatively, to point to 'the content of a devotional life' (page 62). In the second article (page 96) he diagrams his view of the partition of reality according to an Aboriginal scheme. There, things he defines as of the order of religion only represent a portion of the lived order, overlapping with, but of lesser extent than, things of the social order. Insofar as social and religious orders can be distinguished in this way, Stanner views the social as providing a language of 'shapes' (page 133) through which religious reality is expressed (see also page 301on the importance of distinguishing between the nature of symbols and the 'things of ultimate religious concern' for which they stand). All experience is encompassed within the ontology of the Dreaming.

The character of the devotional life is sacramentalist; that is, men act through signs which, he asserts, betoken dependency on an endowment and flow of benefits (totemic in character), and such actions are performed also under a plan for distributing the flow of benefits among men. Thus, Stanner defines the main parts of what he terms the religious economy (page 100) as: the totemic endowment with its flow of life-benefits; the exchange of signs (in rite); and the plan of distributing the flow among men (social institutions). Though the entire religious economy is set within and suffused with the ontology of the Dreaming, the focus, or high points, of the religion are the rites in which signs of the endowment (e.g. sacred objects such as the bullroarer, sacred designs, etc.) are manipulated and exchanged. In the initiatory rites discussed in the first article, for example, it is shown that there is a passing on of rightful knowledge of the efficacious signs from seniors to juniors, initiators to initiands, conceived as a conferring of understanding and adulthood.

Not all socially significant acts are sacramental; that is, not all involve devotional use of signs of the endowment. Stanner notes, for instance, that 'neither birth nor marriage attracts rites and ceremonies of a sacramental kind', so that these occasions, in his sense, are not treated as 'religiously significant' (page 103). Thus, though all religious practice and, in theory, all the instituted forms of life are encompassed within the foundational Dreaming, not all of social life is, in his definition, religious in character.

In his discussions of rite throughout the essays, Stanner describes the 'exchange of signs' and, as well, there is discussion of aspects of the 'distribution of the flow' among men (see e.g. page 298 a reference to a 'ruling stratum' of older men, and to the ascendancy of men over women). His portrayal of the distribution, however, tends overall to be a-political in character: though he observes (page 321) that 'political force was used to impose and maintain' received tradition, his broader assumption is that because there was a 'notion of an original endowment of each clan with the means of life', their relation in the religious rites could only be one of support, not of competition: 'There could be no struggle for a division of what had already been divided' (page 323). He concedes the possibility of individuals acting to maximise their own interests, but sees this as a perversion by which the religion itself should not be judged.

Finally, Stanner explores the totemic endowment partly through discussion of what he calls 'existence classes', that in linguistic description (Walsh 1976) are called 'noun classes'. Stanner, however, would not be happy with this narrower view of them as grammatical phenomena, the nature of whose relation to conception is more or less indirect. He describes the classes as 'ontological conceptions' which 'divide all significant matter in the world into classes' (page 170), so that the 'very language through which the more mundane things of life are dealt with is itself dense with symbolical import' (although he adds, in a way that distinctly lessens the impact of such an assertion, 'it may be somewhat indeterminate'). The claim that these classes are imbued with significances relating to the constitutive patterns of the Dreaming goes, I believe, well beyond anything he is able to establish. But it is also his claim, here (page 177) and elsewhere, that symbolisation in the medium of language is not privileged in the practice of Aboriginal religion. With that, let us turn to consider the senses in which Stanner's approach is, and is not, concerned with issues of symbolic analysis.

Symbolisation in Aboriginal Religion

A large part of Aboriginal religion, Stanner remarks, is focussed upon 'the rightful possession and dutiful use of the efficacious signs' (page 85). But with some exceptions (see e.g. comments on the significance of human hair, page 251) Stanner does not embark on a minute analysis of the detailed sign elements of rite and myth (though there are extensive reports of the contents of both, especially in essays IV and V). His reason for not focussing closely on the symbolisms is perhaps best summarised in his remark that he thought it more important to 'study the symbolised rather than the symbols' (page 308). His general view of the relation between social phenomena and religious expression, a form of problem inherited from Durkheim but in some ways an inversion of Durkheim's reflectionist proposition that religion is a projection of the form of society, is that rite and myth present people with images of the unknown and mysterious in the terms of the 'known and non-mysterious—the social order' (page 135). Thus, for Stanner, the ultimate objects of religion lie beyond the social order: 'The society was not the real source and object of the religion' (page 300). And in any case, considerable difficulties stood in the way of pursuing the study of the meaning of the religion through the elicitation of close comment from the Murinbata.

Stanner describes the difficulty of eliciting exegesis of meanings from informants, and concludes that there is a general attitude of 'uninquiring acceptance' (page 150) of things that would appear to be symbolic in character, standing for something beyond themselves. The religion involves expression in diverse media, and all present difficulties in this regard. Song words are often obscure (page 156). The meaning of spatial motifs of rite, as well as the denotation of many visual signs, often cannot be successfully probed by direct inquiry (page 156). People will make some comments on myth, but beyond these 'The usefulness of both direct and indirect questions falls off sharply' (page 123). A lack of explicit teaching is also typical of those aspects of the secret-sacred Karwadi ceremony which have to do with the initiation of young men (page 92). **Discursive** (i.e. explicit, indigenously made and recognised meanings) do not predominate, while in the brilliant use of music, song, mime and dance, **presentational** symbolisms—indeterminate in sense and reference, but still powerful vehicles of effect—abound (see page 168 for Stanner's application of this distinction, developed by Susanne Langer). If understanding of rite and myth is to pass the threshold of resistance to interpretation, 'then it must be by other means' (page 151) than the usual forms of inquiry. Ultimately any inquiry about rite, myth and things of religious significance results in comment from Aborigines that they are done to 'follow up the Dreaming'. There is an adherence to things and patterns laid down, but obscurity pervades inquiry into them, and Stanner senses that mystery is an important part of Aboriginal feeling for them.

Stanner warns us we should not, on account of the obscurity, make the old mistake of thinking that Aboriginal religion is 'lifeless adhesion to a deadened routine' (page 150). For participants there is 'rapt absorption in things that have emotional appeal and give aesthetic pleasure' (page 149). In Stanner's view, the simple Durkheimian sacred-profane dichotomy is inadequate to yield understanding of the complex and 'crescive' (page 313, i.e. cumulative and overlaid) symbolisms. What form of analysis can yield some understanding?

In relation to the multi-media expression of Aboriginal religion, and even to different tokens of the same type of medium (e.g. different myths), Stanner develops a notion of 'congruent symbolising':

> Act, myth and spatial forms belong to distinct orders. We are thus not discovering the same phenomenon under different names. What we find by analysis is a set of congruences between components of a whole which are expressed according to the technique and system appropriate to each mode of symbolizing (page 168).

He summarises the congruence among forms of religious expression even more pithily, thus:

> It is one of **analogous** elements arranged with **similarity** of form or pattern and having a **commonness** of import manifest in different **types** of symbolism (page 181).

What is that whole of which the various types of expression are components; what is the commonness of import into which religious expression permits a view? Stanner tells us that the religion expresses the insight of a complex sense of people's 'dependence on a ground and source beyond themselves', a sense inherently of 'good-with-suffering', 'order-with-tragedy' (page 165), a 'fatal impairment' (page 323) from the beginning, and thus subjection to the 'joint **imperium** of the good and the bad' (page 147); and that this insight is considerable (though it is his opinion that the intuition of moral freedom or perfectibility is an even greater one, page 145); and that in the religion the insight is expressed with a 'certain nobility that transcends the strange symbolisms' (page 147). Thus:

> The symbolistical activities do not manipulate objects of life but express the valuations placed on them, and the desires for them (page 92).

The Method: Congruence of Myth and Rite

Confronted by the difficulties, already sketched, of gaining indigenous exegesis, Stanner remarks that many anthropologists might feel that they must transpose the study to phenomena of the unconscious mind (page 151). But in a dismissal perhaps typical then of those of British social anthropological background, Stanner tends to see such a psychological approach as mutually exclusive with an anthropological one:

> ...the symbolisms are constituents of collective acts of mutuality, with a logical structure, a detectable range of meanings, and an aesthetic appeal as well as a premial place in the social development of individuals. These relations may be appropriately studied by the methods of anthropology (page 151).

In the first article Stanner discusses the ceremony of Punj or Karwadi, in II the associated myth, in IV and V the myth of the Rainbow Serpent or Kunmanggur, the rite of male initiation, mortuary rite, and the myth of Kukpi, the Black Snake-Woman. Important to Stanner's mode of analysis is that in only some cases are a rite and a myth presently linked: the rite of Karwadi and the myth of Mutjingga, the Old Woman, form such a clearly associated pair. In other instances we have 'riteless myths' (i.e. myths, even apparently great and portentous ones such as that of the Rainbow Serpent, which are not associated with rite), and 'mythless rites' (e.g. male puberty rites).

The problem of the relation between rite and myth was of long standing in the study of religion. Stanner was obviously influenced by Robertson Smith, who saw rite as fundamental and myth as a secondary development in relation to it. Yet Stanner was not wholly satisfied with this view. Despite a measure of disbelief (page 185) that an important myth such as that of the Rainbow Serpent should never have been associated with any known rite (he cites in partial support of his incredulity the apparent association of the myth with two major rock art sites in the region), Stanner is inclined to give definitive priority to neither form. (He does, however, later suggest that myth may have a longer life than cult, page 304). Rather one may, with due caution, adopt the method of looking:

> within presently dissociated myths for the structural forms that would enable them to be compared with myths still demonstrably connected with rites, and to elicit from myths of both classes their kerygmatic elements—the statements of abiding truths about life—for comparison (page 186).

For Stanner has no doubt that:

> Each myth has something to say—something significant, said beautifully and tragically—about the first and last formula of things, the ultimate conditions of human being, the instituted ways in which all things exist, and the continuity between the primal instituting and the experiential here-and-now (page 186).

And there is evidence of improvisation, innovation, vitality, in religious tradition. The Aborigines are not, as T.G.H. Strehlow (1971) would have had it, decadent in a social-evolutionary sense, a people in decline living off the spiritual capital of the past (page 189).

Having segmented and compared the various forms of myth and rite—rite and myth together, mythless rite and riteless myth—Stanner is willing to take an interpretive 'leap in the dark' (page 210) to hypothesise: there is a congruence of structure among all of them. The reader must examine the divisions into phases, and the posited structural parallels among myth and rite forms (e.g. page 212) to determine whether the segmentations, and the alleged parallels, seem apt; Stanner makes no effort to justify them closely. That he senses possible difficulty here is shown by an early comment that, when it is ontology that is under study, 'some degree of implicit valuation' is unavoidable (page 96); and a later one, that there is the 'problem of reducing the impressionism of the approach' since the materials 'transcend controlled methods' (page 273). But he asserts that it is a methodological improvement over the social structural analysis he criticises because it 'arranges for further study the empirical similarities' rather than postulating holism (page 268).

At some level of abstraction from the actual narrative content Stanner proposes that all the forms show a common design with this patterning of content:

> Someone is sent or withdraws from a safe, habited place to a place of solitude. In the second place—the place of removal, or in the place deserted—wildness or terror, and a sort of corruption, become ascendant. Something—trust, young life, innocence—is destroyed there. Then, after a pause, there is a return to the first place. But it is now not the same as before; there has been a change; the old is not quite annulled and the new not altogether unfamiliar (page 224).

And at an even higher level of abstraction, Stanner finds that all exhibit the formula, very similar to the van Gennepian one: there is a setting aside, a withdrawal, a transformation and a changed return (page 268). All rites and myths may be seen as varying 'material manifestations' of the structure (page 269).

What are the meanings of such a structure? Though Stanner makes some observations concerning this in a number of places (see e.g. on the one hand, his noting the demands made upon young males, page 224; and on the other, the emphasis upon transience within forms of permanence), it is really in the final essay, subtitled 'Cosmos and Society Made Correlative', that he makes a sustained effort to put together a portrait of the ontology of which this structure is part, and the limits of the kind of meaning he attributes to it become clear.

The Dreaming

According to the ontology as Stanner interprets it, all that exists does so in terms fixed 'once-for-all' (page 296) by the acts of mythic creator figures in an 'everywhen' time/event dimension (Stanner 1965). (This dimension has come to be called the Dreaming, following some Aboriginal usage, both in English and some indigenous languages; and the mythic figures themselves are called 'dreamings' by Aborigines in many parts of the continent). Existing things belong to types established by the founding creative dramas, and also persons and places are linked to and defined by their relations to those mythic events, relations expressed largely in an idiom of totems, forces which continue to be immanent in the landscape which they created. In the terms of these concepts, the very existence of things is proof of their links to the founding creative acts: what is, is true (page 308) and bears witness to those acts, in which things simultaneously became determinate and endowed with meaning. There was instituted a pattern of relevances and a moral order 'such that the totality of life was a cosmological structure' (page 297). Not only the 'structures and process of life were settled' by the founding creative dramas, but 'man's whole lot, including the possibilities of his life' (page 302). Besides the 'archaist outlook', 'reactionary temper' and 'conservative impulse' associated with such a deterministic conception in general, in Aboriginal society older men in particular comprised a 'ruling stratum' who 'enforced a general assent to the terms of life which they... had adopted at pain and cost' (page 298).

Throughout the essays Stanner finds evidence in myth of a dominant theme of 'immemorial misdirection' (page 118), or 'irreparable injury to man at the beginning of life under instituted forms' (page 319), exemplified by the cruel treatment of youth entrusted to the care of the Old Woman of the myth associated with the rite of Punj or Karwadi.

The major rites simulate the events of the founding dramas and thus are symbolic affirmations (page 299) of them:

> Each ritual occasion vivified in the minds of celebrants the first instituting of the culture, deepened the sense of continuity with man's beginnings, and reaffirmed the structures of existence (page 298).

The rites dramatise and make manifest the possibility of assent to the instituted conditions of life, despite its inalterable element of tragedy:

> The myths are evidence that they reflected and felt a fatal impairment, but the rites are evidence that they met the issue in a positive way. They brought the inexorable within the total economy of living and put positive values upon it, so as to integrate it with social actuality and actuality's values (page 323).

During the founding dramas, two domains of life became distinguishable but remained interdependent: the corporeal and incorporeal (page 298).

> The principle of the religion was to make fleshly, determinate and social life correlative with the spiritual cycle (page 317).

A human life as spirit was subject to movement along an inexorable course at the same time that 'it had to be given value and status appropriate to progressively developing functions of its worldly life' (page 318). The segmentation of the spiritual course was not entirely fixed and underwent historical change, and as part of this process there occurred changes in the allocation of social value. The possibility of developmental change in Murinbata religion is an important theme mentioned in several of the essays, and below we return briefly to Stanner's ideas about the evidence that myth and rite provide for it.

As a result of the conjoint, social-spiritual definition of necessity within the scheme of once-for-all foundation, the 'person himself was treated as helpless' (page 318), required to surrender to imperatives dramatised and embodied in the symbolisms already sketched, of removal from human fellowship, transformation, and restoration, accompanied at each stage by the removal of social value, status and functions, their destruction, and the conferring of enhanced value, status and functions (page 318).Throughout these essays Stanner argues against views of Aboriginal social life as static, and of the religious practice as adherence to a lifeless routine. But his writing distinguished from this, and brought into focus, Aboriginal valuation of continuity and the imposition upon events of an image of persistence 'as the main character of reality' (page 321). In the final essay he suggests some sources of change in Murinbata religious tradition that were compatible with the forms of permanence of the established ritual life. These are revaluations at two loci in the rites which make and keep correlative the corporeal and incorporeal domains: first, change in the relation between 'life-situations' (page 317, stages of human development) and their ritual recognition; and second, change in the recognised value of ritual transformation (and ultimately, in keeping with this, changes in the valuation of particular kinds of rite with respect to each other). In relation to the first point, Stanner cites the preeminence of admission to the rite of Punj over, for example, circumcision: the latter is said to simply confer adulthood or, in the Aboriginal expression, to 'make men', while the former is more highly valued in that it is meant and said to make men understand (page 103). Stanner sees the higher valuation of understanding over the attainment of manhood/adulthood through initiation as the last major historical development in rite before European influence set in (page 317). He sees as a possible kind of change the valuation as of ritual significance of birth and perhaps other life-situations, but he finds there is no evidence of this. There is some direct evidence of changes in Murinbata ritual tradition (see e.g. mention of the obsolescence of formerly great rites, page 141), yet there also appears to be considerable historical persistence of ritual form. Partly on the basis of the evidence of changes, Stanner returns to the problem of what is to be made of the existence of great myths dissociated from rite, and of rites without myths. Suggesting that perhaps the true function of such myth is to rationalise the exalting of things to the status of cult objects, he concludes with an hypothesis of the historical relation of myth and rite, namely that myths not attached to any recent or extant rite are 'memorials of old formations of cult' (page 304). As undemonstrable as this may be from the Aboriginal material, it is part of Stanner's continuing preoccupation with what he was able to distil and make sensible to others as a crucial feature of Murinbata orientation to lived experience, namely, the constant working to assimilate change to the instituted forms of permanence. He saw this as possible within terms of life encompassed by the Dreaming.

The Contribution of 'On Aboriginal Religion'

Not in sympathy with structural-functionalist attempts to define society, Stanner was more interested in the tenor of sociality—which, as Radcliffe-Brown noted, is not any kind of **entity** (page 115)—and, incipiently, in what we might now call socio-cultural constructions of meaning. But he had chosen to work with a people for whom discourse about significance was not a typical or preferred mode, except at levels so abstract (e.g. the rite of Punj is done so that men will understand) that they seemed to provide little analytic leverage.

From a slightly different angle, Stanner deplored the treatment of Aboriginal religion as something else—as totemism, and in particular, as an epiphenomenon of the nature and form of society. It was his prime conviction that 'The first duty of anthropology in dealing with Aboriginal religion is to try to elicit the kind of reality the facts of study have for the people responsible for them' (page 95). But secondly, he ordained the sort of reality this must be: 'natural facts of human conviction about the ultimates of life' (ibid). Hence the tone of profundity and moralism that pervades 'On Aboriginal Religion', some would say giving it a distinctively Stannerian rather than recognisably Aboriginal tone, and hence also the degree of divorce in the work of religion from social structure, upon which Keen (1986) and Morphy (1988:243) have both commented.

Despite the weaknesses this divorce introduces into the work, Stanner's insistence that religious reality must be of that lofty nature enabled him to accomplish something with his Murinbata materials that no previous study of Aboriginal rite and myth had, and that few have since. Leaving behind any framework which would merely assign trivialising functions, or uni-dimensional structure, to the religious order, he pioneered a way of placing the study of 'religion' into broader interpretive study of Aboriginal life. He sought to identify through religious expression the encompassing dimensions of what he called the 'ontology', and by this route succeeded in formulating propositionally many of the overt attitudes and less explicit orientations towards lived experience with which many subsequent attempts to describe Aboriginal ways of life resonate profoundly: faithful belief in the fixed once-for-all foundation of the lived-in world, but yet the absorption of transience within these forms of permanence, and others.

How did this mark a watershed? Aboriginal 'data' always had an extremely important place in the development of sociological-anthropological theory. But many of the early theoretical uses of Aboriginalist material relied upon the particular kinds of evidence gathered by such avid collectors as Spencer and Gillen. Their descriptions of the rites—the Intichiuma, the Wollonqua, and many others—assumed the cardinal institution of totemism, its familiarity and naturalness as an object of study in 'primitive' society. However, one reads dozens of pages of these accounts with the growing realisation that there is little there of 'the kind of reality the facts of study have for the people responsible for them'. Wading through the detailed descriptions of rite is like restricting one's observations of foreign cuisine to the preparation of an elaborate meal of many and strange ingredients: enough **can** be assumed so one thinks one knows what is going on, but at the end, one must acknowledge that the dish remains unpalatably odd, and one has gained little grasp of the overall occasion at which it is to be eaten.

As Malinowski did for the Trobrianders, subsequent major descriptivist accounts of Aboriginal religion (see e.g. Elkin 1964) tended in one way or another to urge that, despite the strange symbolisms, the rites were socially 'functional', the orientations and motives of individuals understandable, and some of the social institutions functionally comparable to our own. But such assurances always come from a perspective that remains unremittingly external to what is under study. Stanner, instead, made 'sense' of the Murinbata material, and recognising significant Aboriginal commonalities, through it also indicated possibilities for understanding of Aboriginalist material more broadly, by developing it in relation to a cosmology, which he described solemnly and even reverently. Of the recognition of his achievement, Morphy (1988:243) has recently written: 'Hiatt (1975:11) was undoubtedly right when he wrote that: 'There would be a wide agreement among Australianists that [Stanner's] *Oceania Monograph* 'On Aboriginal Religion' is the most sensitive analysis of the subject to have appeared'. Morphy adds, however, that the work has been little cited and only recently the subject of critical review (in Keen 1986). This leads us to try to spell out how a thoroughgoing sociological insufficiency appears in the work as the negative side of Stanner's effort to transcend a reductionist structural-functionalism.

Stanner reacted against the limitations of structural-functionalism against the background, which he shared with Radcliffe-Brown, of a pervasive Durkheimian influence (see Stanner's 1967 critique of Durkheim). Stanner attempts to transcend Durkheim's conclusion that the most elementary form of religion is a projection and celebration of the segmental form of society, contending instead that the objects of Aboriginal religion, of myth and rite, are things of ultimate concern. Society is not its object; instead, the religion provides the nearest approach to the encompassing 'ontology', which is the basis of Aboriginal reality. Religious rites are 'acts towards whole reality, myths are allegorical statements about it, and social customs are acts within whole reality' (page 98).

Stanner's formulation, while seemingly opposite to the Durkheimian original, remains **fundamentally** of the same kind as Durkheim's in their shared representationism, that is, in the claim that complex practices encompassed in the term 'religion' may be understood as being **about** some more or less easily defined object. As we have seen, in Stanner's view the religion is about a founding 'paradox, antinomy or dualism common to all the structures of existence' (page 319), of which myths are allegories, and to which rites are a positive response. For Stanner, instead of closely reflecting society's form, 'the religion appeared as the society's completion' (page 319), the mysteries and irreparable injury of the human condition 'adumbrated by means of symbolisms couched in familiar idioms' (page 299).

Thus Stanner shaped the terms of debate inherited from Durkheim as an opposition between the determination of religion by society, or the transcendental character of religion in relation to society. This was certainly not a matter to him of pure theory, but given earlier extended debate on the nature of totemism and primitive religion, he construed it also as an ethical and philosophical issue of the worth to be accorded to Aboriginal life and culture generally. It is because he constructed the issue, with moral overtones, as one of whether Aboriginal religion is greater or lesser than society, and answered it resoundingly in the former way, that he did not develop themes, for which much material is present in his text, of the religion as complex social phenomenon. Stanner's representationism, a curious form of reduction given the vastness of what religion is about ('things of ultimate concern'), gives to his characterisation of the religion an intellectualising, contemplative quality (cf. Keen 1986:44), as if its practices were essentially signifying ones, conveying some importance or consequence of which they are the mere expression. But it is a credit to Stanner as ethnographer the extent to which material that would be needed to develop other themes is suggestively present in the work, as Hiatt's following Introduction also attests.

We may now return to the earlier statement that the reasons for which this work is not more widely known are complex. Though Stanner had criticisms to make of notions of social structure, he did not refine any alternative concepts through the Murinbata material, and in that sense leaves one major initiative in the work unrealised. But though his major concern is to elucidate **Aboriginal** religion, he achieves something of far wider anthropological significance in his suggestion of what he called the 'sacramentalist' religion, with its associated human and cosmic relations, as part of a particular form of life which he depicts in part. Because Stanner makes no concession to simple notions of function, and rejects outright simplifying notions of structure, the definition of the religion, and the human-cosmic forms of relations associated with it, cannot be stated formulaically as an easily repeatable, single 'idea' (cf. Morphy 1988:243); and so the work falls foul of the canon that what is to be perceived as widely applicable must be simple and crystalline. But in the attempt to characterise the interpenetration—rather than simple functional or structural relation—of the religion with other aspects of the form of life, lie multiple strands of connection which Stanner chose not to explore, which however are suggestive not only for students of Aboriginal social life in particular, but also for those many more concerned with developing better understanding of the social grounds of religious phenomena in general.

Acknowledgments

I am grateful to Milton Singer, Alan Rumsey and Les Hiatt for reading and commenting on an earlier draft of this essay.

References

BARWICK, D.E., J. BECKETT and M. REAY. 1985. W.E.H. 'Stanner: An Australian Anthropologist' in D.E. Barwick, J. Beckett and M. Reay (eds), *Metaphors of Interpretation: Essays in Honour of W.E.H. Stanner*, pp. 1–52. Rushcutters Bay: Australian National University Press.

BOURDIEU, P. 1977. *Outline of a Theory of Practice.* Cambridge, London: Cambridge University Press.

DURKHEIM, E. 1954 [1912]. *The Elementary Forms of the Religious Life.* London: Allen and Unwin.

ELKIN, A.P. 1964. *The Australian Aborigines.* New York: Doubleday.

HIATT, L.R. 1975. 'Introduction' in L.R. Hiatt (ed.), *Australian Aboriginal Mythology*, pp. 1–23. Canberra: Australian Institute of Aboriginal Studies.

KEEN, I. 1986. 'Stanner on Aboriginal Religion' *Canberra Anthropology* 9:26–50.

MADDOCK, K. 1985. 'Sacrifice and Other Models in Australian Aboriginal Ritual' in D.E. Barwick, J. Beckett and M. Reay (eds), *Metaphors of Interpretation*, pp. 133–57.

MORPHY, H. 1988. 'The Resurrection of the Hydra: Twenty-five Years of Research on Aboriginal Religion' in R.M. Berndt and R. Tonkinson (eds), *Social Anthropology and Australian Aboriginal Studies: A Contemporary Overview*, pp. 241–66. Canberra: Aboriginal Studies Press.

RADCLIFFE-BROWN, A.R 1930–31. 'The Social Organization of the Australian Tribes', *Oceania* 1(1–4), Oceania Monographs No. 1, Sydney.

RADCLIFFE-BROWN, A.R 1952. *Structure and Function in Primitive Society.* London: Cohen and West.

RADCLIFFE-BROWN, A.R 1957. *A Natural Science of Society.* Glencoe, Il.: The Free Press.

SANSOM, B. 1980. *The Camp at Wallaby Cross: Aboriginal Fringe Dwellers in Darwin.* Canberra: Australian Institute of Aboriginal Studies.

SINGER, M. 1984 [1973]. 'A Neglected Source of Structuralism', Radcliffe-Brown, Russell and Whitehead. *Semiotica* 48:11–96.

STANNER, W.E.H. 1934. 'Culture Contact on the Daly River', MA thesis, University of Sydney.

STANNER, W.E.H. 1938. 'Economic Change in North Australian Tribes', PhD thesis, University of London.

STANNER, W.E.H. 1958. 'Continuity and Change among the Aborigines', *The Australian Journal of Science* 21:99–109. (Presidential Address, Section F, ANZAAS 1958.)

STANNER, W.E.H. 1965. 'Religion, Totemism and Symbolism' in R.M. and C.H. Berndt (eds), *Aboriginal Man in Australia: Essays in Honour of*

Emeritus Professor A.P. Elkin, pp. 207–37. Sydney: Angus and Robertson.

STANNER, W.E.H. 1967. 'Reflections on Durkheim and Aboriginal Religion' in M. Freedman (ed.), *Social Organization: Essays Presented to Raymond Firth*, pp. 217–40. London: Frank and Cass Co. Ltd.

STANNER, W.E.H. 1968. Radcliffe-Brown, A.R. In D.L. Sills (ed.), *International Encyclopedia of the Social Sciences*, 13:285–90. New York: The Macmillan Company and the Free Press.

STREHLOW, T.G.H. 1971. *Songs of Central Australia.* Sydney: Angus and Robertson.

WALSH, M. 1976. 'The Murinypata Language of North-west Australia', PhD thesis, Australian National University.

On Aboriginal Religion: Stanner's Work

L.R. Hiatt

Although in a broad sense Stanner's monograph is based on the research he carried out in the Daly River and Port Keats region between 1932 and 1959, there is no doubt that the rich observational material forming the empirical core of the thesis was obtained during a brief but critical period in 1935. In June of that year Roman Catholic missionaries set out from Darwin to establish a mission among the Murinbata at Port Keats, and Stanner accompanied them. He had previously encountered individual members of the Murinbata tribe at the Daly River, but this was his first trip to their homelands.

The Aboriginal population in the vicinity of the mission was about 150. Despite depopulation caused by disease and migration, the ceremonial life remained vigorous. Stanner stayed at Port Keats for two months (1936:192). By the time of his next visit, after World War II, traditional religious practices had been 'replaced by a systematic education in Christianity' (Falkenberg 1962:19).

Prior to the monograph *On Aboriginal Religion*, Stanner had published only one full-length article on the Murinbata. This was 'Murinbata Kinship and Totemism', which appeared in the December issue of *Oceania* in 1936. Here the Murinbata are described as 'the most important remaining tribe in the salt-water country on the north-west of North Australia' (p. 186). They once occupied a territory of some 500–700 square miles between the Fitzmaurice River and Port Keats (see Map). In 1935 the tribe was still nomadic, few people spoke English, and the people were regarded as 'uncivilised' (p. 187).

'Murinbata Kinship and Totemism' has been widely quoted because of its account of the adoption of the subsection system by the Murinbata (see especially Lévi-Strauss 1969:125, 152–55). The only reference it makes to ceremonial life is a brief statement on increase ceremonies, including a reference to 'the culture-hero of the Murinbata – Kunmanggur, the Rainbow-Snake Man' (pp. 193–94). An article on 'Djamindjung Kinship and Totemism', published in the June issue of *Oceania* in 1936, offers brief comparative notes on Murinbata conception beliefs, cult totems, and the 'bull-roarer cult at secret initiations' (pp. 448–51). The only other published references to the Murinbata prior to World War II occur in 'Aboriginal Modes of Address and Reference in the North-West of the Northern Territory' (*Oceania*, March 1937). Stanner notes that postulants for initiation are referred to as 'wild dogs' (p. 313), and he makes a passing reference to the revelation of *karwadi* bullroarers (p. 313).

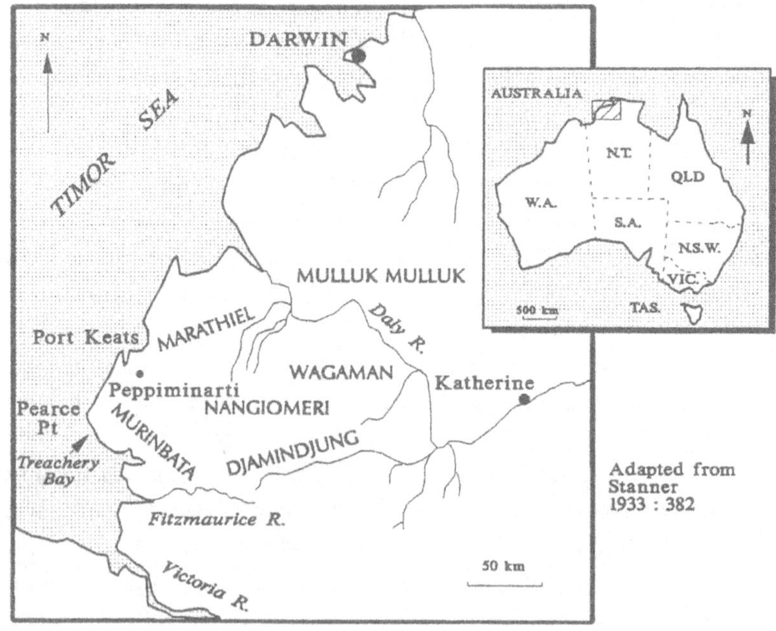

Daly River and Port Keats area

Stanner returned to Port Keats in 1952. The visit revived memories of the ceremonial life he had witnessed seventeen years earlier, much of it now rendered inactive by the mission regime. Some time in 1953 or 1954, after returning to Canberra, he sketched plans for a book on ritual, to include chapters on 'valuation by expressive signs', 'institutional transactions', 'the All-Mother', and 'the Dreaming' (Barwick *et al.* 1985:283). All these topics feature prominently in *On Aboriginal Religion.* Stanner's celebrated essay on 'The Dreaming', first published in an anthology in 1956, was probably based on the relevant chapter of the projected book. Although obviously informed by first-hand experience, it makes no explicit reference to the Murinbata or their congeners.

Stanner made three further visits to the Daly River and Port Keats region during the 1950s. The first published intimation of the empirical content of *On Aboriginal Religion* appeared in several passages of 'Continuity and Change Among the Aborigines', Stanner's Presidential Address to Section F of ANZAAS in 1958 (reprinted in Stanner 1979 from the *Australian Journal of Science*). In section 4 of the paper Stanner summarises the myth of Kunmanggur, the Rainbow Serpent (see below), adding 'A book could be written – indeed, I cannot promise not to write it – about the symbolisms of the myth' (1979:55). He goes on to suggest that the decline of the cult of Kunmanggur and the rise of the cult of Mutjingga (see below) should be seen as a response to colonisation: Kunmanggur is the All-Father who failed his people, Mutjingga is the All-Mother who brings new hope (1979:61).

Stanner spent part of 1959 at Port Keats, and it was during this visit that he drafted his first article in the *Oceania* series 'On Aboriginal Religion'. In the same year, he wrote his splendid biography of Durmugam, a man of the Nangiomeri tribe he had known since 1932 (published 1960, reprinted in Stanner 1979). Here Stanner gives further substance to the view that colonisation provided the critical context for the fall of the All-Father and the rise of the All-Mother. He goes on to relate the circumstances of his own admission to the cult of the All-Mother, which he describes as 'messianic' or 'nativistic', and comparable with Melanesian cargo cults (1979:85).

In mid-1961, after four of the six articles had been published, Stanner presented a paper to the Association of Social Anthropologists (Australian Branch) in which he sought to clarify his objectives. Entitled 'On the Study of Aboriginal Religion', the paper began by setting out four 'self-imposed restrictions', which later appeared as the second paragraph of the introduction to the monograph. After rejecting the approaches of Durkheim and (more peremptorily) Freud, it made a plea for an anthropology 'not of men, or men-in-roles, or men-together-in-groups, but of men-acting-jointly about things of value and doing specifiable things in identifiable situations of life with ends in view' (p. 11). It ended with a pronouncement that the highest Murinbata ritual has as its centrepiece the Mime of the Blowfly, symbolising corruption or living on corruption.

Stanner's last statement on Murinbata religion is an unpublished document entitled 'Big Sunday at Peppiminarti'. In 1978 ten Aborigines from the recently-established Peppiminarti settlement (see Map) visited him in Canberra. They had heard that he was not expected to live much longer and wanted to see him before he died. They were also keen to obtain from him any ritual objects from the Daly River that might be in his possession, for use in a forthcoming Punj ceremony. In the event Stanner made the journey to Peppiminarti for the ceremony itself, where he presented three bullroarers he had received as gifts during the 1930s (one of them from Durmugam). Despite illness and an inability to write, he formed impressions that, on returning to Canberra, he recorded with characteristic sensitivity and candour.

Much remained as he had witnessed it in 1935. Some of it even struck him as the most powerful and suggestive 'theatre' he had ever seen. But the objectives of the cult now seemed to have taken on a political cast in the context of inter-tribal rivalries. Stanner noted a degree of severity in the treatment of novices that seemed to express a greater desire to impose the authority of the cult upon them than to inculcate 'understanding, a sense of mystery or the other loftier things' (p. 11) he had attributed to it in his monograph.

Last, but perhaps not least, the Mime of the Blowfly was missing from the repertoire. In its place was a new performance, the Mime of the Aeroplane.

In 1980 Stanner drafted plans for a book entitled 'The Murinbata: a Religious Aboriginal Society' (Barwick *et al.*, 1985:307). The name 'Murinbata' is a conjunction of *murin*, 'language', and *bata*, 'good' (Falkenberg 1962:11). Chapter 1 was to be called 'The People of the Pleasing Tongue'. The book was never completed.

The Ethnographic Contents

The main raw materials of the monograph, in order of presentation, consist of (a) the bullroarer rite (Punj or Karwadi; p. 92); (b) the myth of Mutjingga, the Old Woman (p. 118); (c) the myth of Kunmanggur, the Rainbow Serpent (p. 183); (d) the circumcision rite (p. 230); (e) the death rite (p. 245); (f) the myth of Kukpi, the Black-Snake Woman (p. 256); (g) the season-changing rite, (Tjimburki p. 279); (h) pre-puberty initiation rites (Karamala and Djaban; p. 285); (i) the myth of Crab and Crow (p. 301). Interspersed between these segments are accounts of Murinbata totemism, noun classes, religious concepts, and modernisation. The empirical materials are subjected to analysis and woven into an original and well-integrated argument.

The three most important beings in the Murinbata pantheon at the time of Stanner's research in the 1930s were Mutjingga, Kunmanggur, and Kukpi (see p. 207). Mutjingga was central to the bullroarer ceremony, but neither Kunmanggur nor Kukpi figured directly in contemporary cults.

In offering a precis of the monograph, I shall begin with the main ethnographic components. I shall then summarise Stanner's interpretations and line of argument.

The Bullroarer Rite

This is a post-circumcision rite inducting youths into the cult of the Mother. The ceremony traditionally took place annually and lasted for one or two months.

1. The postulants are led by a senior man to a secret clearing. Initiated adult males have already assembled. When the youths arrive, the initiates enclose them in a tight circle. They sing a psalm which ends with an invocation of the Mother. The men return with the novices to the main camp, where the latter sit in a position of honour.
2. Before dawn on the following day, the lads return to the ceremonial ground. The day's proceedings begin with singing and institutionalised obscenities (*Tjirmumuk*). The rest of the morning is devoted to singing, the novices again encircled by the initiates. In the early afternoon the youths set out on what they believe is a hunting expedition. Once away from the ceremonial ground, their guardian instructs them to remove their clothing and ornaments. From now on they are referred to as 'dingoes', and their personal names are not used. They are informed that soon the Mother will arrive and swallow them alive, then vomit them up. The initiates perform the Mime of the Blowfly, making small agitated movements and a low-pitched buzzing sound. The postulants are then covered with blood, which they are told comes from the Mother but which actually comes from the veins of their future wives' brothers. After more singing, the men return to the main camp. The novices are kept out of sight, while initiates engage in raucous horse-play, obscene joking, and mock food theft.
3. The postulants return to the secret ground before dawn. Ritual obscenities are followed by the Mime of the Blowfly, and then singing. When the time comes for the youths to be anointed with affinal blood, men in hiding swing bullroarers, whose noise is said to be the voice of the Mother. This, combined with the simulated fear of the assembled initiates, produces in the novices a state of terror. Suddenly the men in hiding leap into full view, exposing the secret

of the bullroarers. Brothers-in-law come forward, each bearing a bullroarer covered with his own blood, which he thrusts between the thighs of his sister's future husband at the angle of an erect penis.

4. Each day, from now until the final day, proceedings follow a regular pattern: singing in a tight circle, ritual obscenities, the Mime of the Blowfly, songs and dances celebrating totem ancestors. On the penultimate day, the impending conclusion of the ceremony is signalled by a particularly vigorous engagement in obscene horse-play, following by a graceful dance.
5. On the morning of the final day, the youths are anointed with blood and presented with gifts or apparel by their brothers-in-law. They are no longer 'dingoes' but fully-initiated men. All the men then proceed to the main camp, where the female kin and affines of the newly-inducted youths have been assembled. The men form two long lines, one for each patrilineal moiety. On a signal from the elders, the youths emerge from concealment and crawl through the tunnels formed by the legs of men of the opposite moiety from their own. On emerging, each youth sits for a moment in front of his mother, while all the assembled women wail and lacerate their heads. The lads then return through the tunnel of legs, and all the men rush back to the ceremonial ground. A week after the end of the ceremony, the youths bathe and have a cryptic insignia of the bullroarer painted on their bodies. They return to the main camp to resume normal life, except that from now on they must not go near their mothers' hearths. After a couple of years they are judged to be ready for marriage.

The Myth of the Old Woman

In the Murinbata language, *mutjingga* is the generic term for an old woman. The myth of Mutjingga is about an ancestral Old Woman, otherwise designated as 'the Mother of us all'. She is the Mother of the bullroarer cult just described.

The myth tells how, in ancestral times, the people decided one day to go on a honey-foraging expedition. Before setting out, they asked the Old Woman to take care of the children. After bathing in the river, the children gathered around their minder, who suggested a mutual delousing session. Taking up each child in turn, the Old Woman swallowed them one after another and then departed.

The parents returned and realised what must have happened. The men set out in pursuit and overtook the Old Woman as she crawled underwater along a creek bed. A man called Lefthand speared her through the legs, while another called Righthand broke her neck with a club. When they cut open her belly, they found the children alive and well in the Old Women's womb. The two men lifted them out, washed and adorned them, then returned them to their mothers.

The Myth of the Rainbow Serpent

The Murinbata know the Rainbow Serpent as Kunmanggur. In the beginning Kunmanggur was a beneficent culture hero, a man of superhuman size and powers who was transformed into a huge serpent associated with the rainbow.

Kunmanggur had two daughters and a son (Tjiniman, the Bat). One day the daughters set out on a hunting expedition. Tjiniman followed them and proposed sexual intercourse. They indignantly refused but, under duress, submitted to his rapacious demands.

The following day the two sisters escaped and later enticed Tjiniman to climb after them up a cliff-face by rope. As he neared the top, they severed the rope and he fell onto the rocks far below. By magical means he repaired his injuries and returned home.

Disgruntled by his experience, Tjiniman invited the people to a ceremony in honour of Kunmanggur ('the Old One', 'the Leader-Friend'). As the dancing drew to a close, the son speared his father in the back. He ran off, wondering what people would do, but no one took revenge. Kunmanggur, in great agony, died slowly, performing various miracles before disappearing into the sea.

The Circumcision Rite

When a boy reached puberty, he was publicly circumcised. The Murinbata used a number of regional song-and-dance styles for the accompanying ceremony, but the basic procedures remained constant.

6. On a pre-arranged day, people gather at the camp of the boy's father. Close relatives form a cluster in a central position, while singers, musicians and dancers perform for several hours.
7. On cue, the music stops abruptly and a future wife's brother of the novice steps forward and places a hand on the lad's shoulder. He may utter the words: 'Now I take you to make you a man'. Amidst wailing and self-mutilation, the boy is led away by his affine from the cluster of close kin.
8. The brother-in-law takes the boy on a tour of neighbouring and distant communities, accompanied by singers and dancers. The journey might last several months, during which the novice enjoys the excitement of seeing new places and people. At the same time he is subject to new disciplines, including food taboos and obedience to his guardians and mentors.
9. The escort party dramatically announces its return by throwing a ceremonial spear into the centre of the home community's circle of camp-fires. At the sight of the white tuft quivering in the firelight, the boy's close kin give forth with lamentations.
10. On the afternoon of the next day, following a morning of growing excitement, a long line of decorated men appears about 500 metres away, heading towards the main camp. After a series of advances and retreats, over several hours, they bring the novice to within 50 metres of his close kin. Weeping profusely, the latter rush forward and attempt to wrest the lad away from his guardians.
11. The men interpose themselves between the boy and his mother, and form a dense screen around the novice. Four of his classificatory brothers-in-law interlace their legs to make a platform on which the boy is placed and held while a surgeon removes his foreskin.

12. For several weeks the circumcised youth stays in the care of his brother-in-law, though provided with food by his mother. Then he is ritually cleansed and decorated. Food taboos are gradually relaxed.

The Death Rite

The Murinbata practiced a form of double disposal, or delayed final burial, for men. The bodies of women were placed on a platform and left to rot. Children were wrapped in bark and finally abandoned in some sheltered place.

1. After a death, close kin of the deceased paint themselves white as a sign of bereavement. The dead man's hair is removed by clansmen and sent to his brother-in-law. With the exception of his stone axe, which is given to an affine or some other close friend, and of his blanket, all his belongings are broken into pieces and wrapped in a bundle. The corpse is placed on a platform and the camp abandoned.
2. When the corpse has dried out, the forearm bones are removed. The body is then cremated and the ashes given to the deceased's mother (or classificatory mother).
3. Several years later close kin of the deceased invite his affines to a feast at which his possessions are burnt. The guests present their hosts with trade valuables.
4. After a further passage of time, the remains of the deceased are finally interred. To mark the occasion, clans throughout the region assemble. Gifts are placed on the grave, around which men in regional formations parade and utter ritual calls throughout the afternoon.

The Myth of the Black-Snake Woman

Kukpi is conceived by the Murinbata as half-woman, half-snake. She is a great singer and song-maker.

Kukpi went on a journey, looking for a good place to stay. As she walked, she tested the ground with her digging stick, creating springs that exist today. At length she settled down at Purgala.

Soon after she arrived a hunter approached, pursuing a wallaby. Kukpi uttered a magic word, and the animal fell down dead. Kukpi told the hunter to roast it. She then directed him to carry it onto a high cliff. Uttering the same magic word, she caused him to fall to his death.

A kinsman followed the dead man's tracks to Kukpi's place. She told him to keep following them to the edge of the cliff and then look down. She uttered the magic word and he fell.

A third man suffered the same fate. Then Padurutj, a wise old man, ventured forth to discover what was wrong. When he arrived at Kukpi's place, she was singing to the accompaniment of clap-sticks. He realised she was responsible for the death of the three men. He also recognised the songs as secret male cult songs.

On a second visit Padurutj received from Kukpi's son two stone bullroarers with secret markings. These became prototypes for bullroarers made from wood. Subsequently two women went to Kukpi's place and brought back more stone bullroarers. The men killed them with axes.

The Season-Changing Rite

Tjimburki is the name of a defunct secret male ceremony, last performed towards the end of the nineteenth century. It took place over five or six months, during which the participants refrained from all sexual intercourse and verbal communication (apart from singing). Hardly anything of the content or purpose of the rite is remembered, though it was apparently concerned with bringing the Wet season to an end and ushering in the Dry.

The rite began at grass-burning time, when youths were inducted into severe but otherwise forgotten disciplines. All participants were blackened from head to toe with charcoal. They danced around a painted pole erected in the middle of a large circular excavation, while the ceremonial leader swung a bag or basket over their heads. Men slept at the secret ground for the duration of the ceremony. The women provided them with food and at the end of the ceremony greeted their return with wailing and self-mutilation.

Pre-puberty Initiation Rites

The Murinbata adopted circumcision as a puberty rite within living memory. Prior to the innovation, boys were initiated by means of a non-circumcising ritual called Karamala. Following the introduction of circumcision, Karamala became a pre-puberty preparatory ritual. At some later period Karamala was replaced by a ritual called Djaban.

Karamala

When boys were within a few years of puberty, they were taken by their potential future brothers-in-law to a friendly neighbouring community. After a stay of some weeks, their hosts returned with them to their home community, laden with gifts. The lads were ceremonially handed back to their close kin, who wailed and fondled them.

At the end of the ceremony the boys formally presented the gifts to their fathers. By doing so they entered the inter-tribal exchange system. From now on they had to observe certain food taboos and were allowed to sleep together away from the family hearth.

Djaban

Djaban was a more complex and intimidating rite than Karamala.

1. As a prelude to the ceremony, the boys were taken on a hunting trip by initiated men. That night they were told to sleep in the centre of the camp-circle.
2. The next morning the boys were taken to the ceremonial ground, where they were placed under the guardianship of their brothers-in-law. From now on they were referred to as 'dingoes'.
3. Later in the day they were taken to a spot not far from the ceremonial ground, then led back with their heads bowed. On their arrival, one group of singers and dancers erupted into obscene horse-play, while another suddenly appeared from behind bushes and instructed the boys to join them in a dance repeated throughout the afternoon.

4. That night the boys were placed under a speech taboo and fed outside the main camp by the affines. After more raucous horse-play, this time in the camp itself, the novices were escorted to their sleeping positions of the night before.
5. The next seven days were occupied with singing and dancing at the ceremonial ground. Boys thought to be in need of discipline were forced to lie face up in the sun with eyes open.
6. At the end of this phase, the boys were told by a guardian that all the men had left the ceremonial ground to prepare for a fight. Pretending to be concerned for their safety, he led them back towards the main camp. On the way, the boys noticed fires burning close to the path. Suddenly masked men leapt from hiding, grunting ominously and hurling weapons. In fear of their lives, the novices ran widely back to the ceremonial ground where, on arriving safely, they were given fire-drills by their brothers-in-law.
7. That night the men engaged each other in licentious horse-play. The following day the novices were decorated by their affines at the ceremonial ground. They then returned to their female kin through the legs of men of the opposite moiety, as in the bullroarer rite. Returning to the ceremonial ground, they were painted with the insignia of the bullroarer.
8. The newly-initiated boys were not allowed to speak to their female kin for another month. In due course a final rite was celebrated in which affines were presented with gifts of food cooked on fires lit by the fire-drills they had previously given to the novices.

Myth of Crab and Crow

This tells how humans learned to die.

Crab, an old woman, fell ill; and, thinking she was dead, people buried her. After five days she emerged with a new shell.

Everyone was happy, except Crow. 'That is not the way to die', he said, 'it takes too long'. With that, he pecked out the Crab's eyes. Then he fell down backwards, rolled his eyes and died immediately.

The Argument

In his initial article, Stanner argues that the bullroarer rite can be understood as a sacrifice in which the youths are offered to the Mother Goddess. First the lads are consecrated by setting them aside, reducing them to nakedness and anonymity, and anointing them with human blood. They are then assembled in the 'presence' of the Mother, who 'swallows' them. In return, the novices are made 'men of mystical understanding', and society as a whole shares the benefits of their transformation.

The suggestion is not developed in later articles and is only briefly alluded to in the conclusion (p. 317). It should accordingly be treated as tangential to the main argument and not as an introduction or direct entry into it.[1]

The central thesis of the monograph is stated in section 4 of the second article. Here, under the heading 'The Search for a Paradigm', Stanner pithily describes Murinbata religion as 'the celebration of a dependent life which is conceived as having taken a wrongful turn at the beginning, a turn such that the good of life is now inseparably connected with suffering' (p. 116). From this formulation he isolates and amplifies three dominant motifs: (a) 'the celebration of dependence'; (b) 'the wrongful turning'; and (c) 'the connection of suffering and good'.

Dependence is conceived both materialistically and spiritually: humans are dependent on nature for the means of subsistence; nature in turn is dependent upon the creative powers of the totemic ancestors. The

1 For discussions of Stanner's thesis on 'the lineaments of sacrifice' in Murinbata religion, see Worms 1963; van Baal 1971; Maddock 1985; Keen 1986. See also Durkheim's section on 'The Elements of Sacrifice' in Book 3 of the *Elementary Forms of the Religious Life*. Keen's essay is a general review of Stanner's monograph and in important respects is complementary to the present Introduction. Other general (though brief) discussions of *On Aboriginal Religion* occur in Eliade 1973; Hiatt 1975a; Yengoyan 1979; Koepping 1981; Swain 1985; Morphy 1988.

'celebration of dependence' is the solemn yet joyous memorialisation of ancestral powers that constitutes the core of Murinbata ceremonial life.

Although Murinbata religion lacks a clearly-articulated notion of perfection or original sin, it is permeated nevertheless by an inference that, but for the wanton and perverse behaviour of certain ancestral beings, life might have been a lot better than it is. This misdirection in human affairs at the beginning of history bequeathed a life of qualified goodness, a flawed sociality where security is undermined by latent treachery and joy coexists with suffering.

The thesis of the monograph is briefly recapitulated in section 4 of the third article. The Murinbata, according to Stanner, conceive the dependence upon transcendental powers to be of a kind entailing 'good-with-suffering' and 'order-with-tragedy' (p. 165). This conception, expressed symbolically rather than explicitly, is reiterated in the main Murinbata myths and rites and accordingly constitutes a structural core of Murinbata liturgy and exegesis.

The Demonstration

Stanner extracts the elements of his thesis from the empirical corpus and arranges them in a number of tables purporting to exhibit homomorphism. Although the structures of myth and rite are interconnected, some clusters of congruent elements illustrate particular aspects of Murinbata ontology better than others. Thus from Table 5 ('Structural Plans of Three Dramas'), we can see how the notion that benefit is conditional upon loss or suffering is distilled from 'the acquisition of fire through the death of the Father', 'conservation of young life through death of the Mother', and 'attainment of understanding through the pain of initiation'. Table 1 ('Myth and Rite: the Empirical Order of Events') reveals that the perception of life as 'a joyous thing with maggots at the centre' (p. 114) is not only articulated in the myths but played out in the rites as well. The bogus hunting expedition in Punj and the spurious report of violence in Djaban, both preludes to terrorisation of the novices, are offered as examples and placed alongside ritual obscenity and the Mime of the Blowfly.

The apprehension of primal malfeasance is expressed with great dramatic force in the perfidious cannibalism of Mutjingga and Tjiniman's wilful parricide. Stanner gives prominence to both examples. But there is also the case of Kukpi who, under the pretence of goodwill, despatched men to their destruction; and of Crow, who maliciously attacked the regenerated Crab before imposing irrevocable death on humanity by his own example.

Not surprisingly, Stanner spends little time substantiating his characterisation of Murinbata religion as a 'celebration of dependence'. The assumption that human destinies depend on transcendental forces is, after all, a basic feature of religion wherever it occurs. We merely need to appreciate the special totemic forms in which the Murinbata have cast their conceptions of ancestral power and to note that they regard their dependence upon it not as a cause for brooding and anxiety but rejoicing.

Commentary

At the beginning of his monograph, Stanner acknowledges that the bullroarer rite is indubitably an **initiation** rite (p. 67); and, towards the end, he remarks that the Murinbata material in many respects is 'a remarkable confirmation of the worth of Arnold van Gennep's schema as set out in *Les Rites de Passage*' (p. 275). Nevertheless Stanner does not wish to be constrained by this conception. Nor does he wish to be limited by Murinbata interpretations of their own religious culture (p. 169). It is true, he says, that initiation ritual has a powerful socialising effect and that its proclaimed objective is to make young men 'understand'. The challenge, however, is to make sense of features that the instructors themselves do not understand.

The thesis that the Murinbata myths and rites are cryptic disquisitions on the most general features of human existence is thus an attempt to transcend native exegesis, or lack of it, in order to render intelligible what the cultists regard as mysteries. We must now consider whether this ascription of an unconscious or inchoate ontology can be justified.

If we put to one side the ritual and mythological treatment of death, together with the dimly-remembered and hence poorly-documented Tjimburki cult, the remainder of the Murinbata corpus presented in the monograph constitutes an elaborate male induction complex.[2] According to Stanner, the effect of the initiatory experience is to transform boys into men, and then into men of mystical understanding (p. 101, p. 232). In his judgment the second phase or aspect constitutes the critical, albeit enigmatic, element in Murinbata religious life and therefore deserves the main effort of elucidation. The first aspect he regards as secular and unproblematic. Nevertheless, it may help to clear the ground for assessment if we spend a moment contemplating its salient features.

The most conspicuous and colourful roles in a youth's initiation are played by men related to him as *nanggun*. The term recurs many times in Stanner's descriptions and may be glossed provisionally as 'brother-in-law'. As noted above, novices are placed under the guardianship of their brothers-in-law in the Karamala pre-puberty rite and the circumcision rite, and taken on journeys to neighbouring communities. In the circumcision ceremony, brothers-in-law form a platform on which the operation is performed. Men of the *nanggun* category present the novices with firedrills in the Djaban rite and bullroarers in the Punj rite.

2 Although Kunmanggur and Kukpi are not contemporary cult deities, both are clearly related to male initiation. Stanner says that the myth of Kunmanggur could stand in the same relation to the Punj ceremony as the myth of Mutjingga (p. 226). The myth of Kukpi describes how men obtained bullroarers for the Punj ceremony (p. 264). The fact that Stanner thinks it might be an accretion hardly changes its significance. There is, incidentally, an interesting parallel between Kukpi and Mumuna, the Mother-Goddess celebrated in the Kunapipi of south-east Arnhem Land (see Berndt 1951: 148–52; Hiatt 1975b:150–51).

At various times they clothe the novices, feed them, decorate them and even anoint them with their own blood.

At the beginning of the circumcision ceremony, the novice is led away from his close kin by an individual who says: 'Now I take you to make you a man' (p. 237). Ideally the person who plays this role is a brother of the novice's betrothed wife. Stanner gives the information without comment. Yet surely there is a question here worth trying to answer: why is the brother-in-law accorded such a key role in the cultural construction of Murinbata manhood?

Until a boy approaches puberty, his relationships with others are largely confined to members of his own small community, especially his family, other close kin, and male coevals. Initiation ushers him into an expanding social universe: the lad is formally introduced to neighbouring communities, given junior status in the ceremonial trade network, and progressively incorporated into the inter-tribal secret cult milieu of adult males. Somewhat later he marries a woman who may belong to another community but in any case should not be a member of the kin group in which he spent his childhood (Stanner 1936b:197–98). Murinbata culture, it would appear, deems that the most appropriate person to guide him on this journey into a wider geographical and social space, which is simultaneously a biological transition from boyhood to manhood and ultimately fatherhood, in his future wife's brother.

Stanner tells us practically nothing in his monograph about the Murinbata system of kinship and marriage. As Morphy has observed (1988:243): 'It is a pity ... that Stanner's opposition to Durkheim led to a perhaps reactive neglect of the political and social dimensions of Aboriginal religion' But neither does he say much about affinal relationships in his sole article on Murinbata kinship (Stanner 1936b). Fortunately this lacuna in the ethnographic record has been filled recently by A. and J. Falkenberg's book *The Affinal Relationship System* (1981), based on fieldwork at Port Keats in 1950. References to the Falkenbergs' data will be given at appropriate points below. Of particular interest at the moment, however, is their statement that, before circumcision, maturing boys often experiment sexually with forbidden girls of their own patrilineal local clan (1981:77–78). Immediately after circumcision they are warned by senior men that, although they are now eligible for sexual relationships, they should on no account have anything to do with their clanswomen (1981:79; see also Falkenberg 1962:25).

A recent trend in the anthropological study of religion has been to approach ritual as a form of theatre. Turner, for instance, says that 'ritual is, in its most typical cross-cultural expressions, a synchronisation of many performative genres, and is often ordered by dramatic structure, a plot' (1982:81).[3] As a working hypothesis, then, let us suppose that the Murinbata morality play in which Youth is the central character is conceived at some level as a journey from Mother and Sister to Wife. The drama is in four acts.

Act 1 (Karamala) is the first stage in the removal of the boy from his family circle. It is done tenderly, with loving kindness. After a brief sojourn, the lad is returned to his parents laden with gifts. A gentle prelude to more traumatic separations.

Act 2 (Djaban) is the boy's introduction to the secret cult life of adult males. Having been taken to neighbouring communities in the Karamala, he is now conducted to the men's secret meeting place. Until the end of the ceremony, the novices are called 'wild dogs'. In the initial stages they spend the day at the secret ceremonial ground, sleeping at night in the centre of the general camp, and are fed on its outskirts by their brothers-in-law. They are subjected to painful disciplines, though their brothers-in-law are permitted to comfort them. In the penultimate stage their anxious attempt to return home is blocked by men grotesquely disguised as warlocks, and they flee in terror back to the security of

3 See also Turner's posthumous essays in *The Anthropology of Performance*, with a preface by Richard Schechner. It is perhaps worth noting that the approach to male puberty rites as a form of drama was developed at some length in a dissertation submitted for the degree of Doctor of Philosophy at Yale University in 1943 by Lucille Charles (see Charles 1946). This in turn was inspired by an earlier work from Yale on 'primitive theatre', Loomis Havemeyer's *The Drama of Savage Peoples* (1916).

the ceremonial ground. Here they are presented with fire-drills by their brothers-in-law, who must ensure that the fires produced are used only by the novices. The ceremony ends when the novices return to their female kin through a tunnel of legs formed by men of the opposite moiety. Their mothers and sisters wail and lacerate their legs. A month passes before the boys are permitted to speak to them again. Later the lads cook food for their brothers-in-law and commit their fire-drills to the flames.

Act 3 (Circumcision) begins when the boy, having reached puberty, is ceremonially led away from his family and close blood relatives by his future wife's brother. From this point until the end of the ceremony, he is known as 'wild dog' or 'penis person'. The guided tour extends his range of contacts beyond those established in the earlier excursion. In the wake of a festive homecoming, his guardians shoulder aside his weeping mother and enclose him inside a tight circle of men. There a surgeon removes the protective cover from the head of his penis, thus putting an end to boyhood and conferring upon him the badge of manhood.

Act 4 (Punj) is the induction of the now-circumcised youth into the cult of the Mother, from which all women are excluded. Symbols of his humanity are temporarily withdrawn, and again he is referred to as 'wild dog'. Each day begins with a formal exchange of obscenities between 'affines' (see below). At the climax, the novices are anointed with the blood of their future wives' brothers, threatened with destruction by the Mother, and finally presented with bullroarers by their brothers-in-law. The curtain falls as the youthful initiates bid farewell to their grieving mothers.

Let us now see whether the main dramaturgical and mythical metaphors are consistent with the hypothesis:

Wild Dog

In the whelping season, Aboriginal hunters often took dingo pups from their mothers in order to tame them (Meggitt 1965:14). The analogy with novices (who are regarded by adult males as 'egotistical and refractory', p. 71) may thus be a direct one. In a more abstract mode, it could be said that to designate novices as 'wild dogs' is to highlight their liminality. The dingo was not normally hunted for food; rather, it scavenged around camps for food left by hunters (Meggitt 1965:11). Even pet dingoes sooner or later returned to the wild (Hamilton 1972:294). The species is thus marginal, neither a part of human society nor yet entirely outside of it. The novices, too, are marginal: expelled from boyhood, but not yet fully qualified for manhood. Their quasi-exiled status is underscored by divesting them of their personal names and clothing.

Firedrills and Bullroarers

To be a husband, a man must be able to make fire. A campfire is the centrepiece of Aboriginal domestic life. But there are also explicit figurative associations in Australia between fire and male sexuality.[4] Firedrills are symbols of virility par excellence: they produce fire by friction when one stick (often designated as 'male') is inserted vertically into a hole in the second, horizontal stick ('female') and twirled.[5]

Bullroarers are also often associated with masculinity.[6] Their ithyphallic status in the Punj rite is transparent.

Bearing this symbolism in mind, we can say that the following sequence occurs in Act 2 (Djaban) and is repeated in Act 4 (Punj): youths are separated from their close female kin, placed in terrifying circumstances, and then presented with symbols of sexual potency by their future wives' brothers. In Act 3 (Circumcision), this same category of men forms a platform under the novice while his penis is physically made ready for sexual intercourse. In terms of our hypothesis, the message seems redundantly clear: 'the road back to the Mother is fraught with danger; you must not seek your manhood there; return

4 See Morton 1987:107; Spencer and Gillen 1899:446. Basedow (1925:292) reports a cave painting near Murinbata territory depicting a flame linking a man's penis with the vagina of an ancestral woman.

5 Cf. Roheim 1974:154–55.

6 For example, Roheim 1925:156, 1974:150–51; Strehlow 1947:89.

briefly only to say goodbye; then, with the impetus received from your affines, and the guidance of the male cult, proceed along the proper path towards the goal of conjugality'.

Cannibal Woman

This too is a widespread motif in Australia (Waterman 1987:90–95). The key to its deployment in the Murinbata initiation complex is provided by the Mutjingga myth: the devouring Mother has to be killed, as 'the condition of the perpetuation of human life through its children' (p. 181). Immediately following the denouement of the mystery of the Mother in the Punj rite, each youth sees springing from his loins an erect bullroarer anointed with the blood of his future wife's brother.

Tunnel of Legs

Metaphors of parturition occur regularly in Aboriginal initiation dramas (Hiatt 1971, 1975a, 1975b). In essence men take boys from their mothers so that they may be symbolically killed; then they reproduce them as adult males. In the Djaban and Karwadi rites, youths crawl out from between the legs of men of their mother's moiety, emerging in front of their real mothers. Stanner thinks the purpose is to humble the lads (p. 80), but maybe the inference should include their mothers as well. In other words, the mime is intended as a commentary on the role of women: men take the raw products of natural parturition (cf. dingo pups) and effect their metamorphosis into fully-fledged cultural beings.

Reciprocal Obscenity

The ribald relationship known in the Port Keats area as *Tjirmumuk* is between quasi-affines: individuals, that is to say, who address each other by affinal terms but who are not related by true affinity. The categories involved in *Tjirmumuk* are 'wife's brother'/'sister's husband', 'wife's father'/'daughter's husband', 'wife's maternal uncle'/'niece's husband'.

True affines are exempt: 'there is an unwillingness to risk offending men intimately linked by actual marriages' (p. 72).

The prominence of *Tjirmumuk* in the Punj ceremony is consistent with the central role played by the brother-in-law. Each day at the ceremonial ground proceedings begin with a demonstration of unity and harmony, as the initiates sing together in a close-knit circle. The singing comes to an end with an exclamatory cry 'Karwadi' (secret name of the Mother). Immediately afterwards the choir breaks up as *Tjirmumuk* partners snatch at each other's genitals, trade sexual insults, and otherwise seek to outdo each other in outrageous persiflage.

Licensed obscenity between quasi-affines is not peculiar to the Murinbata (Hiatt 1965:60–62). Presumably it functions in some way as a counterpoint to the punctilio and reserve characteristic of relationships between true affines. Brothers-in-law are expected to be the best of friends.[7] Yet the subject they must never discuss, and that must never be discussed in their presence, is the very thing that unites them viz. the sexuality of the woman who is the wife of one and the sister of the other. The two aspects of the relationship, overt solidarity and unspoken sexual transactions, are thus beautifully symbolised in the 'intimacy, altruism and unison' (p. 155) of the choir and then parodied through the 'anti-structure' of ribaldry, horse-play and obscenity in *Tjirmumuk.*

Mime of the Blowfly

In Australia circular excavations on secret ceremonial grounds are often symbols of female reproductivity.[8] In the Punj rite, the hole is conceptualised as a nest or wallow in the sacrosanct place 'where the real presence of the Mother is supposed to manifest itself' (p. 124). Each day initiates cluster inside the excavation and emit the humming sound of the blowfly. The association is with rotting flesh (p. 73).

---

7 Stanner was classified as the 'brother-in-law' of his great friend Durmugam (Stanner 1979:83). See also Falkenberg 1979:47ff.

8 See below, p. 65. Also Roheim 1945.

We may infer, then, that the mime signifies the death of the Mother or, more precisely, the dissolution of links with the Mother's flesh as a condition of virility and admission to the male domain of the spirit. Such an inference entails an inversion of subject and object in Stanner's initial thesis: it is not Youth who is sacrificed to the Mother for the sake of the general good, but rather the Mother who is sacrificed by Youth in order to achieve Manhood.[9]

Sibling Incest

The most conspicuous behavioural element common to the Murinbata Rainbow Serpent Myth and its impoverished Wagaman and Nangiomeri variants (p. 191) is sibling incest.[10]In the Murinbata version, the Son consummates a lust for the Sisters in the immediate wake of circumcision (p. 196), then kills the Father. The myth thus stands as a regressive 'antithesis' to the transformative process; an acknowledgement at a psychological level of the 'primal' forces that need to be resisted and overcome if the journey from Mother and Sister to Wife is to be made successfully.[11]

9 I am grateful to my student Philip Taylor, who formulated this inversion in an essay on Stanner's theory of sacrifice in 1988.

10 In the Wagaman version, the Rainbow Serpent steals the wives of his brother-in-law, who presumably are his sisters. In the Nangiomeri version, the Rainbow Serpent's sisters desert their husband and return to their brother 'with sexual intent' (p. 193). Cf. Falkenberg 1962:192–93.

11 The myth of Kunmanggur is such obvious grist for the Freudian mill that one wonders whether it had anything to do with the fact that sometime during the 1950s Stanner drafted a polemic against Totem and Taboo (see Stanner 1982, together with Michael Young's editorial note). It is also worth noting the resemblance between Stanner's summary characterisation of Freudian psychology, which he rejects ('relations flawed through and through by ambivalence, domination, illusion, imbalance, instability, frustration, infantilism'; Stanner 1982:7) and the ontology he attributes to the Murinbata ('at the centre of things social, refuge and rottenness are found together ... an intuition of an integral moral flaw in human association'; see below, p. 124).

Theft of the Bullroarers

Kukpi the Black Snake is an archetypal woman who specialised in creating water (Falkenberg 1962:90) and killing men. She also possessed the bullroarers and sang the songs that are nowadays central to the Karwadi cult. The representation of Woman as monumentally untrustworthy if not treacherous, the primal theft of her sacred property for the purpose of male secret cults, and the infliction of cautionary sanctions on female pretenders together constitute a motif of world-wide distribution and critical significance in the comparative study of religion.[12]

Conclusion

Stanner's monograph *On Aboriginal Religion* is the most important account of an Aboriginal religion written in the modern period. Certainly, no other work has claimed my attention to such a degree. What I have written, however, is not meant to be definitive. In my exegesis I have tried to stay close to the spirit and substance of Stanner's argument, and in my interpretations I have tried to stay close to Aboriginal exegesis. Nevertheless, it is merely one way of reading the thesis and one way of making sense of the materials. I have no doubt there will be many others.

My deliberations, as set out somewhat laconically above, have raised in my mind the question whether Stanner's ontological formulations are superstructures ingeniously, but gratuitously, raised on the more prosaic foundations of rites of passage. Put another way, there is the possibility that the 'discovery' of a higher level of meaning in the mytho-ritual complex has been achieved at the cost of detaching semantics from pragmatics. Whatever awkward silences and inarticulateness are produced by the anthropological quest for a rational metaphysic (p. 307), Aboriginal men are unanimous in their

12 For two recent publications on this theme, see Hiatt 1979; Gewertz 1988.

affirmations that the liturgical arts are 'work' or 'business'; and that, in the case of the induction process under consideration, the object is to 'make men' (cf. Herdt 1982a). To argue that its purpose is to inculcate a world-view that the teachers themselves are unable to articulate seems prematurely adventurous.[3] If in the end we have to cut the cable and enter into free flight, so be it. Till then the sounder procedure is to work within a problematic anchored to exegeses offered in good faith by local authorities. From that perspective, the genius of Aboriginal religion may turn out to lie not in the field of ontology but of applied psychology.[13]

References

AVERY, J. 1985. 'The Law People'. Unpublished PhD thesis, University of Sydney.

BAAL, J. VAN 1971. *Symbols for Communication: an Introduction to the Anthropological Study of Religion*. Assen: van Gorcum.

BARWICK, D., J. BECKETT and M. REAY (eds). 1985. *Metaphors of Interpretation: Essays in Honour of W.E.H. Stanner*. Canberra: Australian National University Press.

BERN, J. 1979. 'Ideology and Domination: Towards a Reconstruction of Australian Aboriginal Social Formation'. *Oceania* 50:118–32.

BERNDT, R. 1951. *Kunapipi: A Study of an Australian Religious Cult*. Melbourne: Cheshire.

CHARLES, L. 1946. 'Growing up through Drama'. *Journal of American Folklore* 59:247–62.

13 With regard to the initiatory complex, induction techniques take effect at three inter-related levels: the re-orientation of libido away from prohibited close female kin towards potential spouses and the male cult (e.g. Roheim 1945; Morton 1985; Avery 1985; Hiatt 1987; cf. Herdt 1982b); the firm delineation of masculine identity (e.g. van Gennep 1960; Mol 1982; cf. Poole 1982); and reproduction of the power and privileges of senior males in relation to knowledge, wealth and women (Maddock 1972; Bern 1979; Keen 1986; cf. Langness 1974).

ELIADE, M. 1973. *Australian Religions: An Introduction.* Ithaca: Cornell University Press.

FALKENBERG, J. 1962. *Kin and Totem: Group Relations of Australian Aborigines in the Port Keats District.* New York: Humanities Press.

FALKENBERG, A. and J. FALKENBERG. 1981. *The Affinal Relationship System: A New Approach to Kinship and Marriage Among the Australian Aborigines at Port Keats.* Oslo: Universitetsforlaget.

GENNEP, A. VAN. 1960. *The Rites of Passage.* London: Routledge & Kegan Paul.

GEWERTZ, D. 1988. *Myths of Matriarchy Reconsidered.* Sydney: Oceania Publications.

HAMILTON, A. 1972. 'Aboriginal Man's Best Friend?', *Mankind* 8:287–95.

HAVEMEYER, L. 1916. *The Drama of Savage Peoples.* New Haven: Yale University Press.

HERDT, G. (ed.). 1982a. *Rituals of Manhood: Male Initiation in Papua New Guinea.* Berkeley: University of California Press.

HERDT, G. 1982b. 'Fetish and Fantasy in Sambia Initiation' in G. Herdt (ed.), *Rituals of Manhood: Male Initiation in Papua New Guinea*, pp. 44–98. Berkeley: University of California Press.

HIATT, L. 1971. 'Secret Pseudo-procreation Rites among the Australian Aborigines' in L. Hiatt and C. Jayawardena (eds), *Anthropology in Oceania: Essays Presented to Ian Hogbin*, pp. 77–88. Sydney: Angus & Robertson.

HIATT, L. 1975a. 'Introduction' in L. Hiatt (ed.), *Australian Aboriginal Mythology*, pp. 1–23. Canberra: Australian Institute of Aboriginal Studies.

HIATT, L. 1975b. 'Swallowing and Regurgitation in Australian Myth and Rite' in L. Hiatt (ed.), *Australian Aboriginal Mythology: Essays in Honour of W.E.H. Stanner*, pp. 143–62. Canberra: Australian Institute of Aboriginal Studies.

HIATT, L. 1979. 'Queen of Night, Mother-Right, and Secret Male Cults' in R. Hook (ed.), *Fantasy and Symbol: Studies in Anthropological Interpretation*, pp. 247–66. London: Academic Press.

HIATT, L. 1987. 'Freud and Anthropology' in D. Austin-Broos (ed.), *Creating Culture: Profiles in the Study of Culture*, pp. 89–106. Sydney: Allen & Unwin.

KEEN, I. 1986. 'Stanner on Aboriginal Religion', *Canberra Anthropology* 9:26–50.

KOEPPING, K-P. 1981. 'Religion in Aboriginal Australia', *Religion* 11:367–91.

LANGNESS, L. 1974. 'Ritual Power and Male Domination in the New Guinea Highlands', *Ethos* 2:189–212.

LÉVI-STRAUSS, C. 1969. *The Elementary Structures of Kinship*. London: Eyre and Spottiswoode.

MADDOCK, K. 1972. *The Australian Aborigines: A Portrait of their Society*. London: Allen Lane.

MADDOCK, K. 1985. 'Sacrifice and other Models in Australian Aboriginal Ritual' in D. Barwick, J. Beckett and M. Reay (eds), *Metaphors of Interpretation: Essays in Honour of W.E.H. Stanner*. Canberra: Australian National University Press.

MEGGITT, M. 1965. 'The Association between Australian Aborigines and Dingoes' in A. Leeds and A.P. Vayda (eds), *Man, Culture and Animals: the Role of Animals in Human Ecological Adjustments*, pp. 7–26. Washington D.C.: American Association Advancement Science.

MOL, H. 1982. *The Firm and the Formless*. Waterloo: Wilfred Laurier University Press.

MORPHY, H. 1988. 'Religion' in R. Berndt and R. Tonkinson (eds), *Social Anthropology and Australian Aboriginal Studies: A Contemporary Overview*, pp. 239–66. Canberra: Aboriginal Studies Press.

MORTON, J. 1985. 'Sustaining Desire'. Unpublished PhD thesis, Australian National University.

1987. 'Singing Subjects and Sacred Objects: More on Munn's "Transformation of Subjects into Objects" in Central Australian Myth', *Oceania* 58:100–18.

POOLE, F. 1982. 'The Ritual Forging of Identity' in G. Herdt (ed.), *Rituals of Manhood: Male Initiation in Papua New Guinea*, pp. 99–154. Berkeley: University of California Press.

ROHEIM, G. 1925. *Australian Totemism: A Psycho-analytic Study in Anthropology*. London: Cass.

ROHEIM, G. 1945. *The Eternal Ones of the Dream*. New York: International Universities Press.

ROHEIM, G. 1974. *Children of the Desert*. New York: Basic Books.

SPENCER, B. and GILLEN, F. 1899. *The Native Tribes of Central Australia*. London: Macmillan.

STANNER, W. 1933. 'The Daly River Tribes', *Oceania* 3:377–405.

STANNER, W. 1936a. 'A Note on Djamindjung Kinship and Totemism', *Oceania* 6:441–51.

STANNER, W. 1936b. 'Murinbata Kinship and Totemism', *Oceania* 7:186–216.

STANNER, W. 1937. 'Aboriginal Modes of Address and Reference in the North-West of the Northern Territory', *Oceania* 7:300–15.

STANNER, W. 1956. 'The Dreaming. In T. Hungerford', (ed.), *Australian Signposts: An Anthology Edited for the Canberra Fellowship of Australian Writers*, pp. 51–65. (Reprinted 1979, 23–40.) Melbourne: Cheshire.

STANNER, W. 1958. 'Continuity and Change among the Aborigines', *Australian Journal of Science* 21:99–109. (Reprinted 1979, 41–66.)

STANNER, W. 1960. 'Durmugam, a Nangiomeri' in J. Casagrande (ed.), *In the Company of Man*. (Reprinted 1979, 67–105.) New York: Harper.

STANNER, W. 1961. 'On the Study of Aboriginal Religion', Unpublished ms, Australian Institute of Aboriginal Studies, 18pp.

STANNER, W. 1979. 'Big Sunday at Peppiminarti', Unpublished ms, Australian Institute of Aboriginal Studies, 21pp.

STANNER, W. 1979. *White Man Got No Dreaming: Essays 1938–73.* Canberra: Australian National University Press.

STANNER, W. 1982. 'On Freud's *Totem and Taboo*', *Canberra Anthropology* 5:1–7.

STREHLOW, T. 1947. *Aranda Traditions.* Melbourne: Melbourne University Press.

SWAIN, T. 1985. *Interpreting Aboriginal Religion: An Historical Account.* Adelaide: Australian Association Study of Religions.

TURNER, V. 1982. *From Ritual to Theatre: The Human Seriousness of Play.* New York: PAJ Publications.

TURNER, V. 1986. *The Anthropology of Performance.* New York: PAJ Publications.

WATERMAN, P. 1987. *A Tale-Type Index of Australian Aboriginal Oral Narratives.* Helsinki: Suomalainen Tiedeakatemia.

WORMS, E. 1963. 'Religion' in H. Sheils (ed.), *Australian Aboriginal Studies*, pp. 231–47. Melbourne: Oxford University Press.

YENGOYAN, A. 1979. 'Economy, Society and Myth in Aboriginal Australia' in B. Siegel (ed.), *Annual Review of Anthropology* 8:393–415.

ON ABORIGINAL RELIGION

By

W. E. H. STANNER

Reader in Comparative Social Institutions
Australian National University

Introduction

W.E.H Stanner

The six articles that form this Monograph are intended to be a contribution towards a general re-examination of Australian Aboriginal religion. That larger task will require the efforts of many scholars. The usefulness of the present work may be increased if I make as clear as I can the viewpoint for which it was written.

The history of the study of primitive, in particular, Aboriginal religion suggested that I should observe certain conditions. In the first place, it seemed advisable to concentrate on a region since there have been few really intensive studies of regional cults, and a better perspective on the continent as a whole can be attained only in that way. Secondly, I thought I should take Aboriginal religion as significant in its own right and make it the primary subject of study, rather than study it, as was done so often in the past, mainly to discover the extent to which it expressed or reflected facts and preoccupations of the social order. That is, study it *as* religion and not as a mirror of something else. It seemed desirable, thirdly, to avoid entanglement with any particular definition or theory of religion and, lastly, to resist any temptation to draw from the single instance any conclusions about all religion. Anyone familiar with the literature on the subject will agree that a good case can be made for such limitations.

Many general statements about the Aborigines rest on a narrow basis of exiguous facts, sometimes on no factual basis at all. That is especially true of statements about their religious life. More intensive regional study cannot alone correct the misunderstandings. A certain reformulation of the whole inquiry is also necessary. For example, it used to be supposed that the Aborigines had nothing worthy of the name of religion. When that viewpoint became modified there was a tendency to assume that the facts could be exhausted by a study of totemism, magic and ritual. Sociologism and psychologism then further confused the issue. They supposed, by and large, that in a scientific study religion must be the dependent variable: the true aim of inquiry was to discover the effect *in* religion of some set of social or psychic variables. The second condition of my work was thus an effort to correct what I believe to be three mistakes: that of theistic-philosophical narrowness; the wrongful identification with totemism, magic and ritual; and the disrespect involved in giving religious facts less importance in inquiry than they actually have in Aboriginal life. Whether the third condition is a practicable one is open to argument. It seems to me that most anthropologists know well enough, for working purposes, what they and their professional associates mean by 'religion.' Slips apart, I have tried to use the word indicatively, for the content of a devotional life. Beyond that, if pressed by the definition-minded to say what I 'really mean' by 'religion,' I would be inclined to point to the facts of Murinbata culture and say: 'That kind of belief and conduct.' It seems to me that definitions of religion—that is, of all religions in all places and at all times—are doubtfully a matter for anthropology at all. No doubt it will one day contribute some of the adequate predicates which philosophers of religion will generalise. But if it is to do so it will certainly have to stop treating religion as the dependent variable of study. As to the last condition, the disinclination to draw from the study any conclusions about religion-in-general, I think I need only say that, like most anthropological studies, the present work deals with some only of the facts of a total culture, examines them partially, and leaves most of its conclusions in suspense.

Anthropology, as an academic discipline, is plainly in transition. I have made as clear as I can the theoretical conceptions that now seem to me important. As far as possible, I have separated the three things—fact, viewpoint and interpretation—which must be separated if others are to use my work. The main theoretical interest seems to me to stem from the changed 'frame of reference.' The general idea of studying human affairs as a dynamic or developmental structure of operations, exemplified in transactions about things of value, has a higher utility and a greater potential than the idea of a persisting structure of enduring relations between persons in role-positions. It forces an analyst to study the historical dimension or, if that cannot be done for lack of evidence, to explain stability, not to assume it. It requires him to develop concepts to apply to the ways in which persons 'work' or 'operate' on other persons, or on things, even on themselves, to obtain valued objects of life. That step alone, if persisted in, would transform anthropology from what it has often seemed to be—a dialogue over abstract nouns—into so to speak a conjugation of verbs. Many younger anthropologists are weary of 'function,' 'process,' 'institution,' 'status,' 'role,' 'position' and other such abstractions. An 'operational' anthropology would substitute a study of real relations—giving, taking, sharing, loving, bewitching, fighting, initiating—and make human sense of their cultural varieties. A direct effect would be a growing awareness that no human social relation can be studied effectively unless it is conceptualised as, at the least, a tetrad: A to B concerning O in respect of Z. The so-called 'dyadic' and 'triadic' relations, A to B, or A to B and C, or some other combination, with no object of life, or situation, or value stipulated, are too virtualistic for profitable study. Hence, the theoretical importance of the relations of association in which classes of persons transact the business of life. It is essentially the emptiness of 'interaction' as distinct from the concreteness of 'transaction' that has made anthropology so often seem abstract and unlifelike. On the other hand, the operational-transactional approach requires that social reality be followed closely; if models are used they must be models of or after reality—'perceptual' models of identifiable real processes, such as initiation. By such means it is easier to find in what respect the processes are 'integrative' and what it is they integrate. The initiations here examined are good examples of processes with integrative functions, and also with structures of such a kind that they allow comparisons between things that at first seemed incomparable. It is an essential purpose of anthropology to make such comparisons and the fact that they can be made in the field of religion, and between religion and the secular field, is an interesting illustration of the value of making a few simple changes in analytical procedure.

It is plainly a mistake to allow inquiry to be ruled by the philosophical notion that religious or metaphysical objects do not exist. They *do* exist for many peoples under study, and the facts of study are what they are because of that. To ignore it is to manipulate the facts illegitimately, in the interest of what may be called philosophical evangelism. If the facts are such, then they must be studied as such.

To deal with many-variable relations in terms of too few variables is also mistaken. It can lead only to stilted artificiality, which has been the fate of the conversion of what, at the least, are tetrads into dyads and triads. My present opinion is that anthropology will not be able to make any serious claim to being a theoretical as well as a realistic discipline until it has found a way to analyse the functional relationships between six variables—(1) operational roles, (2) operations, (3) situations, (4) objects of life, (5) ends, and (6) values. That is obviously a formidable task. In these papers I have taken a restricted field of religious transactions and shown something of the play between (1), (2), (3) and (4). That amounts only to a small expansion and redistribution of conventional emphases of study.

The interest of the transaction concept is that it is a transective concept. That is, it can be used so to speak to cut through the analytic categories 'political,' 'economic,' 'religious,' and etc. Where 'interaction' merely straddles, 'transaction' makes a section. It 'says' several things, which are logically connectable, about any transaction in all fields of life, whether 'religious' or 'economic' or 'political.' Since all things must be studied, at least in the first place, through their structure, it enables one to compare the distinctive structures of operations exemplified in all kinds of transactions in all fields of social life. That seems to me one of the primary objects of anthropology. It does not appear possible of attainment by conventional concepts and existing analytical procedures. The religious transactions are of course the hardest to study, which is why I began with them. They turned out to have an extremely interesting structure, distributed far more widely than I had thought possible.

I

The Lineaments of Sacrifice

1. Introduction

One of the elementary forms of the religious life which Émile Durkheim did not analyse completely in his classical study of the Aborigines is that of sacrifice. Its lineaments show plainly through the cultus of the bull-roarer among the north-western tribes.

The authorities whom Durkheim consulted were not familiar with this region and in any case were not always of the best. Their information was very uneven and much of it had been collected under the influence of ideas which now seem mistaken. Moreover, there are very considerable institutional differences between Central Australia and North Australia, of which he could have known little.

In this article I shall show that there are some very striking resemblances between the form of a bullroarer ceremony and the form of sacrificial ceremonies in more developed religion. The resemblances are not simply those of analogy. The two types are homomorphic and in a deeper sense, which I do not explore, may be isomorphic as well. To reveal the resemblances one must abstract more severely than is perhaps the rule, and also with reference to somewhat different conceptions from those which Durkheim used. The plan I follow is to isolate the operations which the Aboriginal celebrants perform on things, including persons, in the ceremony and to compare the operations, in a general way, with those which are most plain in sacrifice.

Inquiries which I have made into the cultus that surrounds the bullroarer among the Aboriginal peoples of the north-western part of the Northern Territory lead me to believe that what I have found to be the case there may equally well have been so in other regions. If the contention can be substantiated then an extensive re-study of the religious institutions of the Aborigines might well be made. A tradition of study which is of course a good deal older than Durkheim, but which was given by him a formulation of immense influence, would then invite a reconsideration.

It is possible to study the structure of sacrifice as a type of activity from two points of view. First, one may try to find the parts or elements which are organised into a system of activity conceived in terms of human duties: in short, as a system of role-enactments from positions in a social structure. Second, one may try to find the parts or elements conceived as human operations on things, including persons. The two viewpoints are of course connected but may be kept analytically distinct. It is from the second viewpoint that this article is written. The first is a more 'sociological' point of view: an inquiry connected closely with a formed theory about the general character of human society. The second is more akin, at least to begin with, to a natural philosophy or natural history of a type of human conduct.

At the level of natural history the main problems are those of clear description and fruitful classification. In Section 2 I have tried to give as compact a description as possible of the bullroarer ceremony known as *Karwadi* (its secret name) or *Punj* (its public name) among the Murinbata people. But description and classification are not really separable, and classification is or is not fruitful *for* a theoretical intention. The description offered in Section 2 has therefore been made up with the idea of isolating, as clearly as possible; the operations on things, including persons, which may be seen to take place in the ceremonies, or which the Aborigines say take place. One discovery comes very quickly: things are done—i.e. operations are carried out—which the Aborigines perceive only dimly, if at all, since they can offer no explanation of any kind as to the intention of the acts. In such circumstances there seem to be only two legitimate courses: to give a just-so account of what occurs, or to compare the facts with some well-known or at least better-known model of human conduct to which analytical attention has been given. It is obviously absurd to try to relate what is not yet classified to a total system of life—say, to the 'culture' or 'social structure' of the Murinbata—for part of that total system is the very conduct to which not even a good name can yet be given. It was in the search for a well-known or better-known model that, after a good deal of experiment, I found the model of sacrificial conduct most suitable.

Now, the Karwadi ceremonies are very clearly *initiations*, and the Aborigines themselves describe them as such, though in their own words. But the idea of initiation belongs to a family of conceptions by which I do not wish to be limited. It has to do with the socialisation of persons, and while that is certainly a true description of *Karwadi*, the ceremony is not *only* an initiation. It also seemed to me to make for much difficulty in dealing with those features of the ceremony of cryptic or implicit intention. The Aborigines say that the intent of *Karwadi* is to make the young men 'understand'. My problem lay with the features which the instructors themselves did not understand, and thus could not teach. I found that the type of conduct which best fitted all the features were that of sacrificial activity.

When the institutions of sacrifice, bloody or unbloody, are examined the empirical elements may be described as follows. (a) Something of positive value, but of such a substance and nature that it is judged inherently acceptable to its receiver, a spiritual personage, is set aside to an end beyond the common ends of life in such a way that one may speak of its sacralisation or consecration to that end. Something, that is, is made sacred by men. (b) The sacrifice, the thing to be sacrificed, is offered direct or after symbolistical activities have been carried out in such a way that the substance but not the nature of the sacrifice is transformed. One may speak of this as the immolation or destruction, or both, of the sacrificial object. (c) The sacrifice, having been received, or being supposed to have been received, is returned to the offerers with its nature now transformed, and (d) as yield or fruit of sacrifice it is then shared between those who sustained the loss of the sacrificial object. That loss has been requited by a gain, but of an unlike kind, the margin of gain being a motive of the total act.

Such seems to be the kind of core around which the institutions of sacrifice arise, cloaking the core with a rich covering of metaphor, symbolism and metaphysical interpretation. The spiritual insights and æsthetic capacities of impassioned human natures then glorify the cloak. But it is with the core-elements, the basic operations, that I am concerned. The setting aside, the offering, the return, and the sharing are all in some sense the observable acts of actual persons. If these can be found in that order within a well-unified total activity, and if to them can be added an intelligible account of some kind of transformation which is conceived to occur, then a not unpersuasive correspondence has been shown with what is ordinarily called 'sacrifice'. But the extreme unsuitability of that word and its idea should be clear. What it denotes is a gainful transaction between men and their divinities. The word 'sacrifice' mainly denotes what men lose and but vaguely connotes what they gain, and in so doing it puts men's conduct in a better light in their own eyes. But that is perhaps only Gresham's Law at work in the field of connotations.

It is my contention that the *Karwadi* ceremony conforms generically to the operational character of sacrifice as I have sketched it. I do not maintain that there is an exact congruence, but a likeness which cannot be dismissed out of hand and can in fact be shown to be homologous. The fundamental operations, while undoubtedly there, are caught up as a core within a very different cover, and the pattern woven into the cover is an unaccustomed one. Nevertheless, there is an homology.

The *Karwadi* ceremony may be described as a liturgical transaction, within a totemic idiom of symbolism, between men and a spiritual being on whom they conceive themselves to be dependent. The motive of gain is the continuation of a plan of life, given once-for-all in The Dreaming, but in continuous danger of corruption by those who in the course of nature must carry it on. I put this forward as an irresistible interpretation of the symbolism which is enacted day by day in the ceremony. It is this which the older Aborigines try to make youth understand.

The facts of the ceremony are dense with meanings. In this article I can make only a general approach to some of them. The facts are objective enough but they have to be constructed in a certain fashion in order to be understood. Part of the article is therefore given over to the question of the arrangement of the facts for interpretation.

2. The Ceremony of Punj or Karwadi

The *Karwadi* ceremony is extremely sacred and secret. It centres on the showing and presentation of bullroarers to young men who have been circumcised some years before. The bullroarers (*ŋawuru*) have the higher degree of sacredness which we may call sacrosanctity. The word *Karwadi* is the secret name of a provenant spirit also described as The Mother of All or as The Old Woman. The doctrine about her is neither clear nor well-evolved, but the attitude towards her may well be called one of holy dread. She is thought to exercise a rather frightening care of men. The bullroarer is her emblem; the sound it makes when swung is the sign of her real presence; and the emblem is at the same time a vehicle on which complex symbolical conceptions of her are projected.

Ceremonies of the kind are well known in the Australian literature. Some of them have been referred to as fertility cults, but I prefer to describe them as cults of mystery. There is some warrant for such a description in the way in which the Aborigines themselves speak of them: as things they do not really understand but believe in deeply. The Aboriginal doctrine may be summed up in two statements which are accepted as great truths: in the beginning of things, life and death, and all things connected with them, took on the characters they now have because of marvellous events which took place once-for-all; living men should, indeed must, commemorate those events, and keep in touch with the consequences, by acts to signify and symbolise what happened and, somehow, keeps on happening. By such means men 'follow up The Dreaming' through a repeated memorial of it.

Each celebration of the ceremony, which used to occur annually, took from one to two months to complete, depending on the will of the ritual leader (*kirman*), on the number of candidates for admission to the secrets, and on a range of circumstances of a practical kind. There were both secret and public activities. In those which were secret there were due parts allotted to the ritual leader, to senior assistants, to a chorus of singers and instrumentalists, to a body of dancers and actors, and to the initiates. Much the same parts were observed in the public or external activities, but then the women and children—rigidly excluded from the secret phases on pain of the most severe sanctions—were given the somewhat negative duties of an audience.

It was customary for all clans over a large neighbourhood to attend each *Punj*, and thus members of both patrilineal moieties. However, it would not be accurate to speak of 'tribal' gatherings for, in a region of many small tribes, *Punj* might be celebrated by adjacent clans speaking distinct languages. Visitors from distant clans were frequent and welcome. But the two moieties were always represented, members of each having duties towards the other. Unless both moieties were present activities absolutely necessary to *Punj* could not be carried out.

The proceedings had a well-standardised form which I shall now set out. The only terms which need be explained are the following:

***ŋudanu*:** the public name of the ceremonial ground. There is no secret name.

***Kirman*:** the ritual leader. The word is of Djamindjuŋ origin but has been taken over by the Murinbata.

***Merkenu*:** the original Murinbata term for the ritual leader.

***Wanangal*:** wise men with mystical and healing powers who were looked on by their enemies as warlocks.

***Da mambana*:** a hidden place near *ŋudanu* where initiates were secreted.

***Kadu Punj*:** men who have been fully initiated.

***Mada ŋanaŋur*:** the centre of a formally-arranged camp, which has a circular or horse-shoe shape.

The following account may be understood as (a) a narrative of things taking place in the order indicated, (b) my own division of them into phases which are actually observable and, where indicated, recognised or named by the Aborigines themselves, and (c) a minimum of explanatory comment.

1. A few years after circumcision when youths are—in the eyes of mature men—egotistical and refractory because they do not yet understand the restraints of adult life, and do not listen to the prudent counsel of age, they are asked to submit themselves to the disciplines of *Punj* and to learn its secrets. No force is used as at circumcision and pre-pubertal initiation. The youths are offered a discipline which is at the same time a privilege and a means of acquiring status. But acceptance of the discipline is a virtual necessity, for there is a background of mystical as well as human threat.

Secret discussions take place between the older men, including the ritual leaders, and the father of any youth of appropriate age. With parental consent, an older man, usually a classificatory father, having asked the youths if they wish to come, takes them to *ŋudanu* on an afternoon of secret appointment. Here they find all the adult men, known as *kadu punj* (lit. 'persons', 'secret, forbidden, dangerous affairs') already assembled. The youths are gathered together into a tight circle of men who sit, facing inward, while a secret song is sung. The song, repeated many times until sundown, closes with an exclamatory cry—*Karwadi, yoi!* It is the first occasion on which the youths have heard the secret name of The Mother of All. The *yoi!* is an expletive which is untranslatable. It seems to have the character of salutation, perhaps invocation.

At sundown the men and youths return to the main camp which, because of the presence of many clans, takes a formal arrangement as a huge circle of nuclear families divided by fires. The youths are placed within the circle in a position known as *mada ŋanaŋur.* They are not permitted to speak to their patrikin or matrikin, and are required to act quietly and modestly. They eat by themselves, and are handed their needs by old *Kadu Punj.*

When the morning star appears, they are wakened noiselessly by their escort, and are led to *ŋudanu* as dawn is breaking. From now on until the *Karwadi* ceremony is completed they are not spoken to or if at all avoidable even seen by anyone disbarred from *ŋudanu*.

2. The proceedings now assume a somewhat different form. The singing starts as soon as all are assembled but a custom known as *Tjirmumuk* goes on at the same time. It is a kind of horseplay between the moieties or, rather, between individuals in them. Men who stand to each other as cross-cousins, wife's brothers, wife's fathers, and mother's brothers, push and jostle one another, snatch away small personal possessions, pluck at each others' genitals, and in laughing voice shout things which would ordinarily be obscene, embarrassing, and hurtful.[1] The custom is akin to but not the same as *murin tjiwititj* (lit. 'words', 'teasing'), a joking relationship which is a well-marked feature of the regional culture. The initiates watch but do not take part.

When everyone tires of *Tjirmumuk* the men gather the youths within their circle and, without further interruption, sing the song of yesterday. At about mid-afternoon a pretext is made that food is needed and the initiates' escort takes them away to look for it. When *ŋudanu* is out of eyeshot but within hailing distance he commands them to wait. He tells them that they are now at *da mambana*, a hidden and secret place to which they are to be restricted until told to leave.

From this time on their personal names are not used. Anyone who speaks to or about them calls them *ku were* (lit. 'flesh', 'wild dog'). Any flesh which is *ku* cannot be that of persons or *kadu*. The youths are not only made nameless but are symbolically no longer human either. More, their personal ornaments are taken from them, and they are required to be naked. All the external marks or signs of social humanity are thus taken away.

3. Meanwhile at *ŋudanu* the initiated men are preparing the next phase of the ceremony.

---

1 I should here explain that close affines are not attacked in these ways. Men direct their attentions to more distant classificatory relations. There is an unwillingness to risk offending men intimately linked by actual marriages.

The youths have been told that they will be swallowed alive by *Karwadi* and then vomited up. As they wait they are told nothing of what is actually in store for them. At a signal from *ŋudanu*, when all is ready, the escort orders them to stand, to form a line with hands clasped behind their backs, to look fixedly at the ground with heads bent, and to follow him. At least outwardly humbled and often intensely frightened, they make their way to the company of *Kadu Punj*.

Here they find all the initiated men crouched in a circular excavation in the ground. The men, barely recognisable under their cosmetic ochres and bodily decorations of feathers, down and fire-dried leaves, form a close cluster, all facing inwards. They alternately bend until their heads touch—each man being upon his knees—and then sit erect to quiver their shoulders in a quick rhythmic unison. When they bend they make minute restless movements, giving out all the while a low murmurous hum. When they rise the violence of their movements shakes off a small cloud of dried ochre and fragments of their decorations. The youths are taken into the centre of the circle, told to kneel, and to imitate the actions of the others.

This is the mime of the blowfly, with which the proceedings start *every* day, for the whole duration of the celebration, *after* the custom of *Tjirmumuk* has been observed. The esoteric symbolism is *not* explained to the initiates, for no one seems able to interpret it. All that is known, or is now discoverable, is that the proceedings *must* start every day with *Karaŋuk*, the mime of the blowfly, which goes to rotting flesh.

The singing of a song has been carried on meanwhile by a small group of singers, who also use tapping-sticks. When the mime has been repeated several times the singing stops abruptly. The circle breaks up.

4. The escort commands the youths to stand up in front of men—in relationship their *naŋgun* or potential wives' brothers—who have containers of blood. As yet the initiates do not know that the blood has been drawn by right and duty from their *naŋgun*. They are allowed to suppose that it is the blood of The Mother. The *naŋgun* smear them from head to foot with the blood: eyes, ears, nostrils, lips and nose are

all liberally covered, but no special attention is paid to any organ or region except, perhaps, the head.

While this is done the assembled men break into a rhythmic chorus of sound, somewhat reminiscent of birdsong and animal noise. As soon as the blood has been applied fully the youths are told to stand in the heat and smoke of a fire until they are dry. The singing is resumed and goes on for some time.

The sun now being near the horizon, the whole assembly returns with loud cries to the main camp. The naked, blood-caked initiates are kept at a distance, where they cannot see or be seen, while the initiated men leap over the heads of people at the circle of fires and, in the centre, once again act out the custom of *Tjirmumuk*. On this occasion all the former scenes of horseplay are repeated but are dominated by the snatching of food from the classes of affines already mentioned. The aim is to take their food, gobble it with animalian sounds and gestures, and to prevent them if possible from doing the same. The noise and turbulence are extreme, but good-fellowship is nevertheless in evidence, and the bystanders laugh heartily throughout.

The camp settles down eventually. Later at night when the women and children are asleep or at least pretend to be, the escort brings the initiates to their position in the centre of the circle. The initiated men surround them in a cluster and sing over them for some time. With the morning star they are again led to *ŋudanu*.

5. The proceedings come to a climax of tension on this, the third day of the celebration.

Everything follows the pattern of the second day until the time of the anointing with blood. As this starts men in hiding nearby begin to sound bullroarers. The chorus of cries is maintained and, as the roar comes ever nearer, many of the older men, with shouts of well-simulated fear, cry '*Karwadi! Karwadi!* The Old Woman is calling'.[2]

2 One man told me that during the blooding he used to feel weak with fear of the unknown, and that his emotional stress was nearly unbearable when the bullroarers began to sound. It is not unknown for timid youths to lose control of their sphincter muscles.

The secret of the supposed voice of *Karwadi* is made known when the men with the bullroarers spring suddenly to view. The youths then learn also the true source of the blood. At this point the *naŋgun* come forward, each with a new-made bullroarer as a gift of right and duty. Each man rubs a bullroarer on the breast and across the loins of the initiate marked with his, the gift-giver's, blood and then thrusts it between the youth's thighs so that it stands up like an erect penis.

6. The tension over, the character of the celebration undergoes a certain alteration. The disciplines are not relaxed in any way; the youths are still *ku were*; they stay naked and unadorned and nameless; they go apart each day while the preparations for mime and dance are made; at night they wait outside the main camp until *Tjirmumuk* is over; they are escorted in to be sung over and, unspoken to by anyone but their escort, to sleep unwashed and caked with the blood of many anointings, and to leave again before the camp stirs. But now no attempts are made to put them in fear. They are treated rather more as equal fellows within an accepted restraint—and perhaps a mystery—of life. When they go to *da mambana* they take with them their bullroarers to hold across their loins while they wait for the summons to return.

Each day the opening *Tjirmumuk* and the mime of the blowfly are repeated, but are followed by a long series of totemistic mime-dances which have an invariant order. The atmosphere of fear and mystery gives way to one of joyousness in which dancers, singers and painters seem almost to vie with one another for an æsthetic triumph.

7. When the time comes for the ceremony to come to an end—the decision is the *kirman's*—the penultimate day is marked by a very wild demonstration of *Tjirmumuk* at *ŋudanu* and a dance of notable beauty. Again at the main camp the *Tjirmumuk* reaches an unusual vigour.

Early next morning the youths are taken a short distance away, not to *ŋudanu* itself, but to a place which is still considered *da mambana*. There they are blooded and, when they are dry, are given each (again by *naŋgun*) a forehead band, a hairbelt, a necklace and a genital covering. At this point they are judged to be no longer *ku were* but *yuŋuana*.

I have not found it possible to translate the term *yuŋuana* or even to decide as to its morphemes. It is used in direct address and also as a status-title, equivalent to and in many circumstances interchangeable with *Kadu Punj*. It is an absolute signification of mature male status, and is used of and about initiated men until they are of middle age.[3]

At the main camp, which is known in this context as *mununuk* (which connotes 'waiting, with gifts prepared'), the female kin and affines of the youths form an arcuate, seated cluster. The initiated men stand in two lines (one for each patrilineal moiety), with backs turned to *mununuk*. An old man stands at the end of each line farthest from the women and screens the scene with leafy bushes. The youths are ushered towards the old men who, on a signal, throw the leaves to one side. The lined men stand with legs apart and the youths, on hands and knees, crawl towards *mununuk* between the legs of the opposite moiety. Thus humbled, they make their way to their mothers: the conception that it is to the mothers they are going is explicit. As each youth emerges he sits momentarily in front of his mother, with his back to her, but not touching or touched by her, while all the women wail and lacerate their heads to draw blood. As soon as each *yuŋuana* has done so they return together between the legs of the immobile men and, when all have emerged at the other ends of the lines, all men rush together with loud shouts to *da mambana*.

No word has passed between the youths and any females since before *Punj* began, and none may pass for at least a week from the day of first return. The *yuŋuana* continue to stay outside the camp by day and to enter late at night, less escorted now than accompanied by older men. They sleep under the discipline of elders and between a stylised arrangement of fires.

---

3 I was myself inducted into the status of *yuŋguana* by the Nangiomeri, a neighbouring people of the same general culture, in 1934–35. I was addressed and referred to by the term until a few years ago when the sub-section term Djaŋnari, which can also be used as a name, was substituted for it. About the same age-limitation applies to *Kadu Punj* when used as a term of address or reference.

When a week has elapsed they are taken to bathe for the first time since *Punj* began. The last traces of blood are removed, and they are then brightly adorned with cosmetic ochres and charcoal according to a traditional design in which representations of the bullroarer are incorporated, but the import of this motif is (or is said to be) unknown to the women.

Thus marked by the insignia of their new state and position of life they return to the main camp. From now on they are free of it at all times except that they must stay only in their central place, and may not go near their mothers' fires. They may hunt where they will but must not visit other encampments. On their return from bathing, food and comforts are given them—with some show of formality, and with an exchange of set phrases—by their own and their classificatory parents.

After a lapse of two years they are judged ready to marry, but in the meantime have been able to gain experience of sexual intercourse by being allowed to avail themselves of the wives of older clan brothers.

I used earlier of this ceremony the phrase 'dense with meanings', and I do not imagine that many will dissent from its truth. There are thus very many aspects under any of which the facts might be raised for study. After I had worked methodically through a number of these, the question of the interpretation of the symbolistical activities, which seemed to me to have been left far too tacit but at the same time to have been drawn upon in a sidelong way, became unavoidable. It seemed to me possible and desirable to reverse the emphasis: that is, to allow the aspects of social structure, function and organisation, as they are ordinarily understood, to remain tacit, and to concentrate on the aspect of operations in the sense already given. The conceptions needed in this approach are dealt with later.

The construction which may then be put on the *Karwadi* ceremony is as follows.

The Aborigines conceive existence and being to be mysteries. The ancestors evidently understood them, but living men do not. Nevertheless, the mysteries are veritable, but men have only such information about them as the ancestors handed down in the tradition.

Part of the tradition concerns how things came to be as they are, and part concerns what living men must do to control a life so constituted.

In Aboriginal eyes all being, animal and human, corporeal and spiritual, has some sort of unity, but it is a unity of opposites and antitheses. At almost every point men's lives are in touch with this fact. There are both visible and invisible things of power. The invisible things, not less real or less powerful for their invisibility, continually irrupt into the familiar reality of life. At the same time men's this-worldly life is always at risk of disruption by the things men do in the ordinary course of living. Similar things were done by the ancestors with whom there is an unbroken continuity.

The continuity is historical, essential, substantial, and moral. *These* hills and waters of *these* names were made by *this* ancestor. *These* children were born through the action of spirits placed in the waters by *that* ancestor. The physical bodies of *these* men and *these* birds and animals have some kind of substantial identity which is timelessly true of all members of a totemic class constituted by events mentioned in the tradition. The relevance which one thing bears to another was thus *instituted* and made known. The plan of life constituted in this way has been maintained over time. Its continued maintenance is the guarantee of a social life in which relevances are understood, that is, of a moral order. The highest good of living men lies in the perpetuation of what has been found to be the guarantee.

The ancestors taught, and fathers from time out of mind have instructed their sons, that certain actions of *living* are to be carried out in certain ways. Among them are the acts or operations towards the invisible spiritual powers or personages on whom men depend and with whom they are genetically linked. The occasions of such operations arise when youth, because it possesses a nature continuous with that of the first men, is mindful to rebel against the moral system which the first men instituted, though why they did so is the mystery which the Aborigines say they believe but do not understand.

The metaphysic of life which is thus enacted is far from contemptible, and needs only words to evoke the meanings beneath the symbolisms.

The subject will be treated separately in a later article. The immediate problem is to present for interpretation, material which is intrinsically symbolical without mutilating it in the process. I have tried to do so in as neutral a way as I can devise by the use of a diagram (Fig. 1) with explanatory notes. The imagery is geometric but in many ways this seems an advantage.

The conventions of the figure are given in the accompanying notes, but one or two further comments may be made.

The four quadrants are logical divisions of the systems of coordinates and conceptual divisions of the operations, which are all—except for one, the fourth—actual happenings that may be seen. What results is an outline sketch of a model after reality, the reality being drastically simplified.

A time-sequence, a process or task which is assumed and completed, is transposed into a spatial sequence. The principal feature is the path or course of operations which it traces. Along this path older men who have authority to do so move young men from one locus and status to another.

The empirical study, the narrative, shows that certain constituent features of locus and status are changed by the operations in what seems an orderly way. The orderliness reveals the rationale of the operations, which are in a serial or end-to-end relation, a continuous purposive connection. The diagram, it is hoped, condenses the orderliness in such a way that the rationale is made more clear. The broad comparison with the elements of sacrifice is not a theory but an arrangement in the development of a theory.

Now, it will be noted that in the narrative there are eight sections, each representing a phase of the total ceremony. Only six operations are listed. This may seem to some an unhappy discrepancy. There is a very real difficulty on which I should like to comment.

In dealing with such a mass of particulars it is not easy to decide what to include or exclude. I do not think there is any significance in the figures eight and six. Evidently it is not possible to make the number of phases less than eight, and I would not contend a view that my own material shows that there are more than eight. That number seems to me a convenient division of the temporal sequence. I would concede, too, that there are probably many more than six operations. Those listed struck me as central and decisive. The Aborigines have an explicit formulation of all of them. As far as possible I have allowed myself to be guided by their conception. But consider the following problem.

After being made nameless and naked, and thus constituted as 'wild flesh', the youths are taken to the place where The Mother is said to manifest herself. They have a lively dread that they will actually be swallowed and vomited.[4] Now, when those with power force the powerless to go near a superior being, it is—at least in psycho-social terms—the making of a kind of offer. Is one then justified in constructing the facts to the shape of a precious offering? I have no evidence that any such idea is present to the conscious minds of the Aborigines and, for my own part, would say that the construction is quite unjustified. But the same issue arises in half a dozen other parts of the ceremony. I think the point is that we are dealing with a deposit or stock of intuitions only in part revealed by external acts and formed ideas. And of that part which is drawn upon a still smaller part is made explicit. I have tried to cling to the operations which are sharply formulated by the Aborigines themselves, but it is not possible to watch the ceremony without becoming aware of the loom of others. The phases and operations as I represent them are thus not congruent or equalised and, in my understanding, do not have to be.

---

4 Even when they learn that their fear is groundless many youths—at least many have told me so—go on for days or weeks feeling that they may have been lulled into a false security. Several I know could not bring themselves to believe that The Mother did not exist. Full knowledge brought immense relief but I saw no signs of the cynicism one might have expected. Evidently the interior life is so deepened that the inculcation of fear comes to seem to them just and wise.

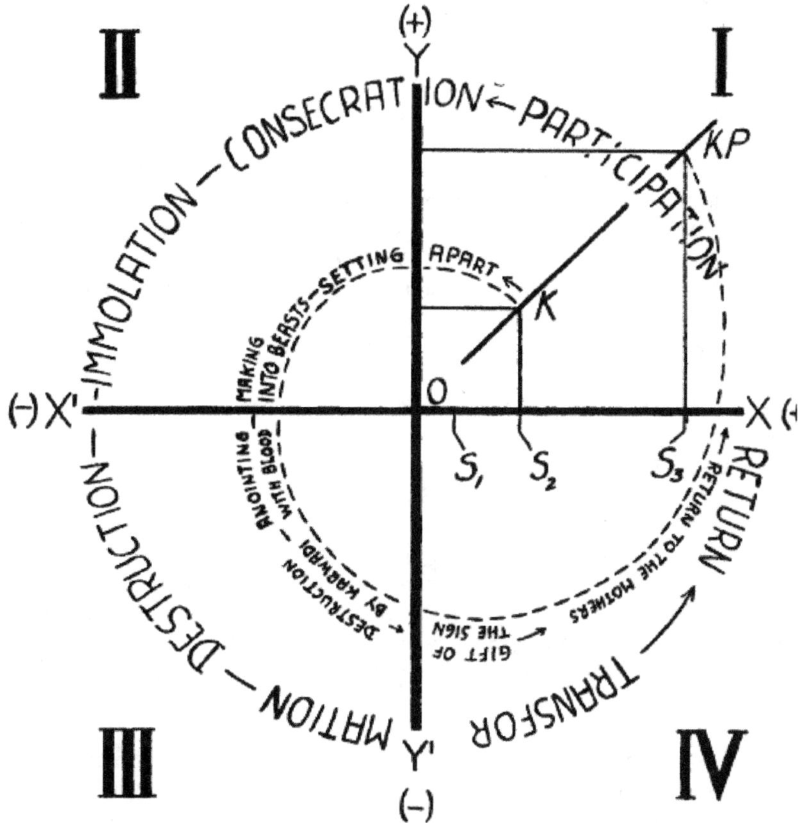

Figure 1. A Comparison of *Punj* with Sacrifice

Fig. 1 is an attempt to use visual means to compare the *Punj* ceremony with the operational structure of sacrifice, no particular sacrifice or tradition being specified.

The *Punj* ceremony is reduced by severe abstraction to two features: (a) a prominent sequence of *acts* or *operations*, and (b) a class of *external signs* exhibited by initiates before, during, and after the ceremony. The acts and the signs are real or objective features in phenomenal association. The invariance, or apparent invariance, of the association suggests a functional interdependence. The use of coordinate systems is thus justified. To use more than two-dimensional coordinate systems is impracticable at present.

From general knowledge it is known that the external signs signify status, and that one of the primary objects of the ceremony is the initiation of youths into a higher status. The coordinates allow us to study, at least with a certain visual clarity, the sign-variation which takes place when transitive operations are set in course with the object of moving youths to a higher social status. We may think of status as a locus in a system of life with associated powers, privileges, duties and a given magnitude of social value. The figure, if logically constructed from clear concepts, should also allow us to look for types of facts which otherwise may not suggest themselves, and to be sharply aware of the need of true connectivity between facts and concepts.

In Fig. 1 the OX axis is used to mark off imaginary positions to each of which corresponds one status-degree and one only. OX is thus a status-scale, reading from O to X. Any point between O and X corresponds to a positive status. The three positions marked S_1, S_2, S_3 correspond in that order to the status achieved at pre-pubertal, pubertal and *Punj* initiation. The facts of *Punj* show that the Aborigines conceive of *negative* status, though their only formulation is symbolical. OX is therefore extended to X´. The hypothetic scale of negative status thus reads from O to X´, in the direction opposite to the positive scale. No negative positions are marked on OX´ in the figure since they are unnecessary for my purpose, but it is possible to do so with warranty of fact.

The OY axis is used to mark off positions to each of which corresponds a given cluster of external signs of status. OY is thus a sign-scale, such that all the Aboriginal world knows immediately, by seeing or otherwise apprehending such a cluster that it signifies a man of a given status and of no other status. In order not to overcrowd the diagram I have not made any entries on OY. The text, I hope, will have made their character sufficiently clear. OY is extended to OY´ in order to provide for the fact of *negative* signs, so that its hypothetical scale reads from O to Y´. The negative scale is left empty for the same reason, and with the same rider, as in OX´.

There are thus four quadrants (I, II, III, IV) of the plane of the figure. Any position in any of the quadrants can be given sets of coordinates within the postulates used, and each set will differ from every other set, and have one of four sets of characteristics: in I (+ +), in II (– +), in III (– –) and in IV (+ –). The two points K and KP in quadrant I denote the locus in the Murinbata system of life (to the extent to which status and signs of status characterise it) of circumcised boys and of men initiated into *Punj*. The coordinates of each locus or position, made in the usual way by ordinate and abscissa in each case, in part *define* each locus and in part *describe* it.

The dotted line drawn anti-clockwise from K to KP is the continuous course of acts or operations, indicated by the script, in the actual order in which they occur, but here somewhat arbitrarily named. To move, within the conventions of the figure, from K to KP, and to pass through all the other quadrants, implies *logically* certain correlated changes of sign and status. Any utility the figure has rests on the correspondence which can be shown to exist between such logical requirements and empirical changes which occur in the course of the ceremony. It is my impression that there is a high correspondence.

I have found the coordinate-type of arrangement of much use in field-situations when, sometimes from over-familiarity with certain facts, and sometimes from their novelty, the puzzles arise which are so inseparable from the nature of the task. With few books and no colleagues at hand, one's mind stales and loses sharpness. The coordinates do not and cannot explain anything but they allow data to be arranged so that one sees more clearly the locus and nature of the puzzles.

The high rationality of Aboriginal customs can be shown by such means. Customs of license, avoidance and joking (which are of mixed characteristics) and of divination and warlockry (which are of negative characteristics) respond interestingly to changed coordinates.

There are four steps in constructing this type of analysis. (a) A frame of reference is set up, in this case the general conception of a system of operations by persons on things, including persons, with objects in view. (b) The development of concepts which fit the frame and conception, in this case the ideas of signed-conduct, of transitive and intransitive operations, and of institutional events as transactions over things. (c) The abstraction of institutional events to prominent features, in this case the two associated features of external signs and operations which can be identified. (d) The application of the concepts to the features so that the connections are made clear, in this case by the use of visual means made up of a geometric imagery.

There is no significance in the fact that the course of the operations is counter-clockwise. It must be so under the conventions of the figure. Curiously, many of the dances which accompany the actual operations trace out circles by movements from right to left.

Between phases 1 and 2 of the celebration, the youths who are to be taught what is only half-comprehended by even the wisest men, are separated physically from all but their teachers. They are then set apart even from these. All the external signs of their former position in life and their state of life are changed in the course of these operations. Their status also becomes negative. I shall say that this is generically an act of consecrating and making sacred.

In phase 3, already changed in locus and state of being, they are brought to the holy and dangerous place where they are to meet *Karwadi*. I shall say, again speaking generically, that they are immolated by blood and offered to The Mother of All. In phases 4 and 5 they are—or at least are conceived or reputed to be—destroyed by The Mother and then returned to life with a changed nature. But they have yet to be given a new state and position of life recognisable by external signs. These operations are distributed between phases 6, 7 and 8. When all is done the youths display on their bodies signs by which all the world knows that here are no longer boys but men, in a new state and locus of life, and with a higher social value. By virtue of the signs they are free to participate in the adult life and bring to it, while sharing, the good of their transformation.

Aboriginal thought is profoundly analogical, and for this reason they are much given to a rude simile and metaphor. Much of the symbolism of *Punj* can be traced to analogies, which seem to the Aborigines vivid and meaningful, between human and cosmic life. Intellectual conceptions are raised by symbolisation on these analogies. This of course is the essential symbol-function. But the development of the conceptions has taken an æsthetic rather than an intellectual course. The Aborigines sing, dance, mime and paint symbolistical conceptions of mysteries brought to their minds by analogical speculation. The *living* of a tradition is always a kind of essay on both principle and circumstance. Apparently a constant circumstance of life for them has been the absence of a specialised intellectual activity. Not that they are incapable of it: the high abstraction of the sub-section system is a convincing answer. But the absence of a class of thinkers has allowed the laws of æsthetic development to take their course guided perhaps only by the intuitive fitting of a symbolistical form to a mystery, which in the first place is perceived through an analogy. I shall deal with this process in a later paper, but a brief illustration is in place here.

In the Murinbata tradition the origin of life as such is not dealt with imaginatively. Life already *was* in The Dreaming. The fact is taken as a datum. To a certain extent the great split of the pristine unity into human and animal kingdoms is explored in mythology, but we are entitled to say that the mystery of life is its perpetuation or continuity after that event rather than the origin or schism.

The bearers of non-corporeal life are child-spirits. They feature in the tradition in a particular way—always as members of classes of pairs. That is, they are paired with (a) fresh water, more especially spring-water, (b) animal fat, and (c) green leaves. The Aborigines see likeness between the members of each pair such that the members are in inseparable connection whenever the context of thought or discourse is the perpetuation or continuity of human life. This seems to be fundamentally an analogical process of thought. A large number of similar classes exist in which natural and social phenomena are paired.

The child-spirits are the object or significatum of which water, fat and leaves are the signs. But the signs are not only indicative: they are efficacious as well. That is, the relation between sign and object is a productive relation. Power over the signs is productive of their objects. A large part of Aboriginal religion is concerned with the rightful possession and dutiful use of the efficacious signs.

What one encounters in the normal course of study is the symbolistical formulation of this and similar facts. That is, the deepening and the refining of the analogical perception. It is the essential function of symbol-systems to do so. Among the Murinbata the raw material of study presents itself in a complex and involuted form. Myth, song, dance, mime, social organisation and institutional practice all lie like so many veils between observer and that mystery which is phrased analogically. These acts in many cases are of unknown intent but they are carried on in love and loyalty. They are ancient things, and for this reason are venerated; they are good things, of which the oldest men are the witnesses; they are mysterious things and beautiful too; and, being enacted in a spirit which has in it something of piety, the intellectual veil over them deepens rather than shallows their meaning. At the same time, however, one cannot be unaware of a consistency which runs throughout. There is some kind of intuitive fitting together of the primary conceptions and their expression through complex symbolistical forms.

An interpretation of all this is inescapably metaphorical: we translate one system of metaphor into another. Perhaps, then, Fig. 1 has merit in that it interposes as few words as possible between things one can see or hear in *Punj* and their translation to paper in an ordered way.

When this is done the likeness between *Punj* and sacrifice, not only in the general fit of act to act and in the sequence of the acts, but also in the outcome, is such that it is not lightly to be brushed aside. The character of the problem then enlarges. I may perhaps avoid misunderstanding by saying first what I do not mean.

I do not mean or imply that there is any historical connection between the institutions. Or that a prime form existed anywhere in history or exists anywhere now. Or that the idea of sacrifice was ever explicit in Aboriginal culture. Or that such an idea is present in the Aboriginal unconscious. The comparison is an elementary one between the known and the unknown, between the named and the unnamed. I have no doubt that an Aboriginal anthropologist would write a paper with the title 'The Lineaments of *Punj* in Sacrifice'.

The two institutions are similar in form but not identical, and belong to different types of system. The respect in which they are homomorphic is an operational one. At the same time there seems to be an isomorphism of a more fundamental kind. This is in the sense in which they both exhibit three classes of conduct. There is a productive activity, an exchange activity, and a distributive activity. In the first, something of value is taken for an end which requires its transformation, all productive activities being transformative. In the second, the transformed object is replaced, or held to be replaced, through a transaction—in this case what we might call a heavenly transaction—by another thing of another nature and greater worth. There is then a distributive activity: the replacement or counter-good of higher worth is shared between those who sustained the original loss.

To assimilate the comparison to an economic model is in no sense to give an 'economic' interpretation. It is simply to avail ourselves of an academic fact: that a very objective, meaningful, and universal model of conduct exists, by the perceptiveness of one discipline, which has some utility in the problems of another. The model has its counterpart in anthropology: the cousinly (and somewhat countrified) paradigm by which Radcliffe-Brown derived his concept of 'social value'. The essence of the difficulties is that, although there has been some growth of the techniques of comparison, they do not allow us to extend *this* model—which is plainly, if remotely, applicable—to the problem in hand. The main reason is that the standing frames of reference of anthropology—structure, function, organisation—require only loose rather than exact comparisons. The exact comparisons require precise analyses of features and operations, which have been attempted only here and there, so that when two or more institutions show some kind of homomorphism we know the properties of the features and operations *for* which they are homomorphic. The apparent isomorphism of *Punj* and sacrifice—their construction after the same fashion as any joint human activity towards an object of value—illustrates the extent to which a strict comparison might be taken.

3. Structure or Operations?

A certain anxiety exists in modern anthropology lest interpretations should not give clear pictures of human persons at the business of life. To the extent to which the anxiety is justified, there seem to me to be three probable sources. One is the use of unsuitable metaphors of interpretation. A second is the use of abstract conceptions of unsuitable logical structure. The third is the habit of abstraction which issues in a virtualistic account, that is, a rough but somewhat misleading approximation, of what is under study. When such trends become orthodox approaches, it is difficult to counter them.

The imageries used in interpretation—like the symbolisms of *Punj*—tend to take on a life of their own. For example, we start with 'structure' and before long are dealing with 'tension' and 'stress' and 'centrifugal and centripetal forces'. A praiseworthy effort to use consistently a useful idea leads to the growth of an interpretative system of metaphors of a physical-mechanistical kind about things which have another nature. The constructions are then projected. There will probably always be two kinds of anthropologists: those who say 'social structures exist', and those who say 'let us construct them'. I shall not deny the first, but say only that the mode of existence is not observable. Radcliffe-Brown, at times a moderate, at others an exaggerated realist, set up the mystical doctrine of 'real structure', but the two aspects of his thought never lay well together. It is ironical that those who assert most firmly the reality of social structure seem to be those who maintain most firmly (as Radcliffe-Brown did not) that belief, including mystical belief, is causal in action. For if the activities which have or are a structure depend on belief there is then no real structure. Its mode of existence is mental.

A second source—the logical character of certain abstract conceptions—has deeply ensnared the discipline. Ideas like 'culture', 'social structure', 'social organisation' and others have little analytic utility, not because they are abstract, but because they are general and collective. Everything collected under them *is* culture, or *has* structure, or *shows* organisation. But to the syntheses which they represent the things which definitively mark off one class from another send no illumination. The attempts to make the ideas analytic are of an additive nature: we may thus emerge with perhaps one hundred varying statements of what culture *is*, each variant introducing a new class of features conceptually connected with different leading ideas and frames of reference. We meet culture, structure and organisation wherever we turn inquiry because we have pre-arranged that we shall do so, but we may be none the wiser how conflict relates to culture, or the rate of interest to social structure, or a trend in art to social organisation. For such reasons it is still difficult to find in anthropology two divisions of inquiry which relate to one another with anything like the clarity which connects, say, the theory of employment and the theory of investment in economics. However, in spite of its immensely broader field, we have in anthropology what few would attempt in economics: a mystical sociology of relations of association ranged in structures of structures; of general organismic functions within complex, compound systems of many interrelated institutions in varying states; and of the total organisation of activities of choice and decision.

A third source is the suppression, or virtual suppression, of the natural triad of person-object-person in favour of person-person relational study. If in the total-system approach the fact of individual persons is made somewhat epiphenomenal, in detailed relational-study the objects of activity become somewhat epiphenomenal. They are illustrative to, rather than integral, in role-and-position analyses.

The abstractly collective and dubiously, if not falsely, concrete ideas like structure, culture and organisation meet, in the same system of interpretative thought, the narrowly analytic and deficiently concrete ideas like role, choice and decision. One must make what one can of this through the veil of metaphor. The structure of anthropological interpretation clearly requires a detached examination if the discipline's wealth of hard-won fact is to have the impact which it merits.

The institution of *Punj* is a notable concentration of well-articulated forms. The aspects which I have left tacit, rightly or wrongly, may be said to illustrate in a remarkably clear way how some well-known principles, or what are taken to be principles—the assimilation of alternate generations, the opposition of interdependent moieties, the dualism of affinity—provide a kind of framework even for religious life. On the level of symbolism, The Mother of All is a kind of equipoise of the Patriarchal Father. Much of the kind might be cited, and with a certain justification. But the intrinsic *ex post* reasoning should be clear. The 'principles' are not principles but descriptions of necessary and enabling conditions of social conduct. The conduct is not consequent upon them so much as that they are part and parcel of the totality of conduct. It is a condition of an act of exchange in a monetary economy that there be a buyer and a seller, but the principles of exchange are something very different. Economics would be a different discipline indeed if, while ignoring the principles of exchange—all the considerations which determine price-quantities of specified classes of goods, both in general and here-and-now—it elaborated an economic structure comparable with the anthropologist's social structure. What reality the conception of social structure has is the reality of its content, and this comes in its entirety from our knowledge of social operations. But that knowledge is partial and uneven for reasons which I have in part indicated. The active search, of which we may see many signs, for a set of conceptions to complement that of social structure is in one sense mistaken: not a complement is required, but something which will make it possible, logically sound, and concretely persuasive. If there is a system of social life then it is probably in the first place a system of operations, and if the structure of the system can be abstracted then we shall best do so by developing conceptions adequate for the study of the operations. At the moment I do not consider that we possess them.

4. Transitive and Intransitive Conduct

I have found some advantages in using the idea of a transaction in place of the less concrete 'interaction', which is again collective and general. The idea of a transaction compels one to deal at all times with what I have called the natural triad of person-object-person. Social life is intrinsically though not exclusively transactional. The *ennui* of this knowledge is possibly the source of the mime of the blowfly in *Punj*, for the Aborigines have a good sense of the two-sidedness of human dealings. Fire, which is for them one of the symbols of sociality, serves and burns. Some of the deepest bitternesses of Murinbata life lie between brothers, who should not transact but share, forced into competitiveness by defections.

In one of its aspects—and that, the sacrificial—*Punj* is, like the Melanesian cargo cults, a one-sided transaction. Men have to deal with a heavenly or spiritual partner. Here we encounter the difficulty of distinguishing 'functional' conduct from the 'symbolical' conduct with which it is usually contrasted. I believe the distinction can be made in a clearer way which is also more widely serviceable. The distinction is between transitive and intransitive conduct. More correctly, between transitive and intransitive operations.

Where activities are made up of transitive operations human intentions are actually transferred, and can be shown to be transferred, to the objects of the activities. The activities we call 'technical' are functional because the operations are transitive. We plant crops to grow food: to eat the yield is the proof and demonstration of transitivity. But there are innumerable objects of life—among them sometimes the most longed-for and highly-prized—of which no proof or demonstration of the outcome of our best efforts is, or seems, possible. If we pursue such objects then we have to proceed in hope, belief or faith. Activities in which the operations, as far as human knowledge goes, are intransitive make up a very large part of anthropology's subject-matter. We describe them as 'symbolical' and often say that they 'depend on mystical beliefs'. Some of the problems of symbolism will be dealt with in a later paper, but I shall say at this point that the second assertion states the relation incorrectly. Symbolical activities attract rather than depend on mystical beliefs, which express human longings and valuations rather than an illusion of technical competence.

Many of the activities of *Punj* really do 'make the young men understand', and can be shown to do so. In this respect they are technical, functional and transitive. But the transfers of other intentions, if real, have to be simulated. I maintain that the simulation occurs because there is suspicion or knowledge that transitivity is not attainable. That is, symbolical or *as if* activity may be carried out in hope but not necessarily with intention of transitivity, and it may well persist in the certain knowledge that there is no basis for hope. The symbolistical operations of the *Karwadi* though intransitive are not therefore less rational or functional than those which are transitive, for their intentions, while obviously complex, belong to an order which is being misunderstood and misrepresented if assimilated to the class of 'technical' intentions.

The symbolistical activities do not manipulate objects of life but express the valuations placed on them, and the desires for them. In this respect they are as rational as any other conduct towards objects of life, in being in logical accord with the perceived nature and value of the objects. Insofar as they impress clear conceptions of the objects on the minds of celebrants and endue them with a lasting sense of the values concerned then, in this secondary sense, the activities are transitive as well. These symbol-functions are indeed carried out with high efficiency by the choice of symbol-vehicles: truly brilliant combinations of mime, song, dance and stylised movements make what seems an indelible impression on those who see them. So much is this the case that there might well be neural or cortical changes as an outcome.

The *Karwadi* ceremony is the third initiation to which youths of the region are subjected.[5] The first takes place at a tender age, usually when boys are between 8 and 10; the second at puberty; and the third at any age from 16 onwards. Each is a variation on the theme of withdrawal, transformation and return. The disciplines are severe and the emotional stresses are high and sustained. In the first ceremony the most obvious intent is to strike fear—of the unknown, of men, and of life—into the hearts of growing boys. The intent of the second is rather to implant in them self-respect, endurance of privation and pain, and a knowledge of their dependence on others. The third has been sufficiently described. The psychology which is applied throughout is highly effective: at the time of fear, there is a protector at hand; at the time of privation and pain, a warm companionship is always there; and, when the youths are most humbled, and perhaps most in fear, the proud things of acknowledged manhood are known to be not far off in time. At each stage the Aboriginal genius for music, song, mime and dance is applied with skill

5 All three were discontinued after the war. I disregard a fourth ceremony which is quite well remembered though abandoned perhaps half a century ago. It *preceded* the three others.

and passion. I have found little evidence of abstract, explicit teaching, and what there is seems obvious and banal, but the affective outcome is most marked. Personality may almost be seen to change under one's eyes. It is not without reason that missionaries of long experience have found boys far less teachable, though not less tractable, after passing through the ceremonies. One suspects a redintegrative effect: responses to given stimuli have become so deeply settled that an Aborigine finds true interest, spiritual ease, and intellectual satisfaction only in that system of life which the stimuli connote. Initiated men learn to live with Europeanism, and even to manipulate it skilfully, but I have met none—except those whose traditional world had utterly collapsed—who were happy with it. It is not difficult to see why.

The symbolical accompaniments of the ceremonies become loved, not for their recondite import, but for their own sake. Many of the songs have no meaning, and the fact signifies nothing: but they are sung not less lovingly. The mimes and dances contain elements one may see in tribes 1,000 miles away in other contexts, of somewhat different meaning, and none the wiser. Even in adjacent tribes the myths associated with *Karwadi* vary considerably. Many of the Aborigines, especially the old, and most especially the *wanaŋgal* or wise men, are aware of and will discuss the more profound aspects of what is done, but a sustained intellectual detachment is rare, and only now and then do the cryptic or implicit elements of the ceremony come under discussion. The vivid symbolism of the blowfly and the wild licence of *Tjirmumuk* persist with almost no doctrine to sustain or explain them. The fact is that *Punj* is something to do rather than to talk about. And it is something to do joyfully: there is no mistaking the rapt participation. In no other circumstances does one see Aborigines so absorbed in a task. If it is a religious task—and, were there nothing else to go upon, the liturgical complexity and lavish symbolism would assure us that it is—here is one instance in which the old jest of the *opus dei* and the *onus diei* is meaningless.

It would be possible, and in many ways desirable, to relate the entire culture and organised life of the region to this single ceremony. In later papers in this series I shall trace at least some of the connections. My concern in this article has been to do two things. The first is to show that what is cryptic or implicit at the ontological level of Aboriginal culture responds at least interestingly to an act of comparison. The second is to show that a study of acts as operations has a useful place in an empirical and comparative anthropology. Indeed, it is perhaps only by such a method that we can bridge those awkward crossing-places which have caused so much difficulty. I refer here to the problems of making a logical and conceptual connection in our interpretations of the explicit and non-explicit elements of culture, and of transitive and intransitive conduct.

In the course of these papers I shall draw extensively on the work of both Durkheim and Radcliffe-Brown and at the same time depart widely from their viewpoints. In particular, I have found it impossible to make sense of Aboriginal life in terms of Durkheim's well-known dichotomy 'the sacred' and 'the profane'. The question will be examined in another paper, with special relation to the custom of *Tjirmumuk*. My narrative will have made plain that the custom, while being an integral part of *Punj*, is in many ways the reverse of which the main ceremony is the obverse. If, with reason, we describe the main ceremony as sacred, or concerned with sacred things, we are obliged by Durkheim's scheme to say that *Tjirmumuk* is an act of profanation. In Aboriginal eyes it most assuredly is not. The native testimony is that it 'belongs to *Karwadi*'.

I have sought to describe *Punj*, or at least its central events, as a liturgical ceremony because it is a kind of work reverential to, though not worshipful of, *Karwadi*, and because it is conducted with the highest formality. It is also a rite because it conforms to a set formulary perennially followed without important variation. We must thus inquire, if Durkheim's dichotomy is valid, in what circumstances a sacred or religious rite can contain its own contrary or opposite as part of itself.

An operational study can of course be as broad or as detailed as one wishes. The gross operations I have mentioned here resolve into constituents, and these too are transitive and intransitive. I leave this question for separate study in relation to the magical content of the ceremony.

II

Sacramentalism, Rite and Myth

1. Some Theoretical Considerations

In the last article, 'The Lineaments of Sacrifice,' I showed that the highest rite of the Murinbata has a marked resemblance to sacrifice, and is therefore a good deal more than we ordinarily mean by initiation. How much more, and how best to interpret the facts, remain central difficulties.

It was apparent also that the rite exhibits other interesting similarities. For example, some of the symbolisms are reminiscent of rebirth and baptism. Observers of many other Aboriginal initiations have noted the same fact.

I concentrated in the article on the structural resemblance to sacrifice since apparently it had not been noticed or stressed by others. What further constructions of the rite may be made?

The first duty of anthropology in dealing with Aboriginal religion is to try to elicit the kind of reality the facts of study have for the people responsible for them. The data might be described as natural facts of human conviction about the ultimates of life. In other words, they are products of human passion, aspiration and imagination. They are what they are because Aboriginal mentality is what it is. In this sense they have their being, as realities studied by anthropology, within what could be called an ontology of life. It is that reality which anthropology must set up for study as best it may (Fig. 2).

In the course of doing so the typical difficulties become rather more marked than when other topics are under examination. The necessary means—abstraction, empirical methods, and an indicative-analytical language—are at all points being transcended by the facts. One neglects some features of reality in order to attend to others; empiricism does not exhaust even what is selected; the chosen language may dry out and at times dessicate what is under study. And in an attempt to outwit the difficulties the analyst can scarcely avoid what Professor Firth has called 'the personal equation,' an implicit valuation of facts under the guise of objectivity. In dealing with the more mundane topics one hardly notices the problems. But they make themselves felt in an acute way when one engages in study the ultimate facts of religious form and concern.

Figure 2. The relations between things of the religious and social orders

Figure 2 is an attempt to represent visually the relations between things of the religious (R) and social (S) orders and ontological reality in the Murinbata system.

When the Aborigines use English they choose the word 'dreaming' (to which I add the definite article) for their totems (*ngakumal*) and totem-sites (*ngoiguminggi*), but also for the time of marvels in the indefinably remote past. But they use the word causatively as well by referring everything to The Dreaming as ground and source and when they say they want to or have to 'follow up' The Dreaming. Again, they dissociate classes and groups of people by saying they have different 'dreamings.'

In their own language, apart from terms like *ngakumal*, there are only two ways of referring to the mythical past as the ground and source of all things. One is by the word *kaduɽɛr* (lit. 'person(s), '? time'), which has the sense of human but marvellous persons of an indefinitely remote past; the other is by the words *da mundak* (lit. 'state of being,' 'past time'). The word for dream (*nin*) is *not* used. Evidently the use of the English word (which is in universal currency from Central Australia to North Australia, and doubtless has passed from tribe to tribe) is an attempt, by metaphor based on analogy, to convey the mystical quality of the relations as being like the relation of dream-life to waking-life. At the same time one must note that, to the Aborigines, an actual dream-experience is agentive and prophetic. Their choice of the English word seems to me a brilliant economy of phrase, covering both the denotations and connotations of the mystical conception of totemism within the ontology.

In Figure 2 the large circle symbolises The Dreaming in its widest sense. In such a sense one may well say that it corresponds to absolute or whole reality, that which comprehends everything and is adequate to everything. It is the total referent of which anything else is a *relatum*.

From within the Aboriginal system of thought the direction of all relations is *from* the circle, the referent of everything, *to* all that it embraces. The shaded and unshaded areas of the outer circle are an attempt to represent that property of whole reality which, in Aboriginal eyes, appears as a kind of duality or as a mixture of dualities. Reality is both visible and invisible, and is both benign and malign. Hence, I believe, the absence of entelechy; the fact that a Golden Age mentality is absent from the myths; the duality of all the main figures of the myths; and the 'human all too human' characteristics of many personages entering into the allegorical constructions. The absence of moral or religious fervour seems to me consonant also with that property.

I intend the figure to mean that the religious and social orders are only analytically separable. There are some social things which are not religious, and some religious things which are not social, but the two orders are connected, and connected with a more comprehensive reality of life and thought.

The placement of R closer than S to the outer circle is meant to show that religious activity brings people closer than does social activity to ontological reality. The successive initiations deepen the interior life and, at the same time, widen the experiential world until, at *Punj*, it approaches whole reality as understood. The 'mystery' of *Punj* is a shape or *nginipun* forming in the field of macro-experience and simply phrased by analogy, metaphor and allegory in a symbolical language drawn from S, the realm of social experience.

The conception which I use is that religious rites are acts *towards* whole reality, myths are allegorical statements *about* it, and social customs are acts *within* whole reality. It is the acting towards The Dreaming which takes the rites upon the ground of macro-experience, the natural ground of mysticity.

In these papers one of my primary aims is to make as explicit as I can aspects of Aboriginal religion which tend to remain tacit in more conventional approaches. To try, as a conscious aim of study, to bring out the onotology of a type of thought and life must involve one, I think unavoidably at present, in some degree of implicit valuation. On the other hand, the distortions made by the spurious ideal of complete objectivity can have even worse consequences.

The tradition of anthropology has always gone beyond the study of man simply as *Homo sapiens* and *Homo faber.* Beyond, too, the rather inelegant conception of *Homo socius.* The analytical construct 'man-acting' has never been more than a convenient travesty. The true subject of study is really *Homo convictus*, to use the term suggested by Zuurdeeg.[1] That is, man to whom it is natural to act socially within a system of life depending on overwhelming convictions about ultimate values.

A certain aridity has lain over anthropological studies of religion for some time. That self-styled 'encyclopæædic inventory' *Anthropology Today* was perhaps a straightforward case of neglect. It did not contain a single paper on the topic and in its index listed only 11 of 929 pages as dealing with central questions. But many studies which are now remedying the neglect are still affected by a kind of theoretic blight. I refer in particular to the presupposition that the social order is primary

1 Willem F. Zuurdeeg, *An Analytical Philosophy of Religion*, London, 1959.

and in some sense causal, and the religious order secondary and in some sense consequential. Thus, studies may issue in general propositions to the effect that religion 'reflects' or 'expresses' the social structure. It is quite difficult to see why such statements seem important or even interesting. They are not clear even as metaphor, since a reflection would be a reversed image, which the theorists do not of course mean, and an expression which is not a concentration—and, in this sense, an elucidation—does not advance analysis. I do not adopt any such formulation, and prefer rather to regard facts of the social order, if they are disconnected from religion, as providing one of the symbolical languages through which ontological reality is conveniently expressed. I have allowed questions of social structure to remain tacit largely for that reason. A few further words may be in place.

Conceptions of social structure seem usually to issue in models *about* human relations. They must be distinguished from models *of* or *after* the observable reality of those relations. The relations of social structure seem usually to be visualised as connections or interdependences between points of force which are characterised as role-positions on a kind of network. The conception is wholly unlike that which I use. One may actually see the constituent operations of *Punj*. One has to infer the role-positions and enactments required to clothe the structural models. I would argue that the operational model is perceptual of or after the matter and constitution of *Punj*, whereas the structural models would be about form and function. They would also be more preceptive than perceptual.

I have sought to avoid using any formulation which would simply be a reversal of the terms of the rejected presupposition. That is, to avoid setting up the religious facts as primary and social facts as secondary, which I do not think is the case. It is thus necessary to examine the relationships between at least three sets of phenomena: the ontological system, the conjoint phenomena of myth and rite, and the main social relationships as continuously interdependent over time.

In this article I shall follow Robertson Smith[2], Roheim[3] and Elkin in making use, though in my own way, of the general idea of 'sacramentalism.' By such means a certain order can be found in the ontology, more particularly with respect to the motivation of rites and the institutions of totemism.

The main rite is marked by the use of external and visible signs betokening men's dependency on otherworldly powers for an endowment and flow of life-benefits. It is the set of relations which obtain between these elements which constitutes sacramentalism. Men act through signs towards the ground of dependency; the flow is accompanied—or is held to be—by external signs signifying that a solidary relation holds between that ground and men; and in this way the acts, signs and flow not only interpenetrate each other but in a long established and involuted religious system compenetrate each other, that is, pervade each other in every part. In such a sense Murinbata religion is sacramentalist through and through. It could be described as a totemic sacramentalism. In order to understand it one has to examine the nature and principle of the endowment (that is, the totemic foundation), the exchange of signs (the rite), and the plan of dispensing or distributing the flow among men (the social institutions). One is dealing with what might be called a religious 'economy.' It is inherently possible to set up comparatively a counterpart of the formulation which, in a particular tradition, deals with 'an exchange of prayers for grace' as a system of determinations within an 'economy of salvation.' Such an economy is not the whole of a religion but is an important part of it.

The relation between rite and myth is one that seems to me very perplexing. Anthropological thought on the matter is quite unsatisfactory. In the main I depend on Robertson Smith's formulations, which seem to me still the most cogent. The myth of *Mutjiŋga* or The Old Woman is now coordinate with the rite of *Punj*, and functions correlatively with it. But the conjunction is a fact of history and, although positive evidence

2 W. Robertson Smith, *Lectures on the Religion of the Semites*, 1889 (1914 Ed.), esp. Lect. IX.

3 Géza Roheim. *The Eternal Ones of the Dream*, 1945.

is lacking, I do not doubt that the myth derives historically from the rite. I take the view that the rite is obligatory and constant, whereas the myth is discretionary and variable. The study is confined to the coordinate and correlative aspects in view of the facts that only speculation would be possible about the historical question, and that there are three other complicating problems: the rite is heavily adorned æsthetically, many systems of symbolism are in use, and the cultus is infiltrated by the political power of men. The historical aspect is certainly important both in relation to the particular facts of Murinbata religion and to the general theory of mythologised rite, but I do not feel able to do more than refer incidentally to it.

An objection has been made (in a private communication) that in the first article I did not specify what *kind* of sacrifice *Punj* resembles. I consider that the criticism is based on a misunderstanding. I used the words 'Lineaments of Sacrifice' precisely because I had elicited an implicit general form, which might be considered a logical and conceptual possibility of the religious culture. The known species or varieties of sacrifice are phenomena of particular traditions, which are much less than fully known. It seems to me a waste of time to try to infer from half-known histories to an eventuality which might have emerged in a history that did not happen.

2. Relations between Punj and Circumcision

The Murinbata distinguish in the most explicit way between *Punj* and its prepubic counterpart (*Djaban*) on the one hand and the circumcision of youths at puberty on the other. The two classes or varieties are—and are seen as—quite distinct in kind, purpose and importance.

In the major rite the veritable signs of The Mother—blood and the bullroarer—are used to transform young men who, if they are to carry life on, must learn the signs which alone have efficacy in drawing the flow from the endowment. The signs are reminders of the past; they have a transformative efficacy in the present; and, somehow, they guarantee what is to come. In such respects they are of the essence of all sacramental observance. The rite itself is episodic and transitory, but it has a permanent effect. It fixes an altogether indelible character on those who are submitted to it. A Murinbata man who becomes *Kadu Punj* becomes one who, in their own language, 'holds something in the ear,' i.e. 'understands.' No one ever undergoes the rite a second time as principal. He attains, irrespective of subsequent conduct, an irreversible state and condition. The distinction between those who have submitted, and those who have yet to submit, is always absolutely clear. The effect of the rite is recognised universally within its region of force and meaning.

The Aborigines are a contemporary people, and the ideas and forms of conduct I am dealing with are also contemporary or recent. It is impossible to know or say anything about the remote history of the forms and ideas. It would therefore be a wrongful procedure to make, or to try to make, a comparison between Murinbata and Christian sacramentalism such that the former is made to appear primitively in a uniform, linear, serial sequence with the latter. To do so would be to narrow what has to be widened, that is, generalised. The viewpoint I adopt has been well stated by Atkins in the observation that 'the deeper fault of all Churchly sacramentarianism is our undue limitation of its meaning' and that the idea of sacrament is 'capable of a vast and helpful extension.'[4] At the same time it is at least of interest to point out how fitting to the Murinbata evidence are some early conceptions of Christian sacramentology. The rite may well be compared to a seal (*sphragis*) which puts an impress on those who submit to and receive it, so that it signs them in a character (*signaculum*) which is indelible. In Murinbata eyes the character or property is one of 'understanding,' and it will be recalled that one of the early comparisons of the effect of baptism was with 'enlightenment.' Indeed, very much as sacrifice may be thought of as a logical possibility of Murinbata religious culture, though a possibility which did not eventuate, so one may say that many conceptual possibilities exist within their ruling ideas. But I feel that

4 G. G. Atkins, *The Making of the Christian Mind*, London, 1929, pp. 214–15.

it is not for anthropology to force the emergence in a speculatively comparative way. We have to study the religion as a sacramentalist complex with differentiations of its own. The pattern of differentiation is distinctive.

A characteristic of the system is that neither birth nor marriage attracts rites and ceremonies of a sacramental kind. The tradition does not select these occasions of life as religiously significant.

The circumcision is not *Punj*, in other words is not a secret, obscure and dangerous thing. Its purpose is to make a youth into a man, whereas the purpose of the rite of the bullroarer is to make a man into a man of mystical understanding. He is a man transformed, one who knows the truth—or as much of the truth as anyone in the tradition can tell him—about a cardinal mystery of human affairs. And nothing like the importance which attaches to the bullroarer rite is attached to circumcision. In this system it would be entirely meaningless to fix on *Punj* any such label as 'spiritual circumcision' in the manner in which a link was made, rather putatively, between baptism and the complex of initiation rites existing before the Christian period. However, nothing I have said implies that circumcision is unimportant among the Murinbata. Far from it. It has high importance, sufficient to override every unconnected activity for days at a time, and to leave lifelong marks on personality, repute and status. It too has the aspects of *sphragis* and *signaculum.* But it is not *nandji ŋala ŋala* (lit. 'thing,' 'big,' 'big,' the duplication of *ŋala* being an intensification), and it in no way ranks in value, or competes in purpose and function, with the major rite. The two are of distinct orders, and are on different planes in that at circumcision mysticity recedes to the far background, and the considerations are dominantly temporal and secular. The fact that it is not intended to make youths 'understand' shows that it is not a spiritual transaction, and cannot be raised to the dignity of a sacrament.

The only other sacramental rite of importance in the regional culture is that attending death. Those which have been called 'increase' rites, intended to regenerate the vital principle of the totems, were not developed to any extent in the region. Nor were the first menses of females marked by elaborate ceremonial.

3. The Sacramental Plan

Aboriginal social life was a volitional and purposive system deferring to traditional data or givens. One may speak of it as tradition-directed. Any order the actualities of life exhibited came from a consistent observance of the givens. That system is now changing fairly rapidly. There are new objects of life to pursue through activities which have no, or very unclear, data to defer to as a means of rationalisation. The younger and very activist generation has yet to find by what to systematise itself. In these articles I am concerned with the traditional system.

The essential point of approach to the religious life of tradition is the phenomenon of totemism. It appears to be the main link between cosmology and ontology on the one hand and the social order on the other. Certainly, it forms the best approach an external observer can make to Aboriginal conceptions of the reality they experience.

An understanding of Aboriginal totemism also allows one to proceed to the stage of theoretical formulation, which must necessarily be stated in terms of a foreign intellectual tradition. I am taking such a step when I refer to a religious 'economy,' with the meaning that the facts are being phrased as those of an ordained (and, therefore, fixed) endowment which is dispensed on a certain plan of entitlement, so that its flow is utilised under conservational forms. As I phrase the formulation, the religious system is sacramental because it is totemic, and it is economic because it is conservational. Totemism is the foundation as well as the frame of the sacramental plan. There are four classical types of totemism in the region, a fifth having been imitated from tribes to the south over the last three generations. The function of Murinbata totemism is to mediate the first ordained order to living people. It may be said to dispense the ancestors' endowment, and to provide channels for the flow. The types will be listed with a minimum of explanation.

1. *Personal or Conceptional Totemism.* Each person has a private totem (*mir*) that links him as an individual with a non-human entity either made by the ancestors or given its first formed relation to social life by them. The totem is identified by means of some notable incident associated with a child's conception. The *ŋaritŋarit* or child-spirit is held to use an incident to draw a husband's notice to the fact that a wife is conceiving a child. The totem is the corporeal agent of the spirit-child. Virtually any entity in the universe—fire, lightning, smoke, the sea, sickness—can be *mir.*

2. *Sex Totemism.* All men as a set are linked jointly with a class of non-human entities, as are all women. Kinship terms are extended to the totems (unnamed except by the names of the species). Thus, all men hold the woollybutt tree as being in a relation of *kaka*, mother's brother, to them. The stringybark stands in the same relation to all women.

3. *Clan Totemism.* All members of each exogamous, patrilineal clan are linked with a large class of animal or natural entities which are thought of as being connected, as species, with particular places within the clan territories. The connection is intrinsic and perennial. The species, if vital, reproduce themselves through the sites, and can also be reproduced there by the totemites through magico-religious procedures.

The nature of the vital principle is obscure. Evidently it lies 'in' the species and not 'in' the association of a species with a place, for it can be stolen and reproduced elsewhere. Units or even fragments of the species (but not the place) are often stolen. The vital principle then works elsewhere. Such thefts are mortal offences. The clan members have an unquestioned right to possession of the totems (*ŋakumal*), the sites (*ŋoigumiŋgi*), the region (*da*), its resources, and any incorporeal correlatives such as songs, dances and emblematic designs. The system may be called 'cult totemism' since the designs, which have public and secret forms, are worn by males at ceremonies.

4. *Moiety Totemism.* All persons, whether male or female, in each patrilineal moiety jointly possess a totem (unnamed except by the names of the species) distinguishing them from all members of the other moiety. Each totem is *pule* (old, senior, authoritative, friend, and in English 'boss') over all totems of the clans constituting its moiety, but the relation is somewhat vague and lacks precise system. Mythology represents the moieties, which are named after *Tiwuŋgu*, the eagle-hawk, and *Kartjin*, the kite-hawk, as composed originally of different orders of people in continuous conflict. Each possessed a vital resource—fire or water—without which the other could not live. They were saved from an animal-like existence and possible death only by co-operation. The moieties compete with each other in games, may abuse each other in conventional terms, and assist in the regulation of marriage. But they are not stressed as such in ceremonies or in camping patterns. The type is logically derivable from (3).

5. *Sub-section Totemism.* All members of each sub-section or *ŋinipun* (in English, 'skin'), of which there are eight, jointly possess a class of non-human entities (named *ŋulu*) which are not connected locally with places. The system was copied from tribes to the south in historic times, and is neither well understood nor assiduously maintained except among the oldest men, who tend to regard it now as one of their secrets.

The effect of the totemic complex as a whole is to parcel out, on a kind of distributive plan, all the non-human entities made or recognised by the ancestors, and given relevance one to another, that is, set up in a moral system. The outcome is that, with the exception of (I),[5] the totemic sets are sacramental corporations of a perennial order.

5 There is no bond between individual persons who have the same *mir*. The only social significance of the totem is that in a limited number of cases it may enable a man to be sure of friendship and safety where otherwise he might find neither. Thus, a man known to me, whose *mir* is fire, received many warm invitations to visit a distant place because, at the time of his birth, a fire had been seen moving strangely from that direction. His spirit was assumed to have come, clinging to the fire, and to have been that of a dead member of the distant clan. Hence the invitations to visit the clan.

It is the associating of a totem with a set of people which makes them into a group, that can operate, or be operated on, in virtue of the totemic sign. Members of the group have a ground of right over the totem and anything it stands for. They are also held answerable for all it imports. The rights are not always clear. In (2) the relation of totem to group does not seem to be much more than emblematic.

The nature of the bond between totem and totemite is best set out in relation to (4). The *ŋakumal* totem is commonly referred to as *ŋatan*, 'brother,' and in English as 'my dreaming.' When the site or *ŋoigumiŋgi* is referred to a possessive adjective is also used. I have not succeeded in finding out the literal meanings of the terms or in separating the morphemes distinctly. In English, the totem place is called 'my dreaming' or 'my dreaming place.' Persons of the same clan are *ŋakumal numi*, in English 'one dreaming,' often intensified to 'one dreaming, one country.' The bond, primarily mystical, can also be said to be 'essential' in that there is an identification of the intrinsic self with the site ('myself there,' 'just like myself,' 'my *ŋjapan* (spirit) there'), and 'substantial' in that a corporeal connection is also asserted. There is the idea of a transmissible biological type, but the what and how of the connection are obscure.[6] In a limited sense the bond is historical, for common knowledge of actual persons who were associated with the place and totem may go back for three generations, rarely more. It is historical too in the longer measure if we accept the pseudo-historicity of myth. But it could not accurately be called 'genetic,' or even 'pseudo-genetic,' for the following reasons.

Genealogical tables of up to six generations are not particularly difficult to make. They are purported to be true and may well be true in part, for a high proportion of entries withstand repeated cross-check between people not in collusion and with nothing obvious to gain by lying. But the tables are worthless as *evidence* of *genetic* fact. There is now, and presumably was in the past, a high rate of extra-marital sexuality;

6 Cases occur of a rudimentary effort to separate types, as when children of markedly different physical appearance are put in different sub-sections in spite of the fact that they are the issue of one woman consorting with one man.

classificatory brothers have a right of sexual access to wives; multiple and short-term marriages by women have been a high proportion of all marriages; no importance whatever is attached to conception or birth outside the clan country; the period of gestation is not known with any accuracy; and there is the immense fact of the mystical theory of procreation. The men who help to construct the genealogies are *not* thinking genetically. What they do is to trace the issue of children from women who were then consorting with men in conditions in which the men had a right of claim to the issue. Murinbata patriliny is the exercise of a political and jural right arising from spiritual agnation.[78]

The *genitor* property of paternity is a function which can be—and, on sufficient evidence, is—performed just as well by a man's brother as by him. A man can institute the *minga* or 'firestick' relation with his brother's child by 'finding' a child-spirit in a dream and directing it to his brother's wife. The *pater* property is the exercise of jural and political right founded on the same mystical ground. The clan is a set or collection of people made into a group, with the unity we try to denote by the word 'clan,' by a sign affixed perennially to them. The sign is the *ŋakumal.* Its referent is the mystical complex 'one dreaming, one country.' Its connotation is a range of rights and duties. The 'patrilineal clan' is patrilineal because there are both a spiritual or essential link and, somehow, a corporeal or substantial link over time between fathers and sons; it is a clan because the sign makes a unified group from a set or collection; and it is perennially corporate in its estate, corporeal and incorporeal, because everything has been from the beginning the

---

7 One finds repeatedly in constructing genealogies that—outside the range of living men who are personally known—no particular importance is attached to an *exact* attribution of children to a *yile*, or 'father,' provided the attribution is made to a man within a set of male siblings of the clan. One is compelled by experience to conclude that the *ngakumal* is a sign which, affixed to a group, generates in its male members a right to the issue of women consorting with them within the rules of marriage.

inalienable[8] right and duty of those who have had the sign from the beginning.

Adoption of members of other clans—especially of the children of captured women—is common. It is fully jural in the sense that there are rules, but no adoptee ever loses his rights and duties *in animum* and *in rem* in the estate of the consort of his mother at or about the time of birth, or acquires those of his adoptor clan. A complete entry into the sacramental corporation by adoption is impossible.

A ground made in this way is a condition of the intelligibility of many events or institutions, for the necessity or requiredness is consequential on totemism. A bare summary may suffice.

The *ku* or *gu* in *ŋakumal* and *ŋoigumiŋgi* evidently means 'flesh.'[91] Birth is the event of arrival, on the plane of the visible, and in the world of the living, of flesh somehow shaped or constituted by a child-spirit (*ŋaritŋarit*) and a soul (*ŋjapan*). The doctrine of the commerce between child-spirit and soul is obscure. But at birth a spiritual duality shows itself in flesh affiliated mystically with a place and a species. The actual birthplace is simply where a baby 'falls' so as to 'make a dent in the ground,' and is otherwise not important. The word 'totemism' conveys very poorly the idea of a ground on which life forms and to which it returns. At death, the former practice coupled platform-exposure of the body with (in the case of men) an eventual rite to free the soul (nothing is said of the child-spirit) to go elsewhere to make a new entry to the

8 After a serious quarrel with an Aboriginal friend of many years' standing, he was much concerned to mend the breach. He made many overtures without avail. In what I took to be an ultimate gesture he went quietly away for several weeks, and made secretly a painting of all his *ngakumal.* He brought it to me at night, hidden under a blanket, offered it with formality and emotion, begged me to tell no one, and to let no one see it. He had come as close as was possible to giving away his 'dreaming.' Later I saw another man, who had finally abandoned his own depopulated country, 'kill' or 'finish' a totem by burning it in a fire, spreading gifts on the ash, and paying for friends to dance on top.

9 I think that *nga* and *ngoi* are possibly archaic forms of *ngai* (I, mine) used as pronominal prefixes, but *minggi* is not recognisable.

visible world. The doctrine allows for the entry of a given spirit into persons of other clans and even of the opposite moiety. The last ashes of the burned remains of the body were then stamped into the ground of the ancestral clan by men of *all* clans. In this way a cycle was completed, but not closed, for the spirit retained its capacity to return to the visible world.

The preferred marriage—with a classificatory cross-cousin—takes that form evidently because at that point the totemic signs of father and mother have lost force sufficiently to be disregarded. The condemnation of marriages which are said to be 'too close' can be analysed to have that meaning.

Trade, which is carried on intertribally, is a transmission between clans of valuables which have been held or touched—'owned' is not the word—in a given sequence by every member of each clan,[10] excluding young children, before being passed onto the next.

Outside the clan there is, with one exception, nothing heritable or inherited. At a man's death his chattels are destroyed, his debts paid, and anything else stays with his clan. If he has the title and office of *pule* (which means in this case seniority in the clan) they too stay within the clan; likewise visionary skills (to see spirits, to dream songs, to divine malefactors) which gifted men like to bequeath to their sons. The exception is the rights of safety, hospitality and hunting-privilege which a man has in his mother's clan-country (*kaŋatji*), which merely lapse. In every other place but his own and his mother's clan-country a man is *kamalik*, a stranger.

I am trying here to give in brief compass an account, not of social structure as it is usually understood, but of the way in which groups are constituted and have a set of functions under what may be called on these evidences a totemic determination. The totemic system has a threefold efficacy. (*a*) It provides a wisdom or principle or *logos* by which the Aborigines conceptualise groups of people. (*b*) It unifies sets or collections of people as more than sets or collections, in short,

10 Wives, who of course are not members of their husbands' clans, also 'touch' and share in the real benefits of trade.

gives them the 'group' property, so that they are supposed to exemplify physically that which characterises them socially in their own eyes and the eyes of others. (*c*) It points two ways through a special class of totems: *back*, to a ground and source which are self-authorised and self-authorising; and *on*, to powers and rights in various classes of functions for the members of groups which have their being—and *a fortiori* the powers and rights—*only* by virtue of the authority set up. The 'necessity' of the relations is a totemic necessity, and totemism is the language of the ontological system.

But there are many such clans, neither solitary nor self-sufficient, ranged in parallel (*Kartjin* clans tend to cluster along the coast) and in series (because the clustering is only a tendency). Their common life of interaction (through marriage, friendship, trade, war, hunting and other types of activity) requires a different method of analysis. The necessities behind these relations are only distantly, if at all, concerned with totemism, but arise from different conditions presupposed for each class. I do not propose to embark on them here. But the principles of such associations are obviously multiple. No one principle—certainly not that of totemism, or that great standby of Australian anthropologists, 'kinship'—orders the totality of interaction. The fact is that the principles of social interaction are conjugate,[11] by which I mean that each is limited in range, true only in given conditions, and to some extent inconsistent with every other. Thus, the spatial principle of 'closeness' or 'distance' modifies the totemic principle sufficiently to allow men to say cynically 'distant sisters are good sweet-hearts,' and to kill without compunction men who, under the terminology of kinship, are 'brothers.'

It follows from the above that, except under hypothesis, Murinbata society and/or culture cannot be set up as 'a unified whole.' The hypothesis seems to me quite unpersuasive. The 'principles' of social interaction do not appear to have a ground of unity which can be stated. Indeed, the metaphysical conceptions which the Murinbata

11 I am following here A. B. Lowell's conception in *Conflicts of Principle*, 1932.

have developed about their own ontology of life are filled with what for the present may be called 'dualism.' It is thus impossible to deal, in any rigorous sense, with *a* social system which is supposed to exhibit *a* structure. The many classes of relations of association exhibit several distinct though connected structures. A brief discussion may help to remove ambiguity.

The relations of association between clans through their members are visible as conjoint acts. These when repeated exhibit form or pattern. One may characterise the form or pattern as a structure of operations. The ceremony of *Punj* is a type-instance. This structure (let us call it S) is a sequence or process of observable features, the acts or operations which are clearly named or identifiable. But a necessary condition of *Punj* is that its principals be guided and guarded throughout by one or more members of a class of *naŋgun*, or wives' brothers. The quasi-genealogical relation is a necessary condition of S, and part of the ceremony may be studied as a relation between referents (*naŋgun*) and *relata* (initiands).[12] In such a case we have also to study operations but, if desired, we can study them as functions of *naŋgun* towards the young principals; and thus, if one likes, as functions between 'positions' in a 'network.' The schema of description, abstraction and interpretation is then quite distinct. A structure of functions in this sense may be distinguished as S, and S, the operations, may be regarded as constituting the matter or content of which *S* is a form. But the persons present on the ground of *Punj* are there as members of families, clans, moieties, sub-sections and the like. That is, as members of groups which form a segmental structure. This structure, which we may call SS, is visible only from time to time and in masked forms. What one *sees* at Punj is the structure of operations (S); one has to infer or construct the structure of functions (S) and the segmental structure (SS). As Professor Firth and many others have shown, the 'structure' idea could be taken a good deal farther.

12 I am using the terms in their formal logical sense. The direction of the relation is from *nanggun* (the referent) to the principal (the *relatum*). But at a later stage the converse relation holds.

If S, *S* and SS are confounded, as they tend to be in many discussions of 'social structure,' an ambiguity which is quite intolerable results.[13] My analysis here is intended to avoid this kind of ambiguity. The objects are limited. I wish to distinguish a class of groups relevant to the religious life (the totemic class); to sketch the types of functions which fall to them by virtue of their constitutive sign; and to show that the acts of sociality taking place between them, and thus forming the 'relations,' may be studied as operations with a distinguishable structure. I believe that 'a structure of enduring relations' must be taken in this sense, as a structure of acts of sociality, when the ontology of the Aboriginal life is under study.

Although the sketch is brief, I hope that it brings out a main point: the totality of Murinbata life is one of multiple principles. Because the principles are conjugate they affect different regions of life which overlap and are in conflict. The sacramental or totemic principle sets an ideal which covers only part of the total field of necessary interaction. If the principles have a unity among themselves I have not been able to find what it is, and doubt if it exists. Certain aspects of Murinbata tradition suggest a working towards a unified system or unified whole. But to utilise a theory in which the fact of a unified whole is a postulate, or even a hypothesis, seems to me to be without warrant.

If one were to try to make a picture of the structure of sociality, it would have nothing in common with the 'network' imagery of structuralist anthropology. The Murinbata themselves make a kind of picture of the articulation of the segmental groups. They use sticks or stones in such a way that what emerges looks a little like a branching tree or a flung fish-net. But it is not a picture of sociality. That picture exists in the dramatisation given by *Punj* in complex symbolisms of mime, song, dance and rite. The ontological reality stated there is not

---

13 'It is the categories of people and the regular forms of relationships between them that anthropologists generally mean when they speak of social structure.' See W. R. Geddes, 'Fijian Social Structure in a Period of Transition,' in *Anthropology in the South Seas*, ed. J. D. Freeman and W. R. Geddes, 1959, p. 202.

reducible to points of force on a network. A 'theory' of that reality would have to be a rationalisation of a reality which, if my account is correct, the Murinbata put to themselves as a joyous thing with maggots at the centre. It takes considerable temerity to try to improve on this imagery.

I shall therefore not extend the sketch, as would be necessary if my purpose were different, to the complex structures and segments of Murinbata organisation, or to the functional classes. Instead, I shall pursue the argument that the religion may best be studied for what it shows itself to be: a celebration of values and at the same time a dramatisation of the moral imperfection of social being. The thesis is much that stated by Höffding[14] many years ago: that religion is determined by 'the fate of values in the struggle for existence.' He was speaking of the precious social values and of religion as their conservation. The view has been described as 'a bad and grovelling philosophy of religion' by a writer[15] from within a particular tradition which itself appears to illustrate the thesis. But Höffding added cautiously: 'if this is so, we must not ignore the possibility that this underlying element of religion may exist and operate without expressing itself either in myth, dogma or cult.' In the traditional Murinbata religion that element finds an expression.

The material which follows lends itself to many uses and interpretations. It can easily be wrought into fancied shapes by those of particular convictions. I would regret such uses though I cannot guard against them. I do not myself regard the facts as giving any weight to general theories of natural religion or to the conceptions of any particular religion.

4. The Search for a Paradigm

The attempt which I made in the first article to draw a picture of the rite of *Punj* resulted in a spiral path or course of connected acts. If the same approach were made to the facts of the two earlier initiations—Djaban

14 Harald Höffding, *The Philosophy of Religion*, 1900, p. 109.

15 J. S. Whale, *The Protestant Tradition*, 1959, p. 267.

and circumcision—and if the three were connected together we should have a whorl-like path or course which gives a kind of total picture of the ritual pattern to be observed in the development of male social personality from tender youth to manhood. As a picture it would have only the worth of its logic and assembled facts. But the totality of a community's life is, as Radcliffe Brown observed, 'not any sort of entity.' The *only* hope of attaining *some* understanding within that totality is by the study of the identifiable processes which *are* entities. In the circumstances even a poor picture is better than none. The initiations are separable and identifiable entities; they are processes or tasks taken on by men of authority, carried through, and ended with well-stated tasks attained. The observation and analysis can be kept at all stages under inductive control. The factual descriptions I have given, while by no means perfect, are not, I believe, greatly in error. The expository device used brings out a property or set of properties of the processes which seems to me to be paradigmatic of Murinbata religious culture. Another approach of the same kind would no doubt produce an equally interesting shape. The task of theory is to enquire into the properties of processes which take on such shapes when pictures are drawn of them. An equal simplicity and clarity are not attainable at present by the use of words and sentences.

Each process is a serial sequence of connected acts. The three processes lie end-to-end in a temporal order. The principle of each is the same: a setting aside from normality, a kind of destruction, a kind of transformation, and a return to a new normality of the same order as, but qualitatively distinct from, the original. A simple word to describe the movement would be 'zigzag,' a more ponderous one 'dialectical.' The facts are quite observable, and if I use 'dialectical' I do so without any reference whatever to the philosophical and argumentative meanings of the word. Nor do I conjure up any images of T. S. Eliot's 'vast impersonal forces.' I am using for things which I have seen, and could have been seen by anyone, a word that describes perhaps better than any other word the form of process in which the things occur. I propose for the moment to leave the usage abstract and allusive, but to try to connect it with a generalisation made by a different approach to the religious culture.

On the facts put forward in these papers, Murinbata religion might well be described as the celebration of a dependent life which is conceived as having taken a wrongful turn at the beginning, a turn such that the good of life is now inseparably connected with suffering. The terms of that statement may now be considered in a little more detail.

(a) The Celebration of Dependence

All the peoples of the region live in what is one of the most favourable environments in Australia. They look on it as abundantly stocked with the means of life. The traditions have little to say of hunger, nothing of famine. Certainly, it is no Polynesia; scarcity makes itself felt; conflict takes place over unlawful use of clan preserves and over the theft of species for magical propagation in places where they are dwindling or have disappeared. But the well-watered countryside has been able to sustain a relatively dense population without difficulty, more easily, for example, than the fertile Murray River Valley. The coastal clans are better off than those inland because of tidal flats and mangrove forests, which are rich in food species. A widely-distributed plant, the zamia palm, provides green or dry nuts as a staple food all the year round. But the clans of the plains, swamps, savannah and hills do not consider their lands less fruitful. Many do not relish seafoods even when available, since the taste does not please them. Every clan tends to boast of the plenty with which the ancestors endowed it.

The idea that living men are lesser beings than the ancestors, and dependent on them, is strongly held. It is justified by a mythology which uses a simple but vivid imagery to show how great the powers which men have lost were. The ancestors stocked the land with rivers, springs, food, weapons and other means of life, raised up hills and mountains, put spirit-children into the waters, used the wind and songs as agencies of will, went up into the sky, provided dreams as a means of communicating with the living, and performed a host of similar marvels. Perhaps the greatest were those by which the ancestors transformed themselves into animals,[16] thus instituting the relationships of totemism, and left life-giving principles in the estates of the patrilineal clans. The nature of the marvels is the measure of men's dependency. But the Murinbata attain a buoyant and even high-spirited attitude to life in spite of its contingency. There is nothing even approximately equivalent to the ancient Nile-dwellers' brooding on 'the carnage of the year.'

In writing of them one is always tempted to use the word 'celebration' instead of 'ceremony.' It would put no strain on the meaning of words to write of *Punj* and *Djaban* in such a way. From all accounts the same spirit ruled the *Karamala*, the first-stage initiation last performed about fifty years ago, and another rite—the *Tjimburki*, on which I have only a little information—which ceased about the same time. The word would even fit, though not quite as well, the expressive quality of the circumcisions, the formal fights between clans, and the games between moieties. I do not of course suggest that 'ceremony' could be dropped. Far from it, since ceremoniousness is the most visible property of the several classes of formal conduct. But 'celebration' peculiarly fits the quality and function of the class of formal conduct which is also religious.

All trustworthy accounts of Aboriginal life have brought out the facts of the vitality and enthusiasm that accompany the religious rites. The account given in the last article was not overdrawn in its suggestion of a rapt celebration of whatever is central to *Punj*.

(b) The Wrongful Turning of Life

It is impossible to say to what extent the Murinbata of the past believed, or those of the present believe, what are put forward as their beliefs.

16 The mythology, unlike that of some other regions, holds that animals are transformations of the original men. But the visual representations often differ. *Mutjingga* may be represented as a grotesque figure only in part recognisable as human. One drawing shows her as half-woman, half-snake. On the whole, animal creation seems to be conceived as humanity transformed and deprived of certain powers. But I regard the question as one which is not now fully determinable.

The older men and women certainly appear to, and scepticism is by no means complete among those who are younger. The mythology, which is well formed, is still widely cited. The element relevant to the inquiry is the persistent suggestion of many myths that there has been some kind of 'immemorial misdirection' in human affairs, and that living men are committed to its consequences.

The myth which is central to *Punj* is not the only one which could be referred to,[17] but is particularly valuable in the present context. It is given here in a contracted form.

> Mutjiŋga, the Old Woman, slept there until morning. The people said, 'we shall leave the children with you while we find honey; you look after them.' The Old Woman said, 'yes, I will keep them here.' The people spread out to hunt.
>
> The Old Woman called to the children, 'go and bathe in the water there, and then come to lie down in the sun to dry.' She showed them how to do so. When they were washed they came ashore, and ran close to her, wanting to sleep.
>
> The Old Woman, herself truly wanting to sleep, made a sleeping place in the shade.
>
> She took one child by the arm, saying '*Kaŋiru*,[18] I will look for lice in your hair. Are you itchy?' The child said, 'Yes, you look for me.' The Old Woman, pretending, said 'you look too for my lice.' Then she swallowed the child, letting it go entirely inside her own body. Then she said to a second

17 Another principal myth, concerning the murder of Kunmaŋgur, the Rainbow Serpent, by his son Tjinimin, the Bat, has the same suggestion stated differently. The myth is mentioned briefly in 'Continuity and Change Among the Aborigines,' my Presidential Address to Section F, at the Adelaide meeting of ANZAAS, 1958.

18 The term designates the relationship of (man-speaking) daughter's daughter, and (woman-speaking) brother's daughter's daughter. All the children were in relationships of the second and third (descending) generations.

child, '*Kaŋiru*, I will make you sleep.' This way, the child disappeared, swallowed like the other.

(The myth then relates, in much the same phraseology, how eight more children, making ten in all, were swallowed).

> A man and his wife, thirsty for water, came back to the camp from hunting. The woman swore violently at her husband, 'I see no children here. Where are they? What did she do with them? She swallowed them! There are no children. Come quickly!' The husband, from a distance, quickly ran to her. The woman, seeing tracks, then said, 'Ah, yes, she went that way.' Then, pointing to the water, she said, 'You run quickly the short way.' Both ran, calling out in alarm, by different ways in the direction in which the water flowed.
>
> All the people, alarmed by the cries, now came together running. They gathered spears and womerahs from every place. Among them, calling out, was a mature man, Left Hand. 'That way, that way.'
>
> Five men ran one way, five another, to come together later at a shallow water-crossing. There was no one there. The water was clear. They ran again as before, and again met. Still the clear water gave no sign. Again they ran and met to no avail, finding clear water only.
>
> The river now went crookedly. The people thought the Old Woman might have crawled along it. Dividing again, they searched as before. Now, meeting, they saw that the water was no longer clear. Ah! The murk stirred up by her dragging fingernails could be seen. Again they divided and ran, meeting to search again. Ah! The water was more clouded still. They divided and ran on the sand to Manawarar. Ah! Here the water was heavily clouded. They were overtaking her. Good!
>
> Now all told Left Hand, because of his great skill, to take spear and Right Hand to take club; the two men ran, one to each side of the water to block the Old Woman's road.

> They came together and looked. No one! Good! They waited and waited ... then they saw big eyes coming, and out came the Old Woman throwing water from each side. Mutjinga was here!
>
> She kept coming, not seeing the men. When she was close Left Hand threw his spear. *Du!* It hit and pierced both her legs. *Yakai!* The Old Woman cried, 'From whom is this?' Left Hand answered 'from yourself! Yours was the fault!'
>
> Right Hand jumped into the water and with his club broke the Old Woman's neck. There, it was done! The men looked. Her belly was moving! Then, slowly, holding her up, they cut her open with a knife of stone. There, in her womb, the children were alive! They had not gone where the excrement was.
>
> Left Hand and Right Hand now pulled the children one by one from the womb, washed them, and came with them to fire to dry them in the smoke. Then they painted the children with ochre and put on their foreheads the *kutaral*[19] which is the mark of the initiated. Then Left Hand and Right Hand took them back to the camp where they now saw their mothers.
>
> Joyfully, the mothers cried, 'they are alive, they are alive. See, the men are bringing them now,' and hit their own heads so that the blood flowed. 'O, children, alas, alas! What did she do to you? She swallowed you!'

Even allowing for differences of idiom, the myth and the rite do not match each other—at least on the analysis so far put forward—in all particulars. There is a good organic connection but, since we are dealing with the myth *of* the rite, we have a natural expectation that the two will fit together. But the respective broad patterns can be narrowed to virtual identity of theme and form: a setting apart of life from normality, an act of destruction, a transformation, and a return to normality in a new

19 A band made of opossum hair.

status and a new locus. Just as the study of the pattern of the rite led in a surprising direction, with its suggestion of depth beyond depth, so does a study of the pattern in the myth.

The myth—like the rite—is obviously dense with import, but not immediately understandable import. There is rich material for analysis within several disciplinary approaches. The immediate task, as I see it, is to try to resolve from the complex what is primary to our purpose, and to leave what—in that sense—is secondary to different studies. The remainder, of course, includes many matters of intrinsic interest to anthropology, e.g. the illumination of relationships of social structure; the adduction to the myth of common-life situations so that they have symbolical meanings; and the syntax and idiom of symbolical conceptualisation. The psychoanalytical schemata are not within my province and, in any case, not every anthropologist is persuaded that truly universal symbolisms have been demonstrated beyond question.

Our first question must surely be: what construction does the Murinbata themselves put on the myth?

With many myths it is often a task of great difficulty to answer such a question. But there is little difficulty in finding out the mentality in this case, since the mature men freely discuss the significance of *Mutjiŋga's* death.

From many conversations with the men the following points emerged quite strongly. (I) *Mutjiŋga* was once *Kadu*, that is a truly human person, not one of the self-subsistent spirits recognised within the theogony. (2) She had primal authority: what she did determined for men much of the subsequent shape of reality. (3) Her death was, and still is, a matter of sorrow: 'she should have lasted a long time'; 'the people did not want to kill her'; 'they wanted to keep her alive for *Punj*.' (4) Her death was the consequence of her own mysteriously motivated act, and was inevitable: 'she went wrong herself'; that is (as Left Hand reminded her) the fault was hers, not the people's; the act was *maŋe nigunu*, 'her own hand.' (5) The loss to man was irreparable: the sentiment is usually expressed by a phrase[20] which is translated into

20 The phrase is *pirimbun madaku*. Its literal meaning is very difficult

English as 'bad luck,' but is possibly better expressed as 'sad finality,' with an overtone of something like 'loss' or 'waste.' (6) *Mutjiŋga's* act was wrong, but apparently only in that it was premature: she should have waited until the children were grown and ready to become *Kadu Punj*; swallowing them would then have been right. (7) Because she died, men now have only the bullroarer, which was made in order to take her place i.e. stand for her and (as I said in the first article) to be her emblem, symbol and sign.[21]

The problem of the 'meaning' of the myth is one to which I have no satisfactory answer. Whatever may be the situation in other societies, in Aboriginal Australia it is impossible to ask questions bearing directly

---

to express. *Pirim* = 'standing,' 'being there,' 'not at rest'; *bun* = vb. suffix, 3rd p. pl.; *ma* = negative particle; *da* = 'camp,' 'place,' 'state of being'; *Ku* = 'flesh.' But *mada* may also mean 'belly' and 'heart.' Being puzzled by the phrase, I asked a very intelligent Murinbata to try to say in English what it meant. He said, 'like you watching someone trying something, like making something; that man not doing good thing [i.e. not being successful]. You say, "You going to try again?" He say, "*Pirimngim madaku!* I finished! I can't do any more!" Like something good, but you don't look after it. Bad luck!' What he implied was a sad recognition of the futility of further effort, that something attempted, or possible, had reached finality in failure. The phrase is very common in everyday situations.

21 The circumstances in which the bullroarer came to men are dealt with in another myth. *Kudapun*, the apostle bird, who was coæval with *Mutjingga* (in spite of her supposed humanness), shaped the first bullroarer after her death. He found that it gave out its roar when swung, but the string broke and it fell into deep water. Two young women at fishing brought it ashore in a net. They were mystified by it, and thought it a bad and dangerous thing. Men took them into the bush (to the first *mambana* or secret place?) and killed them by cutting their necks. Thus, true men became possessed of the bullroarer for the first time and preserved it. The myth justifies the exclusion of women from the secret. They know the myth of *Mutjingga* but—according to the men—not that the bullroarer is her emblem, symbol and sign. The fact is that most adult women do know. Indeed, the 'open' or non-secret name of the bullroarer is *Mutjingga*. Women tell their children that its noise is her voice.

on the matter. There is no way of forming the questions unambiguously in the vernacular, and Aborigines who speak English well not only have nothing relevant to say themselves but cannot phrase the rationalistic-type questions in their own tongue.[22] The usefulness of both direct and indirect questions falls off sharply. Even old men of intelligence and stamina who survive many inquisitions are apt to shrug, and say: 'it is a thing we do not understand.' This always struck me as an excellent definition of mystery.

In the most general sense we are in touch with a world-and-life view beginning to take what would eventually be a credal form. But it is the kind of embodiment which is innocent of detached intellectualism. With such materials Robertson Smith's trenchantly-expressed cautions need to be kept very much in mind. 'The myth apart from the ritual affords only a doubtful and slippery kind of evidence' as to the fixed and statutory elements of the religion. While 'men would not be men if they agreed to do certain things without having a reason for their action' we cannot look to the myths for a statement of those reasons. Nevertheless, accepting the cautions, we may still find at least indirect evidence that to Aboriginal minds the nodal experiences of life—and thus, the primordial formula stated in the myths—have a certain tragic quality. The evidence is rather more extensive than I am able to indicate conveniently here. But one may say that it depicts man-in-the-world as exposed to untimely death, treachery, violence, warlockry and harmful influences of many kinds; as given to malice, bad faith, egoism and jealousy; and in a sense as bereft of justice.

The actualities of life undoubtedly cohere with such an image to a large extent. There is a stratum of living on which much disappointment and bitterness accumulate. Marital infidelity, back-biting, mischief-making, violence, treachery and delict are very common indeed. But the

22 Every anthropologist with knowledge of Australian conditions will be all too familiar with the problem. My best informant said to me: 'It is no good asking the old men why this, why that? All they say is like this: 'Your dreaming there,' and they point.'

mythological conception is on a grander scale than that of the domestic scene. The scale is what I refer to as macro-experience (Fig.1).

To argue that the Murinbata act as they do because they have the conception of life sketched in the myths would be absurd. To argue that the facts of life are the reason why they have the conception would be an undue simplification. It seems to be nearer the truth to say that actuality and conception are variables which have developed together with others. The two cohere, but to say anything of an evidential kind about the development seems impossible.

Ordinarily, Aboriginal religion is not represented as concerned with metaphysical problems. I am not able to share such an opinion, and think that the impression of a rather mindless participation in rites created by some works reflects the outlook of the analyst rather than that of the Aborigines. A prolonged exposure to the rites comes to suggest both a depth and a dignity of outlook which may lack formulation but not reality. The implicitness—by which I mean wordlessness—of the conceptions does not detract from the kind of reality they have. The celebrants of *Punj* cluster in a shallow, circular hole in the sacrosanct place where the real presence of the Mother is supposed to manifest itself. The hole is conceptualised either as a 'nest' or a 'wallow.' The first is a fairly clear symbol of family and sociality. The second is in some sense its reverse. The buffalo, in this region usually a solitary wanderer, makes or seeks a wallow against the heat of the day or to free itself from irritating pests and parasites. The symbol thus denotes what seem like positive and negative statements of the same truth about life: at the centre of things social, refuge and rottenness are found together. In other words, there is an intuition of an integral moral flaw in human association.

Few facts or institutions of living are left without some sort of mythological warrant for being what they are. A supposed past is described in ways which are held to account for the present. The standards of sequence, completeness and logical relatedness attained in the myths are not impressive if the stories are taken in a literal sense. The gaps, variations and contradictions do not allow one to say that, in any rigorous sense, the myths constitute a 'system' of belief. There is also a certain amount of evidence that we are in touch with an historical composite. At the same time we are clearly dealing with a world-and-life view expressing a metaphysic of life which can and should be elicited. But the myths do not allow anything whatsoever to be inferred concerning the remote past with which they purport to deal. What we encounter is a contemporary form of thought about the recent past and present.

(c) The Connection of Suffering and Good

There is nothing like the idea of a Golden Age in the mythology. Some of the evidence that the time of heroes and marvels is not idealised was given in (a) and (b). The absence of such a point of view should mean that on the moral side of mythology there are no entelechies, and this is the case with the Murinbata myths. The ideas of perfection are simply not formed. Indeed, the narration of the myths is sometimes accompanied by laughter among the listeners, and I have sometimes thought it had a sardonic tone.

It might be said that the more important myths are unanalytical essays on acts of will, the motives of the will remaining unstated and rather mysterious. We thus learn of the will of *Mutjiŋga* to put an end to burgeoning life, and of her act and its consequences, but nothing whatsoever of her motive. The same is true of *Tjinimin's* will to kill his father *Kunmaŋgur*, and of the latter's will at death to remove all the fire from the world. Then too there is the will of *Waak*, Old Crow, to die when confronted by the demonstration of *Bali*, Old Crab, that life could continue by casting off its restricting shell. The myths remain tantalisingly silent about the *why* of the acts which had such vast consequences. The Old Woman was killed: and men have to maintain her emblem, sign and symbol as the means of immolating youth. The Father was murdered: and his death at the hands of his son gave men the means of the perennial life which The Mother of All must touch. *Waak* put men under necessity of death: but the vital will of men to persist is evident in all they do; the greatest single cause of human conflict is the attribution of death to warlockry. The facts create a first impression of dualism. To support a thesis of dualism would be easy. There is no suggestion of a first cause, or a spiritual personage who is all-good, or one who is so all-powerful that all are subject to him in all things. There is no independent entity, and none of a wholly unitary nature. *Mutjiŋga* killed, but is mourned. *Kunmaŋgur* was killed but in death gave benison, only to try then to deprive the world of fire so that men would live like animals, eating raw flesh. One could say that dualism in this sense is the norm of the mythology, but it is only an apparent dualism. It is rather a kind of counterpoise, a unity of opposites.

The myths are a sort of statement about whole reality, a declaration about the penalties of private will, and by implication a thesis on the spoiling of possible unity. They also come very close to the spirit of certain insights within other cultures, e.g. The Buddha's observation that suffering is a product of the striving for being. But we simply do not have the evidence from which to infer clearly what *Mutjiŋga* strove for. Why should she have wished of her own volition—*maŋe nigunu*—to end life? This, to the Aborigines, is a dismaying mystery. The case of *Kunmaŋgur* is not easier. *Tjinimin*, The Bat, emerges as a figure again acting *maŋe nukunu*, in self-will for gratuitous motive: He seduced his sisters, but there is no suggestion in the myth that the father knew, or was angry, or reproachful. The Murinbata, thinking it astonishing that anyone, of volition, should have preferred death to life, hold the crow in opprobrium, and hold in contempt peoples who have been known to eat it. We can perhaps say that the evidence shows a dispensation of duality that the formation of familiar being and its constituent entities made for the cohesion of good to bad. But the cohesion is not truly or clearly moralised. The idea of an entelechy has simply not differentiated.

Taken as a whole the myths deal with cosmology rather than cosmogony. That is, they deal less with origins as such than with the instituting of relevances—the beginnings of a moral system—in a life which already was. The tacit assumption invariably is that something existed before the marvels. No imagination is exercised about that aspect. The myths rationalise and justify *familiar* entities, forms and relations. In that sense one may say that they deal with being rather than with existence, or with existence become intelligible by having taken on familiar forms. The enduring nature of the forms is a subject of strong Aboriginal sentiment. The authority of the marvels by which the forms came about or were associated with weighs very heavily. Experience with the traditional Murinbata confirms in every way the impression made on other Australian anthropologists: the Aborigines seem to feel bound by some kind of necessity to what was instituted anciently.

5. Relations between Myth and Rite

The myth of The Old Woman is not *told* as a feature of the rite. It is not, like the rite, a secret. Women know at least something of it. Some men know it better than others. But for all the initiated men it has an esoteric significance which is a male secret. My earlier statement about the myth *of* the rite thus requires qualification. Empirically, we can speak only of an attachment. The anthropological interest lies in that fact, and how it is to be characterised under a theory.

The type of analysis required is one that will link the two within the ontological system as I have tried to sketch it. All the difficulties referred to earlier—the limits of the indicative-analytical language, empirical methods, and abstractive selection—are here at their worst.

An analysis through linguistic categories is not only outside my scope but, in my opinion, is also unsuitable. To be sure, the myth *is* a special kind of language but I reject as inappropriate an analysis *as* a special kind of language. My concern is with the *use* of language or speech-forms *as myth in a situation of rite.* The first aim of study from such a viewpoint is to find similarities between rite as a structure of operations and myth as a structure of comparable or analagous elements. Unless such elements can be brought into an approximation, however rough at first, then there is nothing sufficiently isolate and concrete for concepts to refer to, and in consequence there cannot be any theory of myth attached to rite.

Table 1. Myth and Rite: The Empirical Order of Events

I. Circumcision.	II. **Djaban.**	III. **Rite of *Punj*.**	IV. **Myth of *Punj*.**
A. Secret agreement.	Secret agreement.	Secret agreement.	Public agreement.
B. Escort from camp by affine with token show of force.	Escort from camp by peers who use a trick.	Public act to compel silence and escort to *ngudanu.**	Trustful withdrawal of parents to hunt.
C. Isolation in distant place with guardian and friends.	Isolation from camp in secret place with guardian.	Isolation from camp in secret place with guardian.	Isolation of children in camp with trusted cognate.
D. Token return to camp to be wailed over; prevention of contact with female kin; fondling by male kin.	Fictitious fight; guided flight to camp as refuge; road blocked.	Guarded and secret return to camp at night; act of deception at *ngudanu*; mime of blowfly; *Tjirmumuk.*	Treacherous acts of sociality; mock-search for lice; the deceptive invitation to sleep.
E. Act of circumcision within male screen.	Act of terrorisation by disguised men.	Symbolical swallowing by The Old Woman.	Act of swallowing to the interior of Mutjinga's body†; disembowelling.
F. Gifts of valuables; washing; the return to the camp, with partial exclusion.	Gifts of valuables; washing; the return to the mothers, with partial exclusion.	Gift of the bullroarer; return to the mothers; the washing; partial exclusion.	Restoration to life; washing; the adornment; the return to the mothers under male escort.

* Omitted from description in the first article.

† The myth stresses the fact that the children went into the body as far as the womb.

It is useful at this stage to bring together in a table of condensation the main facts of the rite and myth, and to put alongside them those of *Djaban* and circumcision. Descriptions of the last two are probably unnecessary, since *Djaban* closely resembles *Punj* in all essentials, and the circumcision is of classical type.

Table 1 is an arrangement of the main events or part-events of the four entities set out in columnar sequences which are intended to reproduce the actual processes acted out or told. That is, the order in which the events are set out, from top to bottom of the columns, is the actual order (with certain omissions of detail) in which they occur in the originals.

The tabular presentation makes drastic selection and concentration unavoidable. Each entry is as far as possible a datum, something I have seen, heard or been told. The summary accounts of the myth and the rite already given will enable others to check for distortion.

My aim has been to abstract similarities, and I have adapted the language of description to that purpose.

The table shows three things plainly: an affinity of constituents between columns; a similarity of sequences from the onset to the completion; and a good measure of total congruence. It also shows that the distinction made by the Murinbata between I and II is not true of the structural forms. And it reveals the essential problem: a cryptic similarity between (III) and (IV) across a frontier set up by facts belonging to two distinct order. The similarity is not an effect of the schematic ordering. It is 'in' the facts themselves.

The contents of Table 1 are somewhat more intelligible if considered against certain other relevant facts (Table 2). The first table is an empirical, the second a rational, ordering of facts.

Each of the first three columns of Table 1 denotes an entity—the 'ceremony'—which is also a system of functions and a process. The descriptions are in no case complete. Column (IV) is an imaginative system within a wider system of conduct composed—in the eyes of the Murinbata—of (II), (III) and (IV). The wider system defers to data in part set out by Table 2. It includes invisible as well as visible reality. The functions, if fully analysed, would be a description of the state of the system. The process is the entity seen in time and space.

As I have said, the Murinbata classify (I) separately from (II) and (III) by saying that it is not intended to make young men 'understand' and is not as 'big' or as 'heavy,' thus providing a simple linear scale of their own. They insist that one must know (IV) in order to understand (III), and as best they can expound what they mean by The Dreaming as the condition of understanding (I)—(IV).

It is likely to be fatal to an understanding 'from within' to divide the entity, as by dissociating the use of the language from the acts, or the ideas from the acts, or by setting up beliefs in a causal connection with the acts. Likewise, to impose on the functions a set of organicist or mechanistic metaphors, or to suppose that the process is illumined by treating it as a variable of kin-relations.

Vertically, Table 1 exhibits the activity-aspect of entities and systems of functions as processes over time, each process being distinct and separable from onset to termination. Horizontally, it exhibits what seem to be equivalences. Both axes are fully meaningful only through things which are either not shown, e.g. the symbolic culture, or shown in part only in Table 2, e.g. the data of which each vertical axis of Table 1 is a system. The tabular arrangement has obvious limitations, for at every item one has to consult, as it were silently and by imagination, things which cannot be depicted in this way.

Table 2. Myth and Rite: The Rational Order

	I. **Circumcision.**	II. **Djaban.**	III. **Rite of *Punj*.**	IV. **Myth of *Punj*.**
1. Expressed motive of men in authority.	To 'quieten young boys.'	To 'make them understand' the first tokens of mystery.	To 'make them understand' the full mystery.	*'Mange nigunu.'*
2. Proximate goal.	To 'make a man.'	To 'get ready for *Punj*.'	To 'stop trouble coming.'	'No one understands.'
3. Inferred ultimate goal(s).	To form male ethos; make distant friends; build up desire for premial rewards of conformity.	To instil fear of male authority*; weaken dependence on women†; develop sense of mystification.	To designate formal readiness for marriage; consolidate the male ethos.	?
4. Observed effects.	Growth of male egoism; formation of friendships; developed interest in trade.	Detachment from mother's influence; intensification of restraint with sisters.	Maturation of male social personality.	?
5. Affective intent.	Discipline by pain; attachment to affines; reassurance towards wider society.	Discipline by fear; the demonstration of male power in society; teaching the lesson of 'the wild dog.'	Discipline by fear and mystery; deepening of interior life; the demonstration of the highest sociality.	?

	I. Circumcision.	II. Djaban.	III. Rite of *Punj.*	IV. Myth of *Punj.*
6. Task.				
(*a*) **Structural aspect.**	Submission of one to many.	As in (I).	Submission of one or few to many, and of all to all.	Submission of many to one, and one to all.
(*b*) **Relation between principals.**	Affine and cognate but affine dominant.	As in (I) but influence approximately equal.	As in (I).	Cognate.
(*c*) **Normative duration:**				
(i) Main ceremony.	1–2 days.	2–4 weeks.	2 months.	?
(ii) Total event.	1–3 months.	2–4 weeks.	2 months.	?
(iii) Sequelæ.	6 months.	3 months.	1–2 years.	?
(iv) Degree of secrecy.	Minimal.	Submaximal.	Maximal.	?

* The deliberate terrorisation of boys by older men, who wear disguises, is a notable feature of Djaban, but does not occur in the other ceremonies.

† A growing hostility between boys and their mothers is noticeable before *Djaban*. Stones are flung, bad language used, and authority defied. There is also an increasing constraint with sisters.

There is certainly sufficient natural metaphor on both axes to impel caution in the use of interpretative metaphor suggested by the organicist and mechanical-structural hypotheses. And while the real-life connections between the columns are made by actual persons at the business of life, to select the *classes* of kin-relations as having some kind of primary explanatory power is arbitrary and unwarranted.

6. Analogy; Allegory and Explanation

The art and method of explanation among the Aborigines are to find apt likenesses between the familiar and the unfamiliar. To hear or see this done is one of the most commonplace experiences of fieldwork among them. They take delight in repeating the mistakes their fathers made: how sugar was called 'sand,' flour 'paint,' tobacco 'fæces' and so on. In more complex matters they use the word *ŋinipun* which in this context signifies shape, form, aspect, contour or outwardness: 'general appearance' would be a good translation. I conceive that this process of mind occurs in the making of myth. Things of the social order provide them with *ŋinipun* or shapes or images aptly resembling those which their intuitive minds discern in rite. It is an extension of the process by which one subject, an unknown, is likened to another, a known, the likening constituting a type of explanation. If the main functions of myth are not cognitive and communicative then I doubt very much if we can understand them at all.

In a striking passage[23] Robertson Smith observed: 'As a rule the myth is no explanation of the origin of a ritual to anyone who does not believe it to be a narration of real occurrences, and the boldest mythologist will not believe that. But, if it be not true, the myth itself requires to be explained, and every principle of philosophy and commonsense demands that the explanation be sought, not in arbitrary allegorical theories, but in the actual facts of religious custom to which the myth attaches.'

23 *Op. cit.*, p. 18.

In other words, if there is no theory of rite then there can be no theory of myth. It is a position with which, on the whole, I agree. I do not consider that we can speak seriously of 'a theory of rite' as yet existing in anthropology, and for this reason interpretations of myth remain conditional. But, within this limitation—and it is one which I regard as almost crippling—certain things seem reasonably clear. If the rite of *Punj* has an ontological significance then so has the myth. If the rite expresses something about the macro-experience of living then so does the myth. If the rite has to do with a mystery—and the Aborigines say so in words which are quite distinct—then our concern lies not with the *literal* but with the *figurative* meaning of the myth. The literal language is simply a case of the non-mysterious being used to give shapes or *ŋinipun* to the mysterious. For my own part I see neither true interest nor significance in dissecting the figurative aspect of the myth for 'reflections' or 'expressions' of the social structure. That there are such I do not doubt. What I would think remarkable would be to find myths which did *not* contain such reflections or expressions. For what *other* image or idea-language could be used? One must keep sharply in mind that one is dealing with the symbolical constructions of a people amongst whom there is no class of scholars or detached intellectuals, who know nothing of writing, who rarely if ever ask the *how* or *why*-questions from philosophical motive, and who face a vast undifferentiation of entities and relations which, in such circumstances, can only be intuited. For the same reasons, understanding can founder before it begins if the method of inquiry is controlled by a rational logic which suppresses considerations of an ontological reality that—as is clearly the case among the Aborigines—*has begun to excite feeling*. Both the myth and the rite of *Punj* are evidences of a *something* differentiating, a something the Murinbata say they do not 'hold in the ear,' that is, a mystery.

What one is thus studying is a moment in the development of cult. The historical aspects, for reasons I have already stated, are too nebulous to deal with here, since their significance requires careful, extended reasoning. I will simply interpolate the observation that a large inter-regional study is now required into the wide diffusion of the bullroarer cult, and into the fall or stasis of the significance of circumcision, or its failure to take on the factitious significance of cult in the northern region.

Regarded from the above point of view, the myth of *Punj* appears as an elementary attempt to make an identity between a social reality and a new intuition of a suprasocial reality. The known and non-mysterious—the social order—provides both a literal and a figurative language of shapes by which to interpret the unknown and mysterious. Literally, the myth is a story about people. Figuratively, it is an allegory made up of extended metaphor formed from analogies of resemblance. It is not a fully expressed or explicitly formulated analogy, although it approaches that stage. For the most part it is a mystical and figurative statement; not mystical in the sense of a dreamy confusion of thought, but in the sense of having to do with mystery. Metaphor resting on analogy of resemblance is its necessary means.

On the assumptions that the myth of The Old Woman is a story about one thing under the guise of another, and that the story is thus an allegory, there may be some usefulness in an attempt to extract the allegory in a form which does not simply repeat the story. The procedure can only be arbitrary and rationalistic, and the product is unverifiable, but provided it is done with an informed knowledge of Aboriginal symbolism the result may be not without value.

An allegorical interpretation might run approximately as follows:

(1) Innocence or new life (childhood) in mortal peril (death) from private motive (the act *maŋe nigunu*). (2) Mysterious power (femaleness) using responsibility (seniority) to spoil necessary trust (the people's unavoidable request). (3) The flow of life (the stream) being used as concealment (submersion) after wrongdoing. (4) Life becoming tortuous and secretive (the winding, deepening water) after being simple (shallowness). (5) Wrongdoing, at first untraceable (absence of signs in the clear water) finally becoming identifiable (the murk in the water). (6) Opposed but complementary elements of life (left hand, right hand) by agreement (the plan of search and ambush) and diverse means (the

different routes) which are nevertheless complementary (the successive meetings) attaining their object (the entrapment). (7) The assertion of joint male authority (two men send by all the people) to do justice (the rhetorical attribution of guilt) and retribution (the justified slaying). (8) The persistence of life (the moving stomach of The Old Woman), but its powerlessness to save itself (the disembowelling). (9) The avoidance of contamination (by excrement) as a condition of renewed life. (10) The cleansing of a new life (washing and drying) and bright adornment (by painting) before restoration (escort to camp) in a different status (initiation). (11) The restoration (welcome) to the loving care (weeping) of those with mysterious power over life (the mothers).

The interpretation will seem an exploitation of symbolical obscurities only to those who do not have a developed sense of the Aboriginal power of imagination. A fair degree of plausibility can be given to the general-specific meanings. I do not propose to do so here, or to pursue the approach further since it lies across the main object, but I might point out that the construction is not very much more tenuous than are many statements about the social structure of peoples who—as one distinguished anthropologist has said—may be only dimly aware, or not even aware at all, that they live under such structures. The interest of the construction is that, in conjunction with Table 1, it reveals more vividly, by a change of language, that both the myth and the rite exemplify processes which we can characterise as having a dialectical form. I regard this fact as one of high importance.

The processes are not merely changes or movements over time but *developments* from one state or situation or condition to another, such that new and old belong to the same order but are qualitatively distinct, the old not quite annulled and the new not quite unfamiliar. The developments are also attained through a train or sequence of opposed acts or operations. We thus seem required to characterise the sequence as 'dialectical.' It is certainly temporal; it is certainly also connected or systematic; and it certainly has the appearance—though an obscure appearance, coming through very diverse and complex elements—of motion and direction through opposites which become resolved.

Exactly what a dialectical process amounts to in a society which anthropology tends to regard as more or less stationary is a matter for investigation. The analysis of processes has not been distinguished by clarity or precision, unlike the studies of the morphology of kinship. But developmental processes with such characteristics occur so commonly among the Aborigines—for example, the supposedly static structure of the sub-section system is a type of dialectical form—that once the form is extracted the natural corrective of a static structuralism of approach is provided. However, I do not propose to divert to such matters here.

In Table 3 I set out the materials of Columns III and IV of Table 1 in an effort to clarify some of the details of the form. The *sequences* from A to F are listed vertically, like the vertical arrangement in Table 1. The table is divided by a central line. To the left of it are placed acts of a given class defined as positive (+) for a quality, and to the right of it acts which are the negative (–) of the class. The general conception is that of *signed conduct* referred to earlier. On the far right of the table I have included major entries made in Fig.1 in the first article. The table aims at setting up broad correspondences only. An effort to force the comparison at such points would detract from whatever value the arrangement has. As stated earlier, it must be remembered that we are dealing with a moment in the development of a cult.

Any errors made in the placements in Table 3 are of course transferred to Fig.3. The classes of acts here regarded as (+) and (-) require analysis in respect of their logical characters, a task I have been unable to attempt. Both table and figure are thus to be regarded as provisional. The congruence of the profiles, and a study of the detail of the movements, show that the visual representation of *Punj* given in the first article is at best very notional. The differences of the profiles probably, but not necessarily, indicate incomplete observation or errors of fact or classification. I wish to make clear that I do not regard the facts as perfectly established even though I have taken pains over them.

Table 3. Sequences of Conduct in Rite and Myth of Punj

A.	III.	IV. Public agreement.	III. Secret agreement.	IV.	Initial Situation	↓
B.			Youths made silent.	Mother makes secrect act of will.	↓	Consecration.
	Youths put in care of guardian	Children put in care of guardian.			Setting Apart.	↓
			Youths made 'wild flesh'.	Children bereft of their parents.	Making into Beasts.	
		Children put in safe, known place.	Youths put in secret, dangerous place.		↓	
CD.			Acts of duplicity.	Acts of duplicity.		Immolation.
			Secret return to camp at night.	Mock request to sleep.		↓
E.	The mine of *Tjiir-mumuk*.	The search for lice.			Anointing.	

A.	III.	IV. Public agreement.	III. Secret agreement.	IV.	Initial Situation	↓
	Sounding of bull-roarer.	Mother calls children to sleep.			↓	
			Anointing with blood and symbolic swalling.	Putative swallow-ing.	Destruction and trans-formation.	
	Shoring of bull-roarer.	Entrapment of mother.			↓	Transformation.
				Men kill mother		↓
F.	Youths swing bull-roar-ers.	Men see Mother's moving stomach.			Gift of the sign.	
	Restraints at *ngudanu* relax.	Children taken alive from womb.			↓	
	?	Washing, drying, adornment.				

A.	III.	IV. Public agreement.	III. Secret agreement.	IV.	Initial Situation	↓
	Formal return to mothers.	Formal return to mothers.				
			Formal wailing.	Formal wailing.	Return to life.	Return of countergood.
			Partial exclusion from camp life.	?	↓	↓
	Washing adornment.	?				
	Formal exchange of food with parents and female kin; slow relaxation of restraints; sexual experience; amrriage.	No information but life as initiated persons implied.			Terminal situation = new locus and position.	Terminal situation = new state of life.

7. Myth, Rite and Reality

One of the things that distinguish the myth of The Old Woman from every other is that it is told as a sorrowful story. This and a number of other features put one in mind of the *madre dolorosa* and the Greek cults of mystery. But it is nearer to my purpose here to ask: can reasons be found for the growth of the whole cultus? And, if the process of the rite has been described correctly as dialectical, has it any necessary relation to the cult?

(*a*) The bullroarer existed in the region *before* the rise of the present cult. It was smaller, with a narrower range of types, of different colour (black rather than red-brown), and was decorated externally (by white feathers or down) in a style wholly distinct from the incised patterns which came later. (*b*) There is a dim memory of a great rite—the *Tjimburki*—extending over many months, which celebrated the coming of the dry season, and in all probability was connected with the black bullroarer. The rite was a male secret, and centred around deep, circular excavations in the earth. Traces of the excavations may still be seen. (*c*) Yet another rite, of a distinct kind, was connected with the use of great ovoid or circular stone structures still to be seen in the countryside. Nothing is known of the rite except that it was connected with dancing.[24] Nowadays the stone rings are usually connected—probably in a fictitious way—with *Kunmaŋgur*, The Rainbow Serpent, who *may* have been the subject of an earlier rite. Some Aborigines still connect him rather than *Mutjiŋga* with the bullroarer, and I found this to be so among the Nangiomeri twenty-five years ago. (*d*) There is evidence that songs, dances and decorative designs formerly connected with a senior rite were transferred in the past to the junior rite of *Djaban*, and a probability that those associated with *Djaban* were in turn transferred to the *Karamala* initiation of still younger boys.

24 One is reminded of Lucian's observation that 'no mystery was ever celebrated without dancing.'

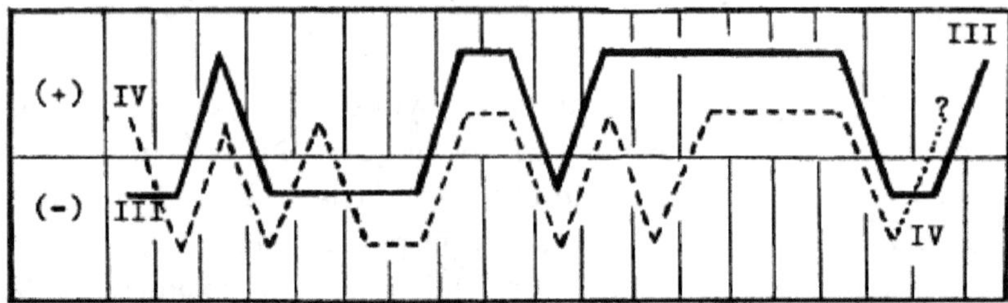

Figure 3. Profiles of sequences in rite and myth. A reduction to visual terms of the entries in Table 3

Facts of this kind strongly suggest an historical succession of cults over a period of perhaps a century. If one adds the indirect evidence of the sacred rock-art the historical perspective is deepened. Some rock-paintings are connected with *Kunmaŋgur* through a myth which still survives strongly, but without a connected rite. Other paintings, which have a strong affinity with the *Wandjina* figures of the Kimberleys, cannot be connected with any rite of which a memory survives.

It seems to me probable that the cultus of the bullroarer, now linked with The Old Woman, is but the last phase of a complex religious development expressing itself through successive transformations of a rite of initiation of constant form. The fact that four ceremonies with an initiatory purpose can be identified gives a peg on which to hang a reconstruction.

On the other hand, the type of process depicted in Fig.2 is thoroughly characteristic of at least three of the initiations, on which I have good information, and probably also of the fourth, the *Karamala*. There is some slight evidence too connecting the *Karamala* with the mime of the blowfly. The facts suggest a crescive and involuted development of theme and form over a fair period of time. The Murinbata live close to the northern boundary of the region where the practice of circumcision ceases, and just beyond the northern boundary of the region where sub-incision ceases. My hypothesis is that the diffusion of circumcision to the region supervened on a system of initiation of which *Karamala* and *Tjimburki* were characteristic, replacing them as the highest cult of the time, only to be superseded in turn by the cult of *Mutjiŋga*. The tradition is that the present cult came from the south through the Victoria River tribes. I propose to examine the evidence for the view in a separate study. A comparison with the cult of *Kunapipi* studied by Dr. Berndt thus becomes necessary.

What emerges immediately is a correction of older views of Aboriginal life as static and unchanging. In terms of the evidence offered here an analytic problem can be rephrased. Instead of the rather bare conception of 'rite,' or of 'rite of initiation,' we may use the conception of *a ritual dialectic of initiation*. A necessary step is the study of the *logical* properties of processes of this type within an ontology of life which predicates many *relational* properties about life in a given world. The symbolical expressions of the metaphysical conceptions of the Aborigines are thus not an optional study for anthropology but a necessity. I regard the questions as absolutely central to theoretical anthropology, but their generality puts them beyond the scope of these articles. I shall attempt a sketch, however, at a later stage.

Each of the *rites de passage* initiated a male *into* a world transcending that in which he had lived hitherto according to the usages proper to his stage and locus of life. But not only were mind and personality widened and deepened by the successive rites. At each stage the subject discovered—or had unfolded to him—a reality of life transcending the former limited reality. On this view the rite of *Punj* widened experience to a terminal. It was, so to speak, the closest approach possible to the whole of life-reality. Hence perhaps the awe and mystification suffusing the rite. The viewpoint at least suggests a *logical* ground for the cognitive and affective states. One may thus construct the initiatory rites, on the metaphysical plane, as acts of thought and feeling towards the whole of reality, and the myths as expressive statements about it. But the history of rites in the region suggest that the conception of reality has been expanding, and with this no doubt there was too a deepening mystification. We may note at this point that there is also positive evidence of an increasing complexity of social organisation at least in part over the same period, e.g. the development of a relatively simple system of patrilineal moieties into the more complex system of subsections which, at least in theory, descend by indirect matrilineality. Many tensions were built up by that process. It is tempting to see in the conjugate principles of matrilineality and patrilineality a possible source of the displacement of *Kunmaŋgur*, the totemic 'father's father' of one moiety and the 'mother's father' of the other, by *Mutjinga*, who is called *kale neki*, 'the mother of us all.'

At all events, the fullness of the *rites de passage* can be apprehended only if they are studied with the Murinbata ontology, and if related to the metaphysical conceptions of a reality being widened and deepened by history. It is in that context also that the ritual dialectic must be studied. The subject requires as its prior condition a careful study of the Murinbata symbolism, and this will form the subject of another article. But I should like to say with care that, since there are so many possibilities of misunderstanding, the argumentative or philosophical senses of 'dialectical' have nothing to do with my usage. Each step in the processes can be checked by observation; the oppositeness of the things related at each step is either implied or stated by the Aborigines themselves; and in the description of such processes from the 'outside'—that is, from the analyst's viewpoint—no better word than 'dialectical' seems available for processes so constituted.

8. The Mood of Assent

The genius of Murinbata religion may be said to lie in three things. It affirms reality as a necessary connection between life and suffering. It sees the relation as continuously incarnate and yet as needing reaffirmation. It celebrates the relation by a rite containing all the beauty of song, mime, dance and art of which men are capable.

That the rite of *Punj* is—whatever else it may be—a high, joyful celebration no one could doubt who has seen it; or that it is at one and the same time a fearful approach to mystery; or that it typifies what in native eyes is an ineluctable condition of men.

The re-enactment of the primordial tragedy brings understanding—or so it is held—to the youths through whom life is to continue. The covenant of duality is thus endorsed by and on a new generation. Each young man is taken out of his empirical and social self, as though to meet his essential self, is touched by something transcendental—The Mother's blood, which is a symbol both of life and of suffering—and is then returned bearing her sign—the bullroarer—to help perpetuate the relation, within a *logos* which gives life and suffering a common source and a joint *imperium*.

There does not seem much reason to doubt that *Punj* could have developed in the appropriate conditions into the species of sacrament known as sacrifice. On the analysis, sacrifice is a logical possibility of the religious culture. Theoretically, it could have differentiated itself. For such a consequence, however, a growth of moral imagination would have been necessary.

One cannot judge an unknown history by its outcome, but there is nothing in Murinbata tradition which suggests an insight that men might be either free or perfectible. They are a people to whom the invisible has been the test of the visible; the unknown has been mysterious and terrifying; the dead have been feared; and men have been bound to the past. One can guess only at the historical conditions, for them, which might in time have suggested that, as St. Paul would have it, the visible is the test of the invisible; or that the unknown is only the unknown, the dead are simply piteous, and living men are able to shape their future. It seems that such ideas have simply not occurred to the Murinbata. Their moral imagination has been stultified.

The logical possibility of sacrifice, inherent in what they do in rite, evidently has had neither occasion nor motive to emerge in events. The emergence has been denied, one would think, by the force of the tradition that first things are also last things.

The ordainment of a once-for-all life puts its terms beyond human initiative. An abandonment of self, as in sacrifice, could not be requited by anything, for the compassion of invisible powers was given once-for-all. Voluntary suffering could not increase merit because the necessity of suffering was part of the founding covenant. The act of sacrifice, to be intelligible at all, needs a ground of moral freedom, one which is understood as such. The motive can scarcely appear until men have seen with clarity that they have no remedy of their own for inherent weakness, and the insight is ineffective unless there is a strong moral conscience.

The Murinbata do not give any significant impression of having, or thinking they have, moral freedom. The sense of the corruption of things lacks sharpness. As far as one can tell from outward show the formations of conscience are not strong.

If rite and symbolism were the only data one might be tempted to see a society 'trembling on the edge of tragedy.' The trouble is that nearly as good a case could be made that it trembles on the edge of laughter. It depends whether one deals primarily with the religious or the mundane life. A sense of tragedy is *co*conscious with the religion, and we can link it—though vaguely—with certain facts of the mundane life, but the latter is far too concerned with the pursuit of food, valuables, leisure, enjoyment, safety, lovers, spouses and other goods of life to have any equivalent concern.

In the mundane life there is an emphasis difficult to state, but in some ways the most revealing of all Aboriginal attitudes. The difficulties are perhaps less in the facts than in our ability to handle them. The character of the emphasis is possibly best stated in the first instance by contrast.

One may say that people have set up a kind of quarrel with life, or with its terms, when they rail against the gods, spirits or fate; or when they threaten or make offertories to the invisible powers; or plead or pray; or shut themselves off from life in hope of inner consolation; or look for final justice to someone or something standing over human history. Such attitudes and types of conduct are alien to Aboriginal mentality. The natural range of human temperament is of course represented, but in the Murinbata ethos one does not find any evidence of a pessimistic, cynical, apathetic or even quietistic tenor. A high intensity of bitterness and violence accompany injury and loss. But the expression is not directed at the self (as in suicide, which to the best of my knowledge never occurs), or in a diffuse way at society, or directionlessly at life or fate. It is directed at people and, to a large extent, along institutionalised lines. A juridical system provides a patterned means of redress for the delicts of actual life. It provides categories of wrongdoing, formal means of accusation, ways of meeting evidence with evidence, a means of bringing wrongdoers to penalty, a code of equivalent injury, and methods of limiting the spread of trouble. It is an elementary and defective system which is deeply undermined by an egoistic insistence on the right and duty of personal retaliation, and by mystical divinations which are often used for other, cloaked enmities. I am unable to embark on these topics here, but will limit myself to the statement that an attitude of 'assent' shows out in the astonishing extent to which the Aborigines appear to forgive and forget *after* the juridical system has worked. Continuous reproach or obloquy are quite uncharacteristic.

If there are an intuition and a symbolism of tragedy, then they do not issue in a quarrel with the proximate terms of life. The motive seems to be the desire to observe the continuity with The Dreaming. This entails the endurance of the joint *imperium* of the good and the bad. One detects no nostalgia for the past or yearning after a perfected futurity. In the tradition no one offered himself to any gods—indeed, there were none—and did not want to be accepted by any. Evidently what was done was done, and much of it was good. The insight that the bad is the condition of the good is not contemptible. In this religion it is expressed with a certain nobility that transcends the strange symbolisms.

The relation between the religious and the mundane life is continuous. It is a functional relation of complex interdependence. A striking phenomenon is the way in which joyous sociality—one might almost say the perfect sociality of laughter and fun, in apparent mockery of almost every stable institution—opens and closes the highest rite. To say that *Tjirmumuk* alone makes possible the parallel celebration of tragedy would be too much. But it is psychologically appropriate that 'good fun' (for that is the way the Murinbata describe *Tjirmumuk*) should make a jointure with ultimate concern. It allows them to assent to life, as it is, without morbidity.

III

Symbolism in the Higher Rites

1. Levels of Awareness

The Aborigines put no important restraints on what a European may see or do when they allow him to attend the celebration of their religious rites. Perhaps they may ask him to keep his knowledge of the more secret matters from the unauthorised, especially from the women and children, but beyond that there are no impediments. Nevertheless, he is likely to feel for a long time unable to pass beyond the anterooms of meaning, because the rites are made up of an infinitude of symbolisms, most of them obscure, for which the Aborigines make no attempt to account and, if asked to, usually cannot. The usages are time-honoured and evidently well-loved, but their significance arouses no curiosity among the celebrants.

In the circumstances the 'cake of custom' of which much was once heard in anthropology might seem to be a reality. But the facts would be misrepresented by any suggestion of mindless automatism, or blind or instinctual following out of a deadened tradition. Nor is there any need to postulate a collective unconscious. One is dealing with a dutiful submission to authority on solemn occasions, and with a rapt absorption in things that have emotional appeal and give æsthetic pleasure.

The young men who are being inducted into the rites are not warned against asking questions. There is no suggestion that they will be put under penalty if they do. A questioning or critical approach would be out of character with the occasion. Those whom I have examined on the matter simply say: 'We looked, we stayed quiet, we did not ask.' But there is more to it than that. The older men use many artifices to induce respect and fear. At various junctures the young men are admonished to comport themselves modestly and deferentially, and commanded to look carefully at what happens so that, when they too are men of authority and understanding, they will know what to do, and to require their sons to do, to 'follow-up'. A guardian is always close at hand to see that they conform to instructions. The form and matter of the rites are thus taught, and doubtless are remembered, in a somewhat rote fashion. The unquestioning attitude in this way is passed between overlapping generations.

What happens on such high occasions is also apprehended in a deeper fashion, and the interior life is shaped in a positive way. All the things seen and done have the authority of ancient, sacred ways (*maŋe mundak*, lit. 'hand-fashion,' 'olden time'). They are also true things (*muṙṙin ḍaitpiṙ*, lit. 'words,' 'lips'). More, they are good things of the utmost gravity (*nandji bata bata, nandji ŋala ŋala*, lit. 'things,' 'excellent,' 'very heavy' or 'very big'). These phrases are commonly used, and every circumstance of context—beauty, drama, excitement, mystery—reinforces them. As well, both young and old, neophytes and instructors, have a lively dread of sanctions of irreverence. It would scarcely be possible to weigh the contributions made by these influences to the attitude of uninquiring acceptance exemplified by the old and emulated by the young. But clearly we are not dealing with a lifeless adhesion to a deadened routine.

It is not particularly difficult to bring the Aborigines to see that many elements of the rites lack explanation. Their response varies from a naïve and somewhat startled surprise to a thoughtful reflection. A means of making them attend to the matter is to build on an example which they themselves see as symbolical. For example, the fact that the bullroarer; in their own words, 'takes the place of' The Old Woman, or, as we might say, 'stands for' her and 'points beyond itself' to her. One may then ask if this is the case with other elements. The inquiry does not lead very far but it helps to adduce some significant details. One comes to two main conclusions. There is a conscious awareness that many elements of the rites designate things of nature. As a case in point, the rhythmic cries that punctuate dances, chants and songs are meant to simulate the calls of birds, the sounds of surf, tides and streams, and the winds. The fact is not at all obvious at first, for the cries do not necessarily refer to anything being celebrated in the rites, or stressed in the accompanying mythology. One is left with the impression that the ritual fashions are compound of old and new elements. The second conclusion is unavoidable: there are several levels of awareness of ritual symbolism. A few usages are recognised clearly as being symbolical; a few more, on the whole of minor importance, are demonstrable as such; but the vast majority are practised without clear recognition of their symbolical character. Direct questioning of the Aborigines does little to clarify the matter, and if understanding is to pass this threshold then it must be by other means.

Many anthropologists, confronted by this situation, might feel that they must transpose the study to phenomena of the Aboriginal unconscious. But the symbolisms are constituents of collective acts of mutuality, with a logical structure, a detectable range of meanings, and an æsthetic appeal as well as a premial place in the social development of individuals. These relations may appropriately be studied by the methods of anthropology. The fact that they are perpetuated apparently without the kinds of conscious awareness or rational consideration that might represent them to the Aborigines as things requiring explanation is not in itself a sufficient reason for thinking them beyond the province of anthropological study.

In this article I propose to examine some of them as conventional signs with practical, logical and expressive functions in the symbolical systems of ritual.

2. The Geometric Idiom of Ceremony

The religious rites involve anything from scores to hundreds of men at a place and time. They are all complex sequences of ritual forms in *unguided* coordination. There is no master of ceremony as such, only a concerting of familiar tasks. One is better able to understand what happens by beginning with the morphic aspect, the visual shape of what may be seen.

The celebrants of Murinbata rites arrange themselves in spatial patterns. These have a geometric idiom—arcs, circles or ovals, points and straight and curved lines. Each rite exhibits a somewhat different combination of the same elements. The compositions give an austere beauty to the inactive phases and an excited vitalism to the active phases. In both they are impressive essays in dynamic symmetry and asymmetry.

A knowledge of the patterns is part of the experience of every man; not, as far as I could determine, as the result of special instruction, but because everyone who passes through the rites becomes familiar with them. Certainly, at the celebrations, everyone appears to fall with an easy confidence into place, stance and posture, and to follow out the sequences of what has to be done to a set formulary.

The formulary is well understood. There is no difficulty in obtaining from informants, by the use of tokens or counters, clear rehearsals or reconstructions. The method of study is rewarding in that it reveals aspects of the rites that are all too easy to miss in direct observation. Some Aborigines, without being solicited, will produce graphic sketches of the positions and movements to which the celebrants must conform. The sketches may resemble the patterns incised on bullroarers, a fact deeply significant in itself.

The spatial plans of the rites should not be allowed to pass as commonplaces of a just-so kind. Each of the shapes has to serve as an arrangement of persons forming a conceptual class, each person and class having parts to play that require a sequence of sentiments, purposes and meanings to be expressed by action or inaction. The combination of shapes has to accord with the logic, the economy, and the æsthetic canons of the ceremony. There is in each combination an undoubted structure—in the terms used in earlier articles, a structure of operations—with a kind of praxis by which the symbolisms indicate, represent and communicate the connected meanings which they express in a sequence, as do the ordered words of a sentence.

My use of the word 'shape' may invite remark. I could not discover any linguistic concepts of the patterns or combinations used in different rites, but there are terms for each of the geometric elements that make them up. However, the word *ŋinipun* is often used of the total patterns, and it can here conveniently be given the meaning of 'shape'[1]. To use it comes very close to the Aboriginal convention.

In an earlier article ('II. Sacramentalism, Rite and Myth') I put forward the hypothesis that familiar things of the social order provide shapes or *ŋinipun* by which religious mystery can be formulated in an understandable way. The same intellectual process seems to be revealed in the spatial configurations of ceremony: familiar things of the physical environment provide shapes or *ŋinipun* for the arrangement of ritual conduct.

I have no direct testimony by the Aborigines to cite as evidence that they wittingly imitate environmental things in their ritual use of geometric shapes, but the indirect evidence of intellectual and æsthetic influence is not unimpressive. (*a*) They are acute observers of their natural scene and little in it escapes notice, particularly the presence of shapely visual form or pattern. Anything that is symmetrically patterned attracts notice, and the same is true of marked asymmetry. (*b*) The word *diṙmu* is applied to a wide range of phenomena: to (i) bodily decorations in dances and mimes, (ii) ancient cave-paintings, and (iii) the spiral, concentric and radial whorls of shells, the segmentation of honeycomb, the divisions of spider-webs, the crystals of rock-minerals, the colour-markings of birds, the skin-patterns of reptiles. (*c*) The usages of the word *diṙmu* make clear that it denotes visual form or pattern, and that it implies (i) the consequences of intent or purpose and (ii) the handiwork of beings, or the outcome of events, significant for man. The conception of non-intentional form or pattern seems foreign to the mentality. (*d*) The elements of *diṙmu* are geometric shapes and it is to the totality of outward form or appearance resulting from a complex of such elements that the word *ŋinipun* is applied.

1 See *Oceania*, Vol. XXX, No. 4, p. 270, for other meanings.

Things that to Europeans are 'natural' forms are to the Aborigines signs that *something happened* long ago, something mysterious, and heavily consequential for the human life that is continuous with the form-making events of The Dream Time. The past is the authority and the organon of the ontology. The 'penetrating, possession-taking faculty' of Aboriginal imagination sees in each shapely excellence of form a consequence which the mythology and totemism then make into a *Gestalt.* My hypothesis is that the geometric forms enter the general system of symbolism as *conventional signs.* Their significance, which is always one of a completed and final action, is a kind of command for an exemplifying action by living men as the appropriate response. The exemplifying is consonant, on the plane of gesture, with the 'following up' of The Dreaming on the plane of conscious intent. In our sense 'natural' signs that become conventional signs, the given forms are in the Aboriginal world a sort of authority gathered up into general symbolism for logical and expressive elaboration. As signs, they *designate* and *indicate* mysterious first things of the long ago, the mythical past; as symbols—that is, when elaborated by language, gesture and music within a system of conduct which is also a system of conceptualism—they *express* and *communicate* first things as last, permanent and continuous things.

An anthropologist encounters them as time-honoured elements of systems which are *already formed* even though, as I have suggested earlier, appearing at the same time to be developmental. In the circumstances, no hypothesis could be brought to 'proof'; one can but raise probabilities. The logic of present conduct utilising the geometric forms, and their rich expressive elaboration, are both evident in the actualities of rites, of which *Punj* is the outstanding example.

The principals at *Punj* cluster for the opening phase in a compact circle. Everyone faces towards the centre. The formation is one in which physical association is intimate. The men sit flank to flank, with knees often crossing, and with arms often flung around the shoulders of neighbours. The kinship and other social categories intermingle without any evident discrimination, except that clansmen often sit close together and, likewise, pairs of men who later are to act boisterously towards each other under the licence of *Tjirmumuk*. While at song, the celebrants vie rather than compete. Some follow the melodic outline while others, without prearrangement, introduce a simple harmony. The men's faces take on a glow of animation and tender intent. At the last exclamatory cry—*Karwadi, yoi!*—everyone shouts as with one voice. An observer feels that he is in the presence of true congregation, a full sociality at a peak of intimacy, altruism and unison.

The onset of *Tjirmumuk* brings a sudden scission. The close circle explodes. The harmony of association disrupts. The men scatter into a new spatial pattern. The solemnity is replaced by ribaldry, the altruism by outward hostility, the solidarity by opposition, and the unison of common purpose by a jostle of similar purposes. But the spatial form is, in a sense, continuous with the old. The celebrants are still a kind of unity. They now act under another principle, from other sentiments, and with a different object. But the changes have the nature of transpositions. An observer has the sense of a negative affirmation of what was affirmed positively in the first phase. It is as though the statement 'everything that is *Karwadi* is sacred' now had the form 'nothing that is not *Karwadi* is sacred.'

The circle as a spatial form is suited by nature to the first phases of the rite. It permits an intimacy of face-to-face relations that no other formation can. It is as well appropriate to the logical datum of the rite: that there should be a unison of men in sentiment and object.

The physical gestures of touching, fondling and embracing between the celebrants express the sentiments after a sign-fashion that is universal to men everywhere. The Aboriginal conventions differ only in the classes of persons to whom the signs are made, and in their symbolical conceptualisation.

The conversational exchanges that go on during the intervals between songs exemplify the unison in the symbolism of language. They exhibit the qualities of good humour and tenderness that conventionally characterise relations between intimates, especially between brothers and between fathers and sons.

The meaning of the songs may be—and usually is—unknown since they, with the dances, come from tribes across the southern boundary of the Murinbata. But the manner of their singing—as with one voice, a harmony being added—reiterates what may be seen on the spatial and gestural planes of symbolism.

Thus, the circle reduces to a minimum the social as well as the physical separation between those who make it up: for a time it makes inappropriate, indeed obliterates, all other social categories; it concentrates a unified totality around a centre. In these ways it makes possible a unison towards a dominating object. Four systems of symbolism—those of spatial configuration, gesture, language and music—are in congruence in this, the phase of congregation. On the facts, the form has a high practical, logical and expressive efficacy.

It was noted earlier that the credal formulation of *Punj* does not deal very explicitly with this phase, or with the second—*Tjirmumuk*—beyond the bare (and, as we shall see, partial) interpretation that the latter is 'good fun.' If the Aborigines consciously appreciate any aspect of the geometric idiom, then it is probably the æsthetic aspect, for its appeal to them from that point of view has some suggestive illustrations. The circular motif has a high incidence in the graphic art. A study of the visual sign-system used in that context shows the circle with a range of meanings. It may be intended to show a camp, a waterhole, a secret centre (such as *Punj*), a sacred totemic site, a yam, a woman's breast or womb, or the moon. The range defines a category, and the ultimate denotation of the sign is presumably the ground or principle of the category. But its nature or definition cannot be elicited by direct inquiry. One can only try to deduce it by observing and comparing the sequences through which the form passes in a sufficient set of contexts, each set occurring within a separable and identifiable process which is an entity in space and time. One such set of sequences may be seen in *Punj*.

The rupture of the circle by *Tjirmumuk* evidently is not—cannot be, if we accept what the celebrants say—intended as a denial of *Punj* in the respects in which that ceremony deals with things that are ancient, sacred, true, and of the highest good and gravity. For the Aboriginal testimony is that *Tjirmumuk* 'belongs to *Karwadi.*' There is no discontinuity of place or persons. It is a matter of one phase of an entity turning into another, within the bounds of a continuous process. The same men who a moment ago were at one are now, in the same place, at odds. But in every other respect it is as though things had been turned upside down. To the reversals already noted we may add that where before there was song, there is now a babble of noise, sometimes simulating the noise of animals. In addition to being 'good fun,' the actions in *Tjirmumuk* are said by some Aborigines to be 'like the wild dogs.' One unusually thoughtful man, trying to meet my repeated requests for an analogy—as I asked him, something that the custom 'took the place of'—pointed to a covey of birds we could see and hear squabbling over a scarce food, and said: 'Like that.'

When the scission occurs, one may note that it is the social categories which, ignored in the first phase, are now stressed; *negatively* stressed, for it is the conflict, not the unity, among them that is expressed. The licence of *Tjirmumuk* is shown essentially between three pairs of classes of men: between (i) the symmetrical classes of classificatory ('distant') wives' brothers (*naŋgun*), and the asymmetrical classes of (ii) classificatory mothers' brothers and sisters' sons (*kaka-muluk*), and (iii) classificatory fathers and sons (*ŋaguluk-wakal*).[2]

Evidently we see again the process of familiar things of social life being drawn on to give shape to less expressible entities and relationships in another realm.

---

2 In the Murinbata system of kinship, affinity and marriage the class of wives' fathers (*kapi*) is a subclass of the class of mothers' brothers (*kaka*), such that any *kaka* who is not a uterine brother of a man's own mother may become *kapi.* Since there is frequently an exchange of sisters in marriage, the wife of *kapi* is distinguished from the class of fathers' sisters (*pipi*) by the (untranslatable) suffix *nginar.* A man's own father's sister's cannot be *pipi nginar* in any circumstances. A brother of *pipi nginar* is distinguished from the class of fathers (*yile*) by being termed *ngaguluk.* This term was adopted from the Djamindjung and, being affected by Murinbata phonetics, is sometimes pronounced *ngawuluk.*

Tension and potential conflict are constitutively part of every Aboriginal social relation, even within the patrilineal clan. In that mystical and perennial corporation, expediency as well as religious and moral sanctions are ranged strongly against division. But common—or at least not uncommon—experience is that siblings of the same womb do fight; that children defy and even strike their fathers; and that fathers reject their children. The fact that conflict is constitutively part of living is in logical accord with the fact that the principles of living are conjugate.[3] No single principle or combination of principles, of social organisation or conduct extends over all the desired objects of living, even for clan-members who, at least in dogma, are a combination, not a competitive association. That is, if they possess, they own or, share, under a tradition that clearly specifies rights *in rem, in personam* and *in animum* so that, again at least in dogma, no conflict should arise. But large fields for the expression of vitality, egotism and selfishness are still left open. These, together with the conjugacy of principles, make clan-unison in part an ideal and in part a fiction. Beyond the clan they issue in an endless clash of interests. The three pairs of classes of actual or potential affines are those between which hostility is overlaid, or could be overlaid, by transacted or transactable interests in women.

The first phase of *Punj* uses a geometric imagery to express the relations of men in combination, at congregation, in unison, and—by the symbolism of many external signs—at one. The second phase destroys the geometric imagery to express the relations of men in association as distinct from combination; men at competition, divided, and—again by the symbolism of counterpart signs—at odds. In the first phase there is something like an element of bravura, a going beyond the mean of social life, which in mundane reality can have such unison only in aspiration. In the second phase, there is something like an element of caricature, a diminution of the mean, which is never one of animal anarchy.

3 See 'On Aboriginal Religion' II. *Oceania*, Vol. XXX, No. 4, pp. 245–78; especially pp. 266 ff.

As the rite proceeds the spatial forms have a somewhat different fashion. A linear motif is now added to them. The youths, being secluded at a concealed point some distance away, are brought in file to ŋudanu. Here they find their seniors crouched within the circular excavation, whether it be 'nest' or 'wallow,' at the mime of the blowfly. The excavation accentuates the crowding together of the celebrants and, visually at least, intensifies the form very much as in the graphic art a set of concentric circles is used to intensify the significance or meaning of its referent. If the celebration is a large one, with many present, the singers form an arcuate line to one side of the circle. The usual position of the youths is between the arc and the circle.[4] At the dances and mimes which follow, the arc and the circle are retained, but the decorated men adopt one of two fundamental linear patterns. They emerge from hiding and, as a body, approach the circle either (i) in a sinuously-curving line, or (ii) as a body less two men, who suddenly appear from concealment at another point, joining the main body by a zig-zag path, pausing in their mime at each change of direction, to make the characteristic quiver of body and shoulders which the Murinbata say is a simulation of birds ruffling their feathers.[5] Both styles issue in a dance before the assembled men enter the excavation.

The form of *Tjirmumuk* having been described sufficiently, we may look briefly at two other occasions when the circular-linear patterns are exhibited.

---

4 My earlier statement that they 'are taken into the centre of the circle, told to kneel, and to imitate the action of the others' is in error. They are taken to the centre of the arc, told to sit, and to 'follow up,' i.e. on future occasions, the actions of the mime.

5 I could discover no evidence that the Murinbata, like the Warramunga of north-central Australia, think of this gesture as setting free spirit-children or any kind of life-principle. Otherwise, they give only technical and æsthetic explanations of the custom. The Murinbata ideology associates *ngarit-ngarit* or spirit-children only with green leaves. The dancers tie to their shoulders, and carry in both hands, bundles of leaves which have been scorched crisp so that the quivering of the shoulders will give out a pleasing sound.

At night, when everyone in the camp (which has a circular form) is asleep, or is pretending to be, the young men are led to it in file, to sleep there unspoken to and unseen. The stealthy entry is the opposite of the sign-convention of *Tjirmumuk* at its camp-phase: the vociferous leap over the heads of everyone. The first tacitly restores a unity, the second dramatically typifies the tensions that are re-entering it.

When the time comes for the initiated youths to be presented to their mothers, the camp assumes the form known as *mununuk* which, as I have said, connotes 'waiting, with gifts prepared.' The close kin of the youths sit in an arc of a circle so that the concave side faces towards the two lines of men, one for each moiety, who stand with legs opened to make passages for the youths as they crawl towards and then away from their mothers.

I have found no way of fixing specific social meanings on the spatial forms. They recur so frequently, however, in the Aboriginal spatial and graphic symbolism that they seem a kind of 'furniture of the mind'[6] (Fig. 4).

I lean to the view that the circle is a naturally-based conventional sign with probably the ultimate meanings of unity or continuity, the line the same type of sign with, probably, the ultimate meanings of action or change, and that the spatial, gestural, æsthetic, linguistic and religious symbolisms raise on them other meanings appropriate to each system.

3. The Problem of Tjirmumuk

The upside-downness of *Tjirmumuk* may incline many to deny it any intrinsic connection with the sacral aspects of *Punj*, and to suppose that in Durkheim's terms it must be regarded as a profane activity.[7]

6 I adopt the phrase from W. H. R. Rivers, 'The Symbolism of Rebirth,' *Folk Lore*, Vol. XXXIII, No. 1. Rivers was discussing the problem of *universal* symbolism, a matter that does not enter into my examination.

7 All references are to the 1915 edition of *The Elementary Forms of The Religious Life.*

The custom is practised in two places, within the secrecy of ŋudanu, and at the open camp to which the celebrants return. At the first place it goes on, not *pro fanum*, but actually on the sacred ground of *Punj*. In the terms of Durkheim's dual categories there is no 'break of continuity' (p. 39). The custom is preceded and followed by sacral actions, so that the continuity is immediate. Nothing overt, or readily accessible to direct inquiry, suggests any 'sort of logical chasm' (p. 40) to break the continuity, or any 'absolute heterogeneity' (p. 38) between the successive activities such that the one set 'radically excludes' (p. 38) the other. When there is such a close and visible succession one cannot say with intellectual comfort that the activities 'belong to two worlds between which there is nothing in common' (p. 39), or that they 'cannot even approach each other and keep their own nature at the same time' (p. 40). The more closely the category of 'the profane' is studied the less suitable it appears.[8]

Before considering the category of 'the sacred' we may rule out certain other possibilities suggested by Durkheim's study. To all appearances, *Tjirmumuk* is not a magical rite 'performing the contrary of the religious ceremony' (p. 43). Some elements of *Punj* are magical, but none in the custom of licence. Nor does it suggest itself as 'a mechanical consequence of the state of super-excitation' (p. 38) following as 'a swift revulsion' (p. 40). On the contrary, there is much evidence of consciously symbolic intent and of consciously patterned conduct. A merely biopsychological explanation could not satisfy.

8 In an as yet unpublished article, I have questioned both the logical adequacy and the empirical warrant of the dual categories. Durkheim gave various meanings to 'the profane': among them, minor sacredness, non-sacredness, dangerous non-sacredness, anti-sacredness, and simple commonness. His system requires, among other additions, the recognition of a third category, that of the common or mundane. His analysis appears to rest implicitly on such a category. Consider, for example, his many references to 'ordinary things,' 'things of common use,' 'the ordinary plane of life,' etc., etc. But he gave the category no formal place in the 'bipartite division of the whole universe, known and unknown, into two classes which embrace all that exists, but which radically exclude each other.'

And it does not appear the more intelligible if treated as an instance of 'ritual promiscuity' (p. 216). The notion of a set formulary, i.e. a ritual, of promiscuity actually doubles the explanatory problem. The three possibilities are to be rejected.

Durkheim's notion (after Robertson Smith) of 'the sacred' as ambiguous and bipolar was based on a postulate that the religious life 'gravitate(s) about two contrary poles between which there is the same opposition as between the pure and the impure, the saint and the sacrilegious, the divine and the diabolic.' In short, that there are propitiously sacred and unpropitiously sacred things and, between them, an incompatibility 'as all-exclusive as that between the sacred and the profane.' We have already noted the elements of duality in *Punj*, and might well use Durkheim's terms, ambiguity and bipolarity. But a cardinal fact should here be underlined: *Tjirmumuk* is as great a contrast with the ordinary life of everyday as it is with the imaginative life of *Punj* in its other manifestations. The contrasts are three-sided, not two-sided. Durkheim's dual categories do not between them 'embrace all that exists.' The *Tjirmumuk* and the *Karwadi* aspects of *Punj* both imply, refer to, and use a symbolic imagery drawn from a third realm, one that is neither sacred nor profane but merely mundane.

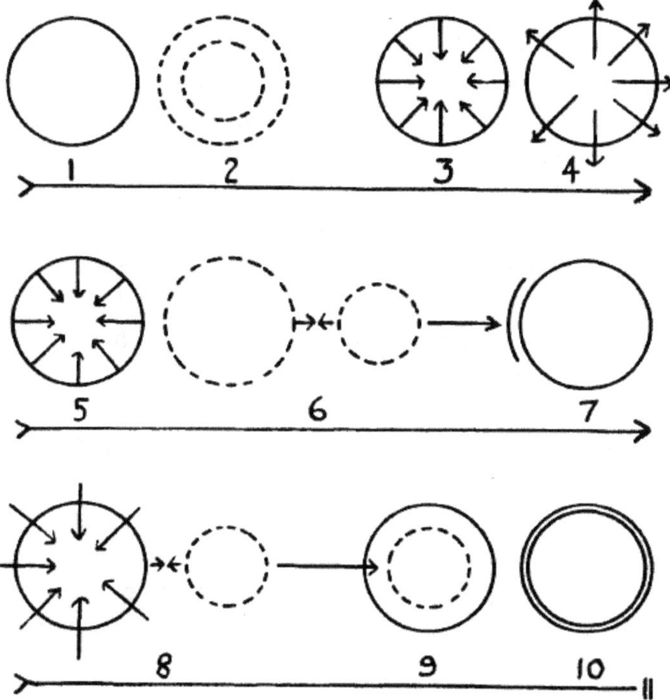

Figure 4. Sequence of Spatial Forms

Figure 4 is in part a schematic and in part an actual representation of the sequence of spatial forms in *Punj.* (1) The initial situation: the undivided camp. (2) The diminution of the camp: mature men withdraw and the youths are segregated. (3) The song-circle assembles at Nudanu. (4) The scission by *Tjirmumuk.* (5) The song-circle reaggregates. (6) The ritual preparations are made in secret while the youths are segregated at *Mambana.* (7) The youths return to witness the rites. (8) The mature men at *Tjirmumuk* irrupt into the diminished circle, while the youths are isolated. (9) The youths enter the camp secretly. (10) The post-initiation camp with the youths, now men of understanding, in a new locus and status.

The 'circles' are schematic in (2), (6) and (in respect of the youths) in (8), but are observable realities in the other cases.

The celebrants return to the mundane world when they practise *Tjirmumuk* at the open camp, leaping over the heads of those who are waiting. The very men who, under the terms of the custom, exploded the close circle of *Punj*, now irrupt into the close circle of the camp. The geometric idiom is thus inverted. In both places they act in ways that seem as far removed as possible from the mundane conventions. The very condition of either demonstration is that there should be, on the one hand, a mean of common life and, on the other, a high order of aspiration and imagination, against which to make the demonstrations. The custom does not profane—by desecrating, violating, degrading, vulgarising, or secularising—either the mean or the higher order. At ŋudanu it breaks up a solidary circle by using a symbolism of animal life to express the hostility underlying mundane relationships. At the open camp it uses the same symbolism, but with inverted geometric forms, to bring the hostility within the circle.

One can scarcely resist the conclusion that there is some kind of praxis and a development of correlated meanings underlying the arrangement of the signs. They are not unconscious; but one must not therefore be understood to say that they are conscious. That dichotomy is not necessarily relevant to the processes of symbolism.

4. Symbolising: Processes and Types

The materials under study are by nature intricate, and the anthropological analysis of symbolism is still in its very early stages. There is advantage in using as simple a conception of symbolism as possible. In what follows I prefer to speak, as far as practicable, of 'symbolising' rather than of symbolism in general or of particular symbols. The reasons for that choice may be stated summarily.

One has to dismember the wholeness of a rite to study it at all, but to study and analyse all the component elements of such a rite as *Punj* is beyond the capability of any single observer. For one must add to the spatial forms just discussed gestures and manual acts in definite sequences, mimes, dances, songs, melodies, bodily decorations, and many specific uses of language. What is selected for emphasis is selected in the light of its supposed significance, that is, because of a thesis.

The thesis of these papers has already been stated: that in the rite of *Punj* the Murinbata express outwardly a complex sense of their dependence on a ground and source beyond themselves. That sense, in my construction, is one of perennial good-with-suffering, of order-with-tragedy. It is a mystery which the Murinbata themselves say they do not understand. But in the words they use, and more especially in the myth of The Old Woman, they are expressing or *symbolising* an understanding. They do so by putting into words a certain conception of what the rite refers to or 'means.' But the rite contains many expressions over a wider range than language and not inherently dependent on it. Language, in this case as myth, is but one of several means or vehicles of symbolising. The spatial forms, the gestures and manual acts, the mimes and dances, the songs and melodies, the decorations and other components, are all symbolising means. Each type of means has—or one may assume it has—an appropriate technique and syntactical system, and for each type of means there is, so to speak, a 'language.' One may reasonably assume also that the rite exhibits a measure of congruence, if perhaps not integration, between the many 'languages,' though one may doubt if anyone will ever find it practicable to demonstrate the assumptions. In the circumstances, a discussion of symbolism-in-general must usually be too vague and of particular symbols usually too precise for the material as it presents itself in Aboriginal Australia. I thus prefer to discuss the particular processes of symbolising which are more observable and recordable.

The symbolising of all types appears to me to be based somewhat arbitrarily—as I suggested in the discussion of spatial forms—on things interpreted as signs and arranged into patterns. The arrangement into patterns exemplifies the process of symbolising. One encounters the already formed systems of symbolism. Now, I have chosen to discuss the spatial arrangements first because it appears to be through them that, to adopt Erwin Schrödinger's phrase, the Aborigines most clearly 'suck in the orderliness' of sign-patterns given in the spatial environment.[9] Arbitrary and conventional meanings are put upon the signs, which—being thus interpreted—are then elaborated by the principles governing that class or order of symbolism. The systems of symbolism are thus made up of anterior signs arbitrarily interpreted, transformed, and hallowed by tradition.

If there were an Aboriginal word for 'nature' then one might say that the spatial configurations are developments of signs drawn 'from nature.' But to do so would be meaningless, for there is no such word or conception. There is only The Dreaming, that which comprehends all and is adequate to all and, like The Deep of Babylonian mythology, 'of old time reckoned a thing of vast importance in the constitution of the world'[10]

The mimes, melodies and songs are as important expressively—and, therefore, to the communication, sharing and teaching of meaning—as the spatial and gestural forms, or the manual acts which I have called 'operations.' In the light of this argument a primary task of study is to try to discover congruences between two or more formed systems of symbolism. Hence my earlier attempts to show, on the one hand, the homomorphism between *Punj* and the better-understood institution of sacrifice and, on the other, between the operational structures of the rite and the myth of *Punj*. I shall now examine the likeness between the operational structure of the rite and the sequences of spatial forms. There too a certain measure of congruence is exhibited.

---

9 Quoted by F. W. Dillistone in *Christianity and Symbolism*, London, 1955, p. 36.

10 F. E. Coggin, *The First Story of Genesis as Literature*, 1932. One might adapt to the Aboriginal use of the phrase 'The Dreaming' the author's remark that 'any name for the material which goes to the making of the world would have been deficient had the *Deep* not been included', pp. 4–5.

5. A Repeated Theme and Congruent Symbolising

We saw, without drawing on the mythopoeic thought of the Murinbata, that the observable acts at *Punj* exemplify a kind of drama on the theme of withdrawal, destruction, transformation and return. The associated myth then showed itself to be, not the pathological 'disease of language' of which Max Müller spoke, but a credal formulation of the same drama. The structural patterns of both sequences of acts were found to be generally conformable.

The acts or operations at *Punj* were abstracted from the larger whole of the rite and necessarily included the spatial forms through which they were done. The forms, further abstracted, show that they too exemplify the drama.

The processes of the rite begin, not at ŋudanu, but at the open camp. Yet an examination starting with the assembly of the celebrants at the secret place reveals something like the familiar sequences going on in a somewhat involuted way within a narrower compass and at the same time within a wider compass. There seem to be three interconnected manifestations. (*a*) The first unison of men at song (the close circle) is destroyed (by the scattering) and then transformed (by the licence of *Tjirmumuk*) before reaggregation (the restoration of the song-circle). (*b*) The new assembly is again dispersed (by the detachment of the youths under a guardian, their isolation at a hidden place, the secret decoration of the dancers, and often the concealment of the mime-dancers) before being drawn together again in a new unity with a radically different structure. A ground-circle is now flanked by an arc and is either filled by masked or decorated men (i.e. in new personalities) or is being penetrated from outside by men performing the contrasted movements which have been described. That formation then dissolves into a somewhat formless unity distinct from the initial assembly. (*c*) The full unity of the whole camp (a circle) is broken by the withdrawal of all mature and young men. Each night, while still reduced, it is transformed into a different character by the custom of *Tjirmumuk* and by the symbolical denial that the youths really visit it or sleep there. It is fully reconstituted again—and then with a *developed* character—only. after the termination of the rite, when the initiates assume their new status.

Act, myth and spatial forms belong to distinct orders. We are thus not 'discovering' the same phenomenon under different names. What we find by analysis is a set of congruences between components of a whole which are expressed according to the technique and system appropriate to each mode of symbolising. A familiar distinction may now be made.

The spatial forms are, in the terms suggested by Mrs. Langer,[11] *presentational* symbolisms. They have somewhat indeterminate meanings imposed on them and, as signs, somewhat indeterminate referents. They have about them something of the character and quality of images or pictures that may be either still or moving. But they are symbolisms because they are vehicles for the conception and expression of the meanings of things, events, or conditions. The process of rite which makes use of them is thus a symbolising process, one of spatial arrangement.

On the other hand, the acts or operations of both the rite and the myth are *discursive* symbolisms. They express mental conceptions which are fairly definite or indefinite. There is clearly a range from high indefiniteness to definiteness. An example of indefiniteness is that part of the rite at which the young men are taken to the spot where The Old Woman is to become manifest. The old men in this way make a gestural and manual sign towards The Mother by taking or compelling the young men to that place. It is *like* offering them. But the sign does not 'mean' an 'offering.' The Aborigines describe what they do but have no clear intellectual conception about it. It is not, therefore, a formed symbolism. On the other hand, there is a clear conception of the blood smeared on the initiates, since it is represented as the blood of The

11 Susanne K. Langer, *Philosophy in a New Key*, 1942. My use of 'discursive' symbolism is also drawn from this source.

Mother and thus symbolises her. One is scarcely more, if at all, than a presentational symbolism; the other is a clear discursive symbolism.

It will be plain in these papers that I depart from the views of some other anthropologists who have discussed religious symbolism. My friend and colleague, the late Professor S. F. Nadel, argued that 'uncomprehended symbols' are not really symbols at all since they indicate nothing to the actors. Thus, they have no interest for the anthropologist.[12]In the sense that 'uncomprehended' means 'unaccompanied by intellectual conceptions' I am not in disagreement. But one can rarely be sure of the uncomprehension or unaccompaniment. One cannot justifiably infer either from implicitness or wordlessness. A methodical search for congruences between ritual facts of different orders may show that an implicit and apparently uncomprehended symbolism of one order is formulated explicitly in another order. On the other hand, Professor Monica Wilson appears to argue[13] that, in order to avoid 'symbolic guessing,' the anthropologist should limit himself to a people's own translations and interpretations of their symbolism. This advice, if followed in Aboriginal studies, would prevent anthropology from going very far beyond just-so descriptions. But in *every* field of anthropological study, a going beyond the facts of observation—a 'guessing' about them—is intrinsic to the act of study, and not even theoretically separable from it.

Ritual symbolisms extend over *all* the orders of facts that are separable as components of human conduct. The symbolisms of the *other* orders are not inherently dependent on the symbolisms of language, though they may receive their clearest expression *in* language. We may see that this is so by referring to the most fundamental categories of the Murinbata language, which are themselves symbolical, though somewhat indefinitely so.

---

12 S. F. Nadel, *Nupe Religion*, 1954, p. 108.

13 Monica Wilson, *Rituals of Kinship Among the Nyakyusa*, 1957, p. 6.

6. The Build of the Dreaming

The Murinbata language designates nine or more classes of entities (Table 4). Each class is known by a name that may be used alone or as a prefix to the name of any member of the class. In common speech, the prefixes are sometimes omitted although grammatical speech requires them to be used.[14]

The classes are not noun-classes in the ordinary sense used of Aboriginal languages. As far as I have been able to determine, there are no grammatical consequences or correlations. It seems best to regard them as existence-classes, i.e. as existential or ontological conceptions, which divide all significant entities in the world into classes which are mutually exclusive.

Table 4. Existence-Classes

Name of Class.	Content of Class.
1. kadu	Human beings, male and female.
	Human spirits other than 6 (i), but probably including *ngarit ngarit* (spirit-children), *ngjapan* (souls), and possibly including *mir* (freed souls?).*
	Subclass:
	(i) *kadu-Punj*: youths undergoing initiation.
2. da	Camps and resting-places.
	Localities.
	Subclass:
	(i) da-*Punj*: places known to be, or to have been *ngudanu* and *mambana*.
	(ii) *ngoiguminggi*: totemic sites.

14 Aborigines often complain that their children speak ungrammatically, pronounce words incorrectly, and use slang.

Name of Class.	Content of Class.
3. nandji	Most natural substances and objects, e.g. stone, minerals, wax, wood. The inedible parts of animals (bones, hair), and plants (leaves, bark). Artifacts, e.g. utensils, implements, ornaments, ritual objects. Certain natural phenomena, e.g. fire, mist, clouds, winds, the heavenly bodies. Urine and human milk. Dances. Subclass: (i) *nandji-Merkat*: any members of Classes (3) and (4) with an exchange-value in intertribal trade. (ii) *nandji-Punj*: any members of Classes (3) and (4) of high ritual significance.
4. tjo	Offensive weapons, e.g. spears, fighting clubs, boomerangs. Thunder and lightning.
5. mi	Vegetable foodstuffs. Fæces. Subclass: (i) *mi-Punj*: any vegetable food forbidden to initiates.
6. ku	The flesh, fat and blood of animals (birds, beasts and fish) and of men. Honey. Subclass:

Name of Class.	Content of Class.
	(i) *kukarait*: human ghosts.
	(ii) *ku-Punj*: any flesh food forbidden to initiates.
7. murin	Speech and language.
	Words, † songs, ‡ stories and myths, gossip and news.
8. kura	Fresh or drinkable water.
	Rain.
	Subclass:
	(i) *kura-mutjingga*: springs and spring-water.
	(ii) *kura-Punj*: ritually dangerous waters.
9. lalinggin	Salt-water.
	The sea.

* There are several classes of spirits which the Aborigines do not classify either as kadu or ku. The distinctions are to be dealt with in a later article.

† I have no evidence of a secret language used by initiates only, although among the Marithiel, a people following a different regional culture to the north-east of the Murinbata, initiates were required to use a special set of words for all food species.

‡ There is no Murinbata word for 'song' as such, though there is for the act of singing. I have not heard the secret songs referred to as *murin-Punj*, but their secrecy, and the condign sanctions of betrayal, are common matters of talk among the initiated.

It is possible (though I think unlikely) that there may be more than nine classes. Some may be unnamed, or it may simply be that I failed to discover them. But those mentioned are readily ascertainable and, with a few minor qualifications, are quite clear in their uses and meanings. The class *tjo* could perhaps be regarded as a subclass of *nandji*, and *laliŋgin* as a subclass of *kura*; on both matters the Aboriginal testimony is a little uncertain. But, with those exceptions, each class is exclusive of every other.

Any attempt to understand the Aboriginal philosophy of life and religion must take the classes into primary account. They are of so fundamental a nature that to try to go 'beneath' or 'behind' them by direct inquiry usually only bewilders the Aborigines.[15] The most fruitful interpretation to be put on them is thus a matter of difficulty. I have come to no final conclusions, but some general truths seem probable.

(1) They apparently embody the character and significance of things that constitute and co-exist perennially in the world, and are thus symbolical. Each class is a distinct and incomparable set of existences, with a type of individuality which the Aborigines generalise. Inference is the only means of discovering the principles of generalisation.

(2) On the evidence of the mythology, the classes as such are not part of the conception of 'the totemistic dispensation' to which reference was made. As far as the Aboriginal outlook can be gauged in this way, they seem understandable as conditions of the dispensation. That is, they already *were* when particular ancestors put these *nandji* and these *tjo* in the *ŋoiguminŋgi* of some clans or dreaming-places and not of others; or found these *ku* and *mi* to be good and not those; or by their exploits named, or shaped the physical properties, of places or *da* where some ancestors went into the ground and the waters, and others flew

15 I mentioned earlier the embarrassment of my informants at the disclosure that Europeans are (at least, were) given the same prefix (*ku*) as the class of beasts and honey. On the same occasion I was defeated—by, among other things, the merriment of my informants—in an attempt to get their explanation of the inclusion of food and fæces in the same class (*mi*). No, they said, it did not imply that anyone ever ate fæces; how could this conceivably be so? It was just a matter of *murin*, of language; perhaps fæces *looked* a little like *mi*; now that I had mentioned the matter, it did seem amusing; but it was not a thing of any importance. The more intelligent men developed a marked interest in my morphemic inquiries, and had some interesting things to say about how words might have been 'built up' in The Dream Time, but the discussions were never of any use in clarifying the existence-classes.

into the sky. Much of the kind suggests the inference that the classes as such are logically anterior, denoting conditions which the dispensation observed. Thus, they do not of themselves bring relation and moral order into the world of multitudinous existences in co-existence: that was done by the ancestors through totemism; what the classes do is to serve as a ground of that dispensation. They are in this sense primary data of life and thought underlying the prolegomena—the discourse on The Dreaming—to the main Aboriginal system of belief.

(3) The list includes all the exterior or sensible objects of life which the Aborigines strive to attain or avoid. Within each class things are valued, negatively as well as positively. The language of the systems of valuation is very simple—a few adjectives expressing crude linear scales—but the systems themselves are multiple. The value-contexts are technical, magical, religious and social, all having negative and positive dimensions. Thus, it is a matter of common experience to see natural objects flung aside with indifference and a disdainful remark '*nandji-wiya!*' (lit. 'thing,' 'bad' =unusable, in this context); or food dismissed as '*mi-wiya*' ('inedible,' 'bad-tasting'); or waterholes pointed out as '*kura-wiya*' ('dangerous'); or to become aware of the hush that falls on a camp at night when an untoward sound in the darkness suggests the presence of *kukarait*. But Murinbata usage suggests that the classes are not simply groupings of *entities*. They are also, at least in part, groupings of *functions* in that the entities have a determinate place in the scheme of life, and of *powers*, in that the entities have efficacies of one kind or another. At the same time they are *generic* concepts of a kind.

(4) Some of the things, considered as entities, have *dir̃mu* and many have *ŋinipun*, but these aspects are not developed significantly to make groupings within or between the classes. The idea of *ŋinipun* is best developed, and then primarily in relation to the eight sub-sections of the class of *kadu*. These are thought to be bi-sexual groups, each having its own bodily conformation generalised (in English) as a 'skin.' The idea is used, but only in a vague and general way, outside that class. The principle of sex is used to a very limited extent outside the *kadu* class. For example, the red ochres (which are *nandji*) have sex-names (*nogan*,

'male,' *miŕŋi*, 'female') according to their brightness, the female ochres being the brighter. The same terms are used for the sex of animals (*ku*). But the classes are not further differentiated, except by secondary classifications: by utility, physical properties (weight, size, colour), age, value-in-exchange, magical efficacy whether benign or malign, and ritual importance.

(5) The factual reference of each class is proximate rather than primary. Certainly, each of them names and groups objects; but not *as* mere objects. Every class is a sort of dualism, sometimes a multiple dualism, that states some principle or principles of the thing's being-there, so that the primary reference is really to pattern 'within' or 'behind' the factual reference. The pattern is relational, and one capable—judging by the lists—of holding contraries together in unity; but to extract the contraries which are related whether as functions or powers, does not seem practicable.

Class (1) bridges the visible and the invisible; (2) unifies the Here-and-Now with The Dream Time; (3) deals jointly with the corporeal and the incorporeal, the disgusting and the pleasurable, the benign and the harmful, the tangible and the intangible; (4) brackets the human and the cosmic; (5) and (6) make classes—a unity of some kind—out of the stuff of sustenance and the vileness of its process in the one case, and out of that which is most corruptible and that which is most sweet in the other case. Perhaps (7), (8) and (9) suggest more clearly functions or powers perennially consequential for man. The effects resemble paradoxes understandable only through the pattern, the relation of the terms, and not through an isolation of the terms themselves, whatever they may be.

(6) The contexts of use suggest that, if we are to understand the classes at all, it is as having a threefold reference. (*a*) They categorise the kinds of *stuff* that make up the external objects of living. (*b*) The stuff took on *pattern* or *constitutive form* of perennial stability at the events of The Dream Time. (*c*) Each of the patterns has its own *import* for men. My earlier observations that both the rite and the myth of *Punj* are 'dense with import,' are thus reinforced; for the very language through

which the more mundane things of life are dealt with is itself dense with symbolical import, although it may be somewhat indeterminate.

(7) There are whole realms of Aboriginal experience and life that lie outside the stuff, pattern and import of the classes, or any combination of them. For they do not embrace the inward or ideal or eternal objects of life, and they assume the actions of men towards or away from those objects.

The analysis has shown that the primary object of *Punj* is to make youth understand a mystery. But for the myth—and the other commentary offered by the Aborigines—we should not have been able to draw any such conclusion from the rite itself. The *aperçu* given expression in the myth leaps beyond the import of anything that makes up the rite. The myth is not the only one to suggest that alternatives existed in The Dream Time but, as I have already stated, it seems to be the only truly sorrowful myth.

Several things are to be noted. The leap forward, the 'going beyond,' is as much in the realm of life-striving as it is in the affective and cognitive realms of experience. It takes the form of a story which seems new and unprecedented, but the symbolising of mystery is commensurate with all the other *concurrent* orders of symbolising. That is, the *spoken* drama of tragedy and suffering is commensurate with the *acted* drama. And this in turn is commensurate—simultaneous in time, congruent in structural form, and evidently common in meaning—with the spatial configurations through which that drama is acted out.

It is as though that inner paradigm of which I spoke earlier—the *ŋinipun* or shapely pattern of setting apart, destruction, transformation and return—being immanent in the whole ritual culture of the Murinbata, if not more widely still, were being given, in the myth, its full import through a brilliant *aperçu*, a new illumination. As though the immanent were being made outward, and being transcended while remaining itself. And this in spite of the fact that boundaries between distinct orders of symbolising are crossed.

(8) The problem of interpreting the classes is made much more difficult by a view that they first have to be made intelligible empirically

and scientifically. It is hard—and, for my own part, I would say impossible—to equate or delimit or satisfy any of the classes by empirical fact as we grasp it. But if one does not begin with the assumption that there is only *one* mode of intelligibility then the difficulties diminish. The classes, like the myth and rite which they subserve, belong to the same order of reality as poetry, art and music. On this, let me repeat and endorse what Professor James has said.[16] Myth, rite, poetry, art and music, 'each according to its own technique, externalises and expresses a feeling, a mood, an inner quality of life, an emotional impulse and interpretation of reality'. Goethe, in his conversation with Heinrich Luden, states our first principle: 'What the poet has created must be taken *as* he has created it; as he made his world, so it is.'

(9) The course of study must evidently proceed from symbolic import through repeated pattern to constituent stuff. But the significance of the entities—among them the most outstanding being such fundamental things as blood, fire, water, earth, winds, songs, holes, leaves, red ochre, fat, weapons, and spirit-children—in part depends on the human actions taken about them. In the myths, which are the main evidence on which to draw, the actions are assumed as often as stated. The act-structure of myths requires the study of an immense number of discrete activities towards and away from the entities: camping, hunting, tracking, dividing and quarrelling over the fruits of the chase, love-making, plotting, fighting, acts of deception, murder, sorcery and the like. The symbolism of the things is certainly wrapped up with the symbolism of the activities into which they enter, and the classes give us *part* only of the furniture of the Aboriginal mind.

16 E. O. James, *Myth and Ritual in the Ancient Near East*, 1958, p. 309. Though developed mainly with reference to other cultures, Professor James's thesis holds true of the Aboriginal material in all essentials. Myth and rite 'give verbal and symbolic form and meaning to the emotional urge and rhythmic relations of life as a living reality, recounting and enacting events on which the very existence of mankind has been believed to depend, and proclaiming and making efficacious an aspect and an apprehension of truth and reality transcending historical occurrences and empirical reasoning and cosmological and eschatological speculations.'

A full understanding of the religious symbolism is to be attained only by a thorough morphemic analysis of the whole language. That study is beyond my technical competence. But until the analysis is made we have not penetrated the true inwardness of the stuff of symbolism. All we have done is to attain a rough idea of its pattern and import. The 'build' of The Dreaming is the product of an intimate interrelationship between all three.

Perhaps we have shown, however, that the fact that many of the dominant symbolisms are not put clearly into words does not condition their valence. It conditions only the capacity to express clear conceptions in words and sentences so that for the most part they remain beyond the symbolism of language. But *not* beyond the symbolisms which are independent of spoken language. The Murinbata have no words for, say, 'sine curve' and 'leftward-moving spiral,' but the celebrants of the rite trace out such evolutions year after year. These and other forms are so clear, dominant, and persuasive in their minds that, as they trace them out, the Aborigines seem to be saying (as R. R. Marett once put it): 'How, if not thus?' They are drawing on a rich stock of conventional signs known and used skilfully without any necessity of verbal symbolism. An observer has to stifle his own mind not to see in them the expression of æsthetic insight and a rhythmic symmetry of design. It is impossible to dismiss them as 'uncomprehended.'

7. The Dominant Symbolism

The telling of Murinbata myths often but by no means always ends with the exclamatory word *Demŋinoi!* A plural form is about as common as the singular: it then becomes *Pirimŋinoi* (sometimes pronounced as *Peremŋinoi*). Both are verbs in the third person and evidently in the past tense. The usage suggests a reflexive verb, but this remains uncertain. No other forms—if there ever were any—survive.[17]

17 I heard one possible exception, the form *pennginoi-nu*, which could be the 1st pers. sing. fut. but there was some head-shaking about it.

English-speaking Aborigines phrase the meaning of *demŋinoi* as 'changing the body' or 'turning' from man (*kadu*) to animal (*ku*). It appears to have certain connotations, at least further suggestions, among them 'spreading out,' 'flying away,' and 'going into the water.' There are distinct words for such activities, but they are seldom used in the myths, *demŋinoi* evidently being able to suggest them. The central meaning of that word seems to be 'metamorphosis,' one that is instant, a voluntary exercise of choice, and at the same time a necessity of overwhelming circumstance. It is clearly a metempirical conception.

One man, trying to clarify the meaning for me, referred to the Murinbata belief that a hunted animal, in order to save its life, may change itself instantly into something else. He said: '*ku-ḍaitpiṙ bamgadu ku-ŋinipun diniḍa ... ḍamul manaka panyatka nyinida nandji-buṙuṙ wada demŋinoi.*' Literally, 'animal or flesh+true—I saw—animal or flesh+shape or body (i.e. having the body or outward form of an animal)—being there—spear—as soon as, at the same time as—I threw—that which is there—inanimate thing+antbed—now, instantly—changed mysteriously.' In other words, 'I saw a veritable animal; I threw a spear; instantly and mysteriously, it changed into an ant-bed.' He put the story forward as an instance of personal experience.

The *demŋinoi* in this explanation could not be replaced, my informant said, by any other word and still have the same sense. For example, by *dinim*, which means approximately 'became' in the ordinary English sense and, in Murinbata, is used when a man becomes a wise man (*wanaŋgal*) as the result of a mystical experience. Or by *baŋambitj*, which means something like 'made itself' or 'was responsible for its own existence,' the word being used for self-subsistent spirits (*kadu baŋambitj*) which are distinguished from the spirits of dead human persons. Or by *yiŋambata*, which means the mystical process by which a totemic ancestor—at the instant of, and also by the act *demŋinoi*—made a spirit site or *ŋoigumiŋgi*.

The conception of a metamorphosis of animals into humans or humans into animals is of course at the very centre of Aboriginal symbolism throughout Australia. The facts that the myth of The Old

Woman does not stress, or apparently even mention, the *demŋinoi* motif and that the transformation of youths during the rite of *Punj* is not consciously likened to that type of transformation, are therefore interesting and in need of explanation. At the same time there is undoubtedly a certain likeness—the kind of likeness that constitutes metaphor—between (*a*) the sequences of mythical events leading up to the 'changing of body' and 'spreading out,' etc., and (*b*) the sequences acted-out in the rite or narrated in the myth of *Punj*. Obviously, a more careful study is needed of the apparent reduction or elision of so dominant a motif, or its possible concealment in metaphor.

It is to be remembered that we are dealing with a *moment* in the development or practise of a religious cultus. The *Karwadi* exemplifies a leap forward from older religious habitudes. By 'cult' one means precisely a going-beyond what was before. In such a cult a hitherto common value may be made sacred, or one that is already sacred made holy. Evidently it is the second step that has been taken in the rite and myth under study. In such a process a kind of chiaroscuro results: the blaze of the holy casts many shadows dimming much that before may have had the highest significance, even blotting it out, since there is nothing so dead as last year's cult. In linguistic symbolism we are dealing with intellectual conceptions making use of familiar imageries. In the linguistic symbolism of cults of the second kind, we may suppose that we shall meet with conceptions that are enhanced in much the same measure as the religious value. The motive of the *Karwadi* cult has been suggested as a discovery, or an illumination, of something in the condition of human life that excites sorrow by its sad inevitability. The particular symbolism through which this is expressed in the myth of The Old Woman appears to be made up of enhanced tropes or embellished metaphors of a conception arranged and expressed differently, but still recognisably, in other myths. The myth of Old Crow tells how men learned to die. The myth of The Rainbow Serpent tells—among other things—how the very condition of humanness, the possession of fire, was at the expense of the death of the father's father of one moiety of men and the mother's father of the other. The myth of *Karwadi* tells, in terms of sorrowful mystery, how young life had to be saved from its guardian. There is no evidence on which to base a chronology of the three myths, but the second certainly antedates the third. The myth of The Rainbow Serpent stresses the *demŋinoi* motif; the myth of The Old Woman does not elide but transfigures it, by changing some elements, by rearranging others and embellishing the same general pattern. In one, the death of a dualistic father one generation removed is the condition of the survival of all humanness. In the other, the death of The Mother is the condition of the perpetuation of human life through its children. The latter is a metaphor of the former, but intensified: the locus of good-with-tragedy is unified in the image of a single instead of a dual personage, and one that is a generation nearer.[18] And the element of sadness within, and evident in the telling of, the myth of The Old Woman has no counterpart, to my knowledge, in the myth of The Rainbow Serpent. We seem thus to meet a consonant development of insight, linguistic expression, and emotion.

It might seem, however, that the congruence of pattern between the myth and the rite under study argues against rather than for the thesis of cultistic development. The relation may be stated more exactly. It is one of *analogous* elements arranged with *similarity* of form or pattern and having a *commonness* of import manifest in different *types* of symbolism. Having examined a rite associated with a myth, I propose in the next article to examine (*a*) a myth *not* associated with a rite and (*b*) a rite *not* associated with a myth. If a pattern can be found constant between all three, then its dominance seems well established, and we shall be better able to ask what evidence should be discoverable if in fact a development of symbolising has taken place around a continuous form. In (*a*) the structure of the myth of The Rainbow Serpent will be studied, and in (*b*) that of a funerary rite which once brought all the clans together to give a man's soul its quittance. Taken together, they seem to me to establish that Aboriginal man, 'the victim of transience in himself and in the forms among which he dwells, is yet endowed with

18 The dualism is not wholly removed for the myth records her remarks to grandchildren.

the power to create forms which endure.' And more, has the power to adapt the work of his imaginative mind to the unfolding of history.

IV

The Design-Plan of a Riteless Myth

1. The Myth of the Rainbow Serpent

It has long been recognised that Aboriginal mythology in many parts of Australia gives great prominence to a being for whom Radcliffe-Brown suggested the title The Rainbow Serpent. Certain elements of belief about that being are so widely distributed that Radcliffe-Brown thought they might 'very possibly be practically universal' and form a conception 'characteristic of Australia as a whole and not of any one part or stratum of it.'[1] The elements he thought 'more essential' are: (1) a conception of the rainbow as a huge serpent which (2) perennially inhabits deep, permanent waters, (3) is associated with rain and rain-making, and (4) is connected also with the iridescence of quartz crystals and mother of pearl. He was inclined to represent The Rainbow Serpent as a sort of guardian-spirit. Its invariable association with water suggested to him that the Aborigines conceive of it as The Spirit of Water.

A myth in which the four elements occur is told widely among tribes on the north-west coast of the Northern Territory. I recorded the Murinbata version in detail but could recover only fragments of the versions known to the Marithiel, Nangiomeri and Wagaman. The account and analysis that follow deal primarily with the Murinbata version, but I include the other tribal outlines as well because of the possible significance of their variations.

Among the Murinbata, The Rainbow Serpent has at least four names, or perhaps it would be more correct to say, one proper name but may be identified in three other ways. The proper name is Kunmanggur, of which no English equivalent can be suggested. Curiously, the name is

1 *Journal Royal Anthropological Institute*, Vol. LVI.

borne by at least one living female although, in the myth, it is the name of a male being, albeit a male sometimes said to have breasts like a woman. In the narration of the myth Kunmanggur is used interchangeably with Kanamgek which, with one qualification, may be admitted also as a name. The qualification is that Kanamgek is recognisable as a compound verb-form, made up of an auxiliary and a root. The auxiliary is *kanam*, the 3rd pers. sing. pres. of a verb (often used as a suffix, but here as a prefix) meaning a repeated, habitual or continuous state of being. The root is the element *gek*, evidently an archaism, and of uncertain meaning, which is just possibly distantly cognate with a current verb meaning 'to spit water.'[2] The third name or word, Dimgek, is a similar compound verb-form, with the same root, but another auxiliary (*dim*), meaning a present instance or state of being. When a rainbow is mentioned in a conversational context, without mythological or religious reference, the word *dimgek* is then used, and may be regarded as the common word for rainbow. But because it is very occasionally substituted for Kanamgek, it should perhaps be considered a name also.[3] The fourth usage is Kulaitj, used here as a sort of name, but in other contexts as an ordinal adjective meaning simply the older or eldest. In the narration of the myth, and in discussions about it, the changes are rung on all

2 The root is heard in other contexts that make this meaning doubtful. For example, (I) *maiyen yibimgek* = 'the road,' 'is-there' (lit. 'lies-down-there')+*gek*; (2) *ngipilin panggoi wurangek* = 'river,' 'long,' 'goes-one-way'+*gek*. As far as I could determine, the root is used only of uniform action along a line or path or in a direction, and takes on a particular meaning from context. The rainbow is usually said to be the tongue or spit of Kunmanggur, but I have heard it described also as water blown from his drone-pipe. Some Aborigines add that the water contains flying-foxes and spirit-children. In the circumstances, one is perhaps wiser to give the root the most general meaning of 'acts.' I cannot say with any surety whether it is transitive or intransitive.

3 The use as a verb-form is, however, more common. When a rainbow appears the Murinbata may be heard to say '*Kanamgek dimgek!*' The coupled words have the sense of 'he who is-acts continuously, now manifest-acts,' subject to the qualifications made in the foregoing footnote.

four words. Kunmanggur and Kanamgek are about equally common; the two others are used occasionally. It would be near the general spirit of the usages to say that Kunmanggur, the main proper name, carries the sense of The Oldest One, He Who Perennially Is-Acts, Is-Acts Now.

It seems remarkable that the myth, which is the longest, the most detailed, and—to a European mind—the most dramatic of the many known to the Murinbata, should have no demonstrable connection with any rite now or recently practised. There could have been some such connection in times gone by, but the Aborigines make no such assertion and, when questioned on the matter, have nothing helpful to say. There is a second unusual aspect: the Kunmanggur of the myth is identified with the being visually portrayed in rock-paintings at Purmi and Kirindjingin, just outside Murinbata territory. The sites of the paintings are mentioned in the myth, and the tradition identifying the two beings is strong; but tradition is not evidence; and there is no way of knowing if the myth and paintings were coeval or not. The paintings no longer have any function in Murinbata life and what their functions may have been in the past is very obscure. As far as I could determine, only one other myth is associated with rock-paintings and it, like that of Kunmanggur, has no ritual connections; but a great many myths are told that have no associations of either kind. In the circumstances an *a priori* assumption that all myths have their genesis in rites—an assumption that Robertson Smith made—is unpersuasive, and the hermeneutic approach in which one looks to the ritual life for the first hints about the nature of truths being stated in myths meets a serious check.

On the other hand, the paintings associated by tradition with Kunmanggur are works of high imagination; it would not be too much to say, of artistic passion. And the myth itself is one of great power. To anyone familiar with Aboriginal life, and especially with its religion, a supposition that two such powerful expressions of Aboriginal insight could have developed without ritual associations has an improbable ring. The somewhat draconic argument of Radcliffe-Brown—that a conjectural history could but confound the problem—is an argument against unsupported history, not against speculation. If his caution is given due weight, one may try justifiably to do the two things attempted here: to look within presently dissociated myths for the structural forms that would enable them to be compared with myths still demonstrably connected with rites, and to elicit from myths of both classes their kerygmatic elements—the statements of abiding truths about life—for comparison.

The manner of telling the myth of Kunmanggur amply supports Strehlow's observation that an Aboriginal language is 'an instrument of great strength and beauty, which can rise to great heights of feeling.'[4] True, many, if not most, of the northern myths are, as he said of those of central Australia, 'rarely elaborate in form' but 'simple and brief accounts of the lives of totemic ancestors of a given group in a tribe.' But that of Kunmanggur is one of three—the others deal with The Old Woman (already narrated) and Kupki, The Snake Woman—which in every way warrant the use of the most sensitive art of translation. All three suggest that an oral literature of expressive beauty may not necessarily be rooted in ritual ground. Many Aboriginal myths seem pointless and inconsequential to a European mind, but these three make an immediate appeal by reason of the incident, texture, structure and climax of their stories. They demonstrate perhaps as well as anything could that although the weight of the past is very heavy on the present of Aboriginal life, and although there is a ready—and, at any moment, uncritical—adherence to 'received opinions and traditions,' the Aborigines do not live an 'unexamined life' in the Socratic sense. Each myth has something to say—something significant, said beautifully and tragically—about the first and last formula of things, the ultimate conditions of human being, the instituted ways in which all things exist, and the continuity between the primal instituting and the experiential here-and-now.

The four elements which seemed to Radcliffe-Brown 'more essential' are actually of secondary importance in the northern myth. Their main usefulness is taxonomic. The Rainbow Serpent does appear to be a kind of guardian spirit, and to say that he is The Spirit of Water is not

4 T. G. H. Strehlow, *Aranda Traditions*, 1947, p. xviii.

inapt. But the quiddity of the myth transcends such characterisation. What it narrates is a religious world-drama: a *drama* because it tells of events that follow in sequence to a unison which is a consummation by catastrophe; a *religious* drama because ultimate things of human being and existence are the concern throughout; and a *world* drama because the import is cosmogonical. The drama has a surface stratum and a deeper stratum. On the surface one hears of acts of incest by a brother; of deceit and parricide by a son; of the gift by a father of perennial water, the means of eternal life; of the attempted deprival by The Oldest One of fire, that which divides men from animals; and of the restoration to all by one man of fire, that which makes men human. I shall put upon these elements a construction consistent with the argument of earlier papers in this series: that they are symbolisations, or sorts of statement about one set of things under the guise of another. The task of analysis is to elicit from a myth that is in no way connected with any rite the masked propositions of life concealed on the deeper stratum.

2. The Problem of Myth-Variation

An important—perhaps decisive—point should be made here. There is no univocal version of the Kunmanggur myth; nor, indeed, in my opinion, of *any* Aboriginal myth. One is not dealing with dogmata or creeds, so there is no question of an authoritative or doctrinal form. Narrators may, and do, start or finish at somewhat different points; omit or include details; vary the emphases; describe events differently and attribute them to different causes and persons. Certainly, there is a sort of standard nub or core, a story with a plot, that all observe broadly. But, in my opinion, there is no accepted or enforced consensus, as in a formulated creed. I began my studies with a presupposition, drawn I know not whence, that for intellectual reasons there *must* be a consensus, a consistency of all versions in all parts. With short and evidently unimportant myths, a high consistency between versions could be obtained. But I failed to do so with the long and elaborate myths. These tax the

Aboriginal memory by reason of their complexity, but the complexity is not the cause of the variation, which seems due rather to the fact that the formula of the nub or core-story allows a wide field in which free imagination can play. The moving shapes of actual life appear to be drawn on to exemplify the formula, and the elements of the core appear also to be open to commutation. Variations of such kinds may be noted in versions of the myth given by individual persons among the Murinbata and also among the tribes of the same cultural region. I did not perceive for a long time the possibility that the variations might be as significant as the postulated consensus; that there might be one or more meaningful structures of variation. Experience eventually convinced me that the variations do indeed have inspirations and a logic of their own. When one is disabused of the misleading notion of a dogmatic version, variable only because of the frailty of human memory or from similar causes, one is compelled to consider the possibility that what keeps a myth 'alive' is not only the intrinsic interest or relevance of its story and symbolism: the dramatic potential is also involved. Every myth deals with persons, events and situations that, being less than fully described, are variably open to development by men of force, intellect or insight.[55] Under such development, motive can be attributed, character

5 One man, of flamboyant personality and theatrical style, and with political gifts of no mean order, narrated the myth of The Rainbow Serpent for me in a particularly striking fashion. He left the personality of Kunmanggur flat and characterless, but developed the part of Tjinimin, the Bat, with gleeful zest. By vivid gestures, by words and poses that were sometimes obscene, and by evil laughter, he exhibited Tjinimin as having a satanic nature. Such an emphasis is decidedly uncommon. But it is implicit in the more conventional narrations. It thus waits to be evoked by a powerful imagination. The same informant gave circumstantial details of supposed conversations which, in the ordinary telling, are indicated by short phrases only. But the conversations were consistent with what the mythical persons *might* have said in such situations. It appeared to me a good illustration of processes by which free imagination and human insight, while still obeying the canons of situation, may greatly change the emphasis and tone of a myth, and may even change its content.

suggested, and events and situations elucidated—or commutated—in a formative way without any actual breach of a tradition. By the same token, elisions can occur. So that unless one is able to compare versions of a myth given by the same individuals, or at least people of the same intimate group, at sufficient intervals, one cannot say with surety much about the status of a version recorded on a particular occasion.

In the above circumstances, I am unable to regard the myths of the northern region as conforming to what Strehlow has said[6] of those of central Australia. He contended that 'it is almost certain that native myths had ceased to be invented many centuries ago'; that 'the present-day natives are on the whole merely the painstaking, uninspired preservers of a great and interesting inheritance'; that 'they live almost entirely on the traditions of their forefathers'; and that they are 'in many ways, not so much a primitive as a decadent people.' My own experiences suggest the opposite of each statement. Mythopoeic thought is probably a *continuous* function of Aboriginal mentality, especially of the more gifted and imaginative minds, which are not few. The notion of a time when myths were, or ceased to be, invented is probably a schematic figment: one could as legitimately postulate the 'invention' of the family, the forms of social organisation, or any institution. Such a vocabulary of thought is wrongly applied to organic growths. In the north, there is every evidence of painstaking adherence to traditions; but the traditions themselves are a continuous inspiration; and adherence is not necessarily dispassion, disinterest, or dullness. The presence of a religious cult, in all probability as one of a succession, does not suggest men who simply live on the spiritual capital of olden times. Doubtless, there was a time when these Aborigines struggled up to the plateau of social and religious attainment on which Europeans found them. Much evidence points, not to decadence, but to a lively and developing life on the plateau. Against, then, Strehlow's view that in central Australia there is an 'attitude of utter apathy and ... general mental stagnation ... as far as literary efforts of any kind are concerned' I can but record my own experience of having heard brilliant improvisation, and my belief

6 *Op. cit.*, p. 6.

that this is part of the process by which mythopoeic thought nurtures and is nurtured.

The telling of a myth, then, is apt to vary with persons, occasions, and times. Many circumstances and, doubtless, many motives may have such effects. An informant's forgetfulness, lack of interest, mentality, prejudice and notion of what a questioner wishes to hear, or should be told, may affect the version recorded. It will surprise no experienced anthropologist to be reminded that jealousy, shame, a desire to shine, and an unfathomable malice not infrequently may affect Aboriginal informants in this as in other matters. Even the best informants on occasions may become a joyous danger for another reason—the mind, voice and imagination of such a person can make deeply exciting a myth left dull by another's. Whose version is one to accept? In many such cases I have no doubt that personal inspiration, leading to improvisation, takes place. Listeners rarely interrupt others' narrations to protest or disagree although, later, and—because of the convention of good manners—in private, may say that the telling was wrong. But their own corrections may meet with the same criticism from others. The anthropologist is thus under a practical necessity to decide on a version, and under a moral and intellectual duty to decide what is representative. But his decision is also one of art.

In the following account of Kunmanggur I have tried to indicate, as best seems possible, the main elements of agreement and variation. The Murinbata record is perhaps best prefaced by the few details I was able to obtain from adjacent tribes.

3. Three Fragmentary Accounts

During the course of field work in 1932–35 I was able to obtain the broad outline of the Marithiel, Wagaman and Nangiomeri versions of the myth. The fragments are worthy of record for the contrasts they afford with the Murinbata myth.

The Marithiel at that time were deeply disturbed, had abandoned their tribal home in the paper-bark forests, were crowding in upon the Daly River, and were at violent enmity with the river tribes amongst whom I was working. I depended on a single informant, a young man who had a poor grasp of his own culture. He told me all he knew.

Lerwin, The Rainbow Serpent, had no wife. Amanggal, The Little Flying Fox,[7] had two wives. Lerwin stole one of the women while Amanggal was looking for food. When he discovered the loss, Amanggal pursued Lerwin to a far country and slew him with a stone-tipped spear. Lerwin cried out in pain, jumped into deep water, and was transformed into a serpent. Amanggal flew into the sky.

My informant could not say what were the relations between the principals, but I was able to gather a few further pieces of information: a lively dread of Lerwin; a belief that, in the serpent-form, he inhabits deep waters, whether salt or fresh; that his tail is hooked ('like an anchor'); that he drowns people by thrusting the hook through a leg behind the heel-tendon, and also that he uses the hook to smash canoes and boats or to draw them under water; that newly initiated boys should not immerse themselves wholly in water lest they be seized and drowned by him; and that there is a close association between Lerwin and the iridescence of pearl-shell.

The information about the Wagaman version was about as sketchy. Only a handful of elderly men of the tribe were then on the Daly River, and they wanted as little to do with Europeans as possible. The main name of The Serpent was given to me as Djagwut, but the Wagaman appeared to distinguish two rainbows, one described as being 'high,'

7 My notes show that my informant referred to Amanggal as the male, and to Agarinyin as the female, one of several varieties of flying-fox. The Marithiel word *agarinyin* is suspiciously like the Nangiomeri *adirminmin* and the Wagaman-Murinbata *tjinimin*, although the four languages are not closely related. Only the Murinbata specify *tjinimin* as a bat, but I am inclined to think that all the terms refer to that creature, and that my informants said 'flying fox' only because of their poor command of English.

one 'low.' I could not be sure if they were making a distinction between the main colour-bands of rainbows, and the spurious bows, or between primary and secondary rainbows. The 'high' (i.e. secondary) rainbow was described as the spit of Djagwut and the 'low' (i.e. primary) rainbow as the spit of Tjinimin. Djagwut was recognised as the source and protector of human life, and as the giver of spirit-children. He was supposed to persist in deep springs, rivers and billabongs, and to be especially dangerous to menstruating women, being able to smell them from afar. The Wagaman assigned Djagwut to the Tjimitj sub-section and Tjinimin to the Djangala sub-section, the two thus being in an affinal (wife's brother) relation.[8] All I could recapture of the myth was that Tjinimin had two wives; that Djagwut stole both of them; that Tjinimin pursued and slew him with a stone-tipped spear while asleep, the spear striking him in the back. Djagwut cried out in pain, jumped into deep water, and was transformed into a serpent. Tjinimin flew into the sky.

The Nangiomeri version, though fragmentary, was a little more specific in some details. The Rainbow Serpent, Angamunggi, was described to me in terms of the familiar All-Father imagery: as the primæval father of men, the giver of life, the maker of spirit-children, and the guardian and protector of men. The decimation of the tribe at that time by disease, and the declining number of children then being born, were said to be due to the fact that Angamunggi had 'gone away' and no longer 'looked after' his people. The Nangiomeri seemed to think of Angamunggi as a dualistic person. They suggested that he had a womb, that a son had died within it and that the 'low' or 'small' rainbow (Amebe) was also his son. He was assigned to the Tjanama sub-section, and Adirminmin (again described as The Little Flying Fox) was assigned to the Djangala sub-section, that is, to the correlative affinal sub-section of Tjanama. The myth as it was told to me ran thus:

---

8 I could not discover the relation between Djagwut and the 'low' rainbow, or between Djagwut and the women. Under the rules of marriage between the sub-sections, either Djagwut or Tjinimin, or both, could have been in the wrong.

Adirminmin went about trying to find good stone for a spear. He went to many places. Finally he went to a spring at Kimul (on the Fitzmaurice River). There he went hunting for kangaroo. He was a Djangala man and took with him two Nangari women who had been given to him by Angamunggi. The two women went away and hid. Carrying a kangaroo, he caught up with them. They were on a high cliff and made a rope to lift him up. The rope broke and he fell down a long way, breaking his bones. The women went to bathe in the salt-water part of the river, and then ran away, with sexual intent, to Angamunggi. Adirminmin mended his broken bones, bathed in the salt-water, and set out to recapture the women. The tide kept on sweeping him back as he tried to cross the river. He went to try to find good stone for a spear. He tried several kinds of stone, but they were not sharp enough. Finally he found a sharp stone called *katamalga*, and put it on a spear-shaft. Then he chased and found the women. He said: 'Ah! Here you two are! I have to pick up my spear.' He sang the song that begins *Kawandi, kawandi*; then he danced by himself; and, after that, went to sleep. Wakening, he found Angamunggi, and threw the spear so that it pierced The Rainbow Serpent's backbone.

4. The Murinbata Myth

I shall now set out, at length, the myth as it is told among the Murinbata. In the form given, it is known only to older people who were adult at the time when the Mission of the Sacred Heart was established (1935).

It is divided somewhat arbitrarily, for ease of reference, into numbered sections, each section being a roughly distinguishable phase. Major variations made by informants are put in square brackets, and my own truncations in doubled square brackets.

(1) Kunmanggur had two daughters, Pilitman, The Green Parrot Women (ornithological identification uncertain). [They were the sisters of Tjinimin, The Bat.] They were with Kunmanggur at Kimul. They said: 'Father, we want to go that way,' pointing towards the sea;

'we want to find food.' Kunmanggur sent them from Kimul towards the island known as Nganangur. He said: 'Take this bottle-tree (*bamnudut*, baobab) and put it on that island.[9] You will find a good place there.'

(2) The two girls went off, carrying digging-sticks. They went to the place known as Mindjini-Mindjini, and there began to gather many pieces of paperbark. Then they went on, to camp at Were-Kurumbunuru, near Maiyilindi. The next day they passed a big hill, and crossed over the big river near Wakal-Tjinang. They gathered paperbark at Paiyer, and divided the sheets of paperbark into two big heaps, one for each of them. Then they went on to Nganangur to look about for fish and crabs.

(3) [Tjinimin lusted after the girls.] One had pubic hair, the other none. They were very pretty. Tjinimin [did not care that they were his sisters or were of the Kartjin moiety, his own; he wanted them, and] meant to follow them. He said to Kunmanggur: 'Father I want to go that way,' pointing in the direction in which The Green Parrot Women had gone; 'I want to see The Flying Fox people.' He was deceiving his father. Tjinimin wore his forehead-band (*daral*). [His penis was still very sore and painful.[10] He followed the girls, but lost their track after

9 Many Murinbata resent being told that horticulture and agriculture are unknown to them. They cite Kunmanggur's instruction to his daughters that 'making a garden' is an old Aboriginal custom. They interpret the presence of any natural species in an unexpected place as an intended result of human action in past time. The baobab grows sporadically, sometimes singly, sometimes in clusters, in unpredictable places, and this fact is taken to be evidence of human intent. It is especially plentiful on Nganagur.

10 A sign of initiation. A subsidiary myth relates how Tjinimin had been subincised by Yuwirnga, one of the Flying Fox Brothers. The brothers, Walet and Yurwirnga, had started from Nganarangga to find a good country. They came to a place now known as Karawupman and there made a dreaming-place (*ngoiguminggi*). At that time Walet had a penis like a man. Yuwirnga took a sharp cutting-stone secretly and subincised Walet, so that he became *ngi madaiyin*. Later, he did the same to Tjinimin, and later still to all the people to the south (*kadu tjiltji*). All *kadu tjiltji* now call those from the north *lamatingi*, and say that they are not truly

Mindjini-Mindjini, where he veered to the west. He took another road passing through Dangaiyer. He killed a rock-wallaby and roasted it quickly because he thought the girls might be close. He put the wallaby on his shoulder to carry it but it burned his neck, so he dipped his burden in water. Then, still carrying the roasted wallaby, he came on the girls' track. On an open place, he saw the paperbark they had left. The girls were not there.

(4) When he saw the paperbark Tjinimin said: 'Ah, this is theirs; they left it here.' He knew they would come back. He took the wallaby to a jungle and hung it in a tree. [Then he made a spear. He went to where the girls had made camp and saw some of their menstrual blood. At the sight, he had an erection.] He took white paint, softened it in his mouth, and painted himself like an initiated man, and put on a pubic-covering. Then he moved the paperbark to another position, smoothing out all the marks where it had lain. He piled the sheets one by one on top of himself so that he was hidden underneath. He crossed his arms on his chest and, breathing through a small hole, waited, listening and sleeping alternately.

(5) After a long time the girls came. They had many mullet with them. They put down the fish and made a fire.[11] They did not see Tjinimin. Then they noticed the changed position of the paperbark. 'Oh, sister,' said one, 'look! a big wind must have done this.' They began to sort out the sheets. 'Whose is this?' 'It is mine; put it here.' 'Whose is this?' 'It is mine; put it there.' At last, only one big sheet was left.

(6) As the last sheet was taken away, Tjinimin leaped out, laughing with glee and malice. The girls were startled. 'Oh, my brother is here,'

---

men. The Murinbata, who practise circumcision, apply the same term to the uncircumcised tribes to the north of the Daly River.

11 Some informants deny that the girls had fire, and say that the fish was to be eaten raw. It was Tjinimin who had fire 'because he was man,' implying that the girls were still birds. The variation suggests some doubt about Tjinimin's moiety, for the mythology holds that in The Dream Time only Tiwunggu people had fire. The implicit suggestion is that he belonged to the Tiwunggu moiety.

said one. 'Why have you come?' Tjinimin said: 'My father[12] sent me to find you two.' 'Perhaps you are pretending? My father did not tell me that.' 'No, my father said to bring you back.' But Tjinimin was deceiving them. [He showed them his erect penis, and spilled semen on the ground. The girls were very frightened. 'What is that you have lost?' said one. Tjinimin replied: 'It is nothing.'] He kept on laughing.

(7) He next told them to get the wallaby. The girls said: 'No, you go for it; we are tired from coming through the mangroves.' Tjinimin did so. He then invited the girls to eat of it. They refused, saying: 'No, leave it until later; we will eat the fish before it is rotten.' He said: 'I will keep it for you. You will eat it bye-and-bye.' They ate the fish, offering some to Tjinimin.

(8) As darkness came, he went for a walk, telling the girls to stay where they were. The sun was going down. [He took off his pubic covering. Hornets came and stung his penis so that it swelled enormously.] With the darkness, he returned to prepare a camp. He told the girls he would copulate with them. They said: 'We cannot do that; we are your own sisters; you are our own brother.' Tjinimin replied: 'It does not matter; it is enough that I came alone; no one is here; no one can see; we must copulate.' He threatened them that if they did not he might do something like *Yerindi*[13] to them. The girls were very frightened. They said to each other: 'Sister, who will go to him?' The younger said: 'I have no pubic hair. You go.' So the older sister went to him. Tjinimin made fire. The

12 One informant, narrating the myth, said at this point, 'Your *kaka* (mother's brother) sent me to find you two.' Later, he reverted to the statement that Kunmanggur was the father of all three. When I questioned him, he was confused, saying that Tjinimin was a 'little bit Tjalyeri,' that is, belonged to the opposite moiety from Kunmanggur. The designation of Kunmanggur as father (*yile*) or mother's brother (*kaka*) seems to vary with the locus of the clan from which informants come. Those from clans nearest the Nangiomeri and Wagaman tend to favour the Tiwunggu moiety as Kunmanggur's.

13 *Yerindi* is song-sorcery, of which even sophisticated Aborigines of modern times remain in dread.

three slept thus: the younger Pilitman between two first, Tjinimin and the older Pilitman between the second and third fires.

He copulated with the older girl, so that she cried out in pain: 'Oh! Oh! brother! Oh! sister, come to me.' The younger Pilitman was asleep; she did not hear. He did it to the older Pilitman again and again, leaving her half-dead. Her sister brought her water, and she slept as though dead. Tjinimin then copulated with the younger girl. She too cried out in pain: 'Oh! Oh! brother!' She called out to her sister in vain.

(9) The next day the girls went to get water at the creek known as Merngoiyi. It was dry. They went back and said to Tjinimin: 'Come, we will all go to-day.' Tjinimin said: 'No, let us stay here another day.' The sisters said: 'No, we had better go; we can sleep on the other side of the creek. We will carry the paper-bark; you can carry the kangaroo.' But they told Tjinimin to wait while they went ahead to make a crossing. On their way through the jungle they danced, and the magic of the dance brought hornets to wait on Tjinimin's path. When he came, they stung him everywhere, all over his body, so that he cried out in agony. But the girls called out: 'Come quickly, the tide is coming.' They stopped its motion by song-magic. 'Hurry,' they called out. Tjinimin was finding the kangaroo very heavy, and asked them to help him. 'No, no,' they called, 'hurry. There is no water yet. The tide is shallow.' When they were on the other side of the creek they ran away. But the tide caught Tjinimin. It swept him away. The kangaroo, and his spear, womerah, pubic covering and firestick were all lost.

(10) Tjinimin, still alive, put his feet on dry ground at Panyida, where there are rocks. He tried to make fire but, being without a fire-stick, failed. Taking [finding?] a new spear and womerah, he killed a kangaroo, and made a pubic-covering from its hair. Then he saw the smoke of a fire a long way away. He suspected that it had been made by the Pilitman women.

(11) He camped twice before he came close to it, and saw them sitting on a high hilltop. He called out to them: 'Which way do I climb up?' The women pointed to a steep cliff, saying: 'You must go there.' Tjinimin tried to climb the cliff by many different ways, but failed each

time. 'You must make a rope and throw it down to me,' he cried out. The women made a rope and let it down the cliff. They said to Tjinimin: 'You hold the rope and we will pull you up.' They pulled him up, up, up, almost to the top. Then they cut the rope. Tjinimin fell on to the rocks far below. He broke the bones of his legs, arms, shoulders and head.

(12) [But he was clever, and full of tricks; the breath did not leave his body. He mended his own bones. Then he stretched himself, trying his limbs and muscles. 'Ah,' he said, 'I had a good sleep. Those two women did not wake me up.'] Now he went another way.

(13) Tjinimin broke a piece of white stone (*malawat*) and with it tried to cut his nose. The stone was too blunt. He tried another; it too was blunt; he threw it away. He went to Tagundjiya, and tried the stone there. It was no good. At another place, Toinying, he found a long stone. It was good; it cut sharply through his nose. He lay down and, by magic, restored his nose. 'Oh, it is good.'

(14) Now he returned to Kimul, where Kunmanggur was. Kunmanggur said: 'My son, *Kadu Punj*, is returning.' Tjinimin stayed for one day. Then he said to his father: 'I am going that way.' 'Where?' Tjinimin pointed to the north. 'I am going for a bamboo' (spear-shaft?, drone-pipe?).

[He found his *naŋgun*, Kiniming, The Black Hawk, at Pulupulu. Tjinimin was troubled by his bones. Kiniming asked him what was the matter. Tjinimin blamed the two women: 'No one looked after me; I fell down on the stones.' Kiniming gave him a bamboo (spear-shaft?) and asked if he had a spear-point. Tjinimin said: 'Yes, I have a spear; it belongs to my father; I will put this stone-point on it.' No one found out that it was his own spear.]

[Tjinimin went to a far place to search for a bamboo spear-shaft. He tried a *malawat* stone; it broke in half. He said: 'I will leave here (to find) a good stone.' Again he went a long way. At the place called Kuradagunda he made another spear but the shaft broke. He tried another; it broke. Then Tjinimin fitted a *malawat* stone to a spear, straightened the bamboo shaft, and bound it with waxed string. Taking the spear he went on and on, to Kimul, to that place where all came out.]

(14) He visited all the people. He said to them: 'Hear! We shall all dance at the open place at Kimul. Kanamgek, The Old One, The Leader-Friend, is there.'

He gathered all the people, and they went towards Kimul. He said to Maminmanga, The Diver-Bird: 'I cannot leave you here; you are the singing-man; you must come with me.' Maminmanga brought a big bamboo for Kunmanggur. Tjinimin called to come Kularkur The Brolga, the skilful dancer; Mundoigoi The Turkey; Tjimeri The Jabiru; The Ducks Laidpar and Ngulpi; and the Black Kalawipi (unidentifiable) for the women's dance (*mamburki*). They all went, and came out at Kimul.

(15) Tjinimin made fire all the way along the tops of hills. Kunmanggur, seeing the the smoke, said: 'Oh, Tjinimin returns.' All the tribes went with him. They were a great many, stretching over a great distance. Tjinimin went first to Kunmanggur, who asked him: 'What news?' (*murin*). Tjinimin replied: 'Many, many people are coming to dance. We shall have a big *waŋga*.'

(16) Maminmanga gave the drone-pipe to Kunmanggur and said: 'I will sing.' Kunmanggur began to play *kidnork, kidnork, kidnork!*, and Maminmanga to sing:

Kawawawandi, kawandi kawandi,
Mutjinga tjalala, purima marata,
Krrk, krrk, krrk, krrk.[14]

(17) Tjinimin danced. All danced. Tjinimin came close. All were dancing. The two Pilitman girls came and sat close to their father. Kunmanggur said to his son: 'Which way have you come?' Tjinimin replied: 'I have come from Mungiri.' 'You have brought something?' 'Nothing.' He had brought only his fire-stick and womerah. He had

14 The Murinbata are unable to give a translation. In all probability the song is in the language of another tribe, or includes archaic Murinbata words. *Kawandi* is reminiscent of the Djamindjing *wandiwandi* (an evil, non-human spirit), but *mutjingga* (old woman) and *purima* (wife) are Murinbata words.

hidden his spear. The two girls were there now, with their father. [They had told Kunmanggur what Tjinimin had done.]

(18) There were many people, and much noise. Tjinimin danced so as to make the women desire him. He and Kularkur were the leaders. With many tricks and artifices, they danced close to the singing-man. Then Tjinimin spoke swiftly in the Wagaman language: 'I am going to kill your father, I am going to kill your father.' People did not understand, and said: 'What is it you say?' Tjinimin answered: 'I told Walumuma to get me water.' Walumuma went to get water for him, carrying it in her hands. Tjinimin spilled the water without drinking.

Again Maminmanga began to sing, Kanamgek to blow his pipe, and Tjinimin to dance. As he danced he called out swiftly: 'I am going to kill your father.' Again he spoke in the Wagaman language and not understanding, people asked: 'What is it you say?' Tjinimin replied: 'I said, 'bring me good water to drink.' ' Walumuma brought him water in a water-carrier. Again Tjinimin spilled it, and again Kunmanggur blew his pipe, Maminmanga sang, and Tjinimin danced. As he danced he drew the hidden spear towards him by his toes. Again he spoke swiftly in Wagaman; again they asked him what he had said; again he said that he wanted water to drink. To himself, he said, without words: 'Not long now. From this place I will throw the spear.' He went on calling for water and when they brought it he would spill it.

(19) Now all were tiring. They said: 'How many more times shall we dance?' They counted three times more. Kunmanggur blew his pipe, Maminmanga sang, Tjinimin danced. 'Soon I will spear your father.' 'What is that you say?' 'Bring me good water quickly for I am hot from dancing.' Walumuma ran and filled a water-carrier. 'How many more dances?' 'Two more!' Kunmanggur blew; Maminmanga sang ... and then he stopped. Tjinimin ran in darkness close to the spear and privily moved it nearer. He said to himself: 'Not long now, and I will throw it.' All said to him: 'What is that you say? Is the water there?' Tjinimin replied: 'Dance once more!'

(20) Now, the other people danced, but Tjinimin ran to the spear, grasped it and came close. While they danced that time, and

Kunmanggur blew his pipe, Tjinimin came close and did that thing. *Prrp!* (the sound of the womerah). *Trrr!* (the sound of the spear). (It hit) there in the back!

(21) 'Yeeeeee!' cried Kunmanggur. He threw the drone-pipe in the water there. *Pub!* (the sound of falling). The Old One, The Friend-Leader, is finished.

(22) Walet, The Flying Foxes, transformed on the instant, flew away into the air, crying 'Eeeee!'. All the birds flew away. The children of Kunmanggur cried out in grief.

[Tjinimin ran from that place, and, standing afar off, looked back, wondering what they would do. But no one revenged themselves upon him.] They all cried out in grief, and went another way (flying, spreading out).

(23) The Old One rolled about (in agony). He plunged into the water at Maiyiwa. *Bu!* (the sound of plunging into water). He cried out to his son, Nindji, The Black Flying Fox: 'Pull out the spear.' Nindji did as his father bid. 'Throw it.' Nindji threw it afar. That spear is now at Toinying.

(24) He stayed at Maiyiwa for one moon. They made fire and put hot stones to his wound but to no avail; it did not heal; and water came out through the fire. 'I cannot recover; better I should go away from here.' So from there he went to the rock shelter at Purmi, where the great baobab is that comes from him. But he was still sick and, taking with him all his sons, The Flying Foxes, he went on.

[The myth then lists a large number of places—of which I recorded thirty—which the dying Kunmanggur visited. At each place he rested, hoping for a soft-lying place, that his wound would heal; but at each place he met disappointment, and felt death coming nearer. At many, but not all, places his wives and sons dug a hole in the ground, made a fire to heat stones, and tried fruitlessly to staunch his bleeding wounds, and at each such place water came up through the flames. At many places Kunmanggur performed many feats of wonder; as at Kulindang, where he left one of his three testicles; or at Kiringjingin, where he left his signs, in the shape of a body and footprints, on the wall of a vast cave; or at Dirinbilin, where his blood still seeps out through the rocks and water. At other places he left personal possessions: his stone-axe and fishing net at Kiringjingin, and his forehead-band at Kandiwuli in a pool of glass-like water. At last he turned towards the sea, eventually reaching a place which the myth leaves uncertain, but somewhere near Blunder Bay on the lower Victoria River.]

(25) Now Kunmanggur said to Pilirin, The Kestrel: 'Hear! I am hungry for flesh-food. You hunt flesh for me!' So Pilirin took his spear and went. He speared a kangaroo, roasting it at Palkanmi. But Kunmanggur was now wearied and angry from his sickness. Slowly he gathered all the fire from that place and stood it on his head as though it were a head-dress (*mutura*). [The people said to him: 'Why do you do that?' He replied to them: 'Stay silent; I shall take this fire forever for myself.'] He entered the water close to Doitpir. Slowly the water rose upon him to here ... to here ... to here ... The people cried out to Kadpur The Butcher Bird: 'He intends to take that fire into the water there!' Kadpur cried out to Pilirin: 'Kai-i-i-i, kai-i-i-i, kai-i-i-i!' Pilirin heard the hail all the vast distance from Palkanmi. 'Someone is calling out from there. What is (the unknown) trouble? I think it is (about) The Old One. I think they have lost The Old One, The Leader-Friend.' He ran all the way to that place, ran without pause, and stopped only when he had come close.

(26) Kunmanggur was now far out. The water rose on him to here ... to here ... to here ... it was up to his chest. He went to the place known as Lalalarda, where he pushed out his legs to make the creek. Kadpur cried out to Pilirin: 'The Old One has taken all the fire into the water. Hasten after him!' Kadpur ran (flew) swiftly to where only the fiery head-dress could now be seen. He ran (flew) to where the water was beginning to cover Kunmanggur's head. *Pit!* (the sound of snatching). He snatched the fire out of the water. But Kunmanggur's fire was out! Finished!

(27) Pilirin ran (flew) close to the people. He made fire with fire-sticks—this was the first time men had used fire-sticks (i.e. the fire-drill). He set fire to the grass on all sides. To this day all that country looks fire-scorched. That is from what Pilirin did.

(28) Kunmanggur thrashed around in the water and made it turbulent with foam. He thrust out his legs! Now a creek is there. That place is Tjuliyel. He thrust out his legs! Now at Purulunjnu and Turubilin little creeks are there. He rolled about! Now came that big creek men call Doitpir. Where he splashed about at Mendiputj men now swim across straightway to Kudunnyinggal.

That place at Doitpir, where he went into the water, is *da lurutj kalegale ya kalegale* ('place' + 'mighty, strong' + 'mother, mother' + intensive particle + 'mother, mother')!

5. Palimpsest and Overscript

Our concern is not with the myth as a tale or fable as such, or even as a literary form. Rather is it with the respect in which the myth is a kind of essay in self-understanding. A difficulty from this point of view is its historical standing.

The fact that many myths may be remembered and told at a given time, or over a period, is not evidence that they all have the same standing. The matter is clearly one that requires caution and an absence of priorism. The dissociation of the myth of Kunmanggur from any extant or recent rite—a demonstrable fact—could suggest its obsolescence. Were that the case then its lack of appeal to the living Aborigines becomes the more readily understandable. The symbolic images through which its truths, whatever they be, timeless or timely, are expressed, themselves being dated, would of course be more than ordinarily obscure. Several lines of inquiry inclined me to conclude that this was so.

In a prolonged study of the myth, I found that it impinged rather more widely and deeply on the mystical beliefs of the Murinbata than any other, but the evidence was diffuse and refractory. I could assign the myth no precise place in the life of sentiment or action. One thing only set it apart from other myths not associated with rites: the well-remembered connection with rock-paintings at Purmi and Kirindjingin.

But the Aborigines who went with me to see the paintings looked on them with no show of emotion. The story of the myth seemed to have an intrinsic interest for the Aborigines but, as far as I could judge from their statements and conduct, perhaps no greater interest than others. However, its narration did not lead to expressions of sorrow and pity, as with the myth of The Old Woman. Many experiments led me to conclude that there was no prospect of settling with certainty a number of matters which, from rational considerations, seemed important: the occasions of telling, the preferences for variant statements, shared notions of significance and import, the classes most familiar with the myth, and the like. On numberless occasions I turned inquiry towards such questions, hoping for the sudden illuminations that so often come if one patiently uses indirect means of inquiry. I left the region not a little puzzled by the standing and function of the myth.

A second, and more puzzling, difficulty emerged. The picture of Kunmanggur built up by the things that narrators of the myth actually said, was perhaps rather flat, but at least it had a certain unity. It was the picture of a beneficent culture-hero, a great man of superhuman size and powers: the ancestor who 'made us all' and still 'looks after people'; the father's father of the Kartjin moiety and the mother's father of the Tiwunggu moiety. That unity was greatly weakened when, in hope to add to the depth, I sought to draw on the large amount of contextual information that resulted from protracted inquiry. Kunmanggur then came to seem a momentary convention of a figure about whose sex, unity and beneficence many doubts clustered. It was as though things written on a palimpsest were emerging to cast into doubt, if not to contradict, what had appeared to be an overlying fair copy. The following summary brings out the dubieties.

(*a*) There was a hint in some statements that The Oldest One may not have been Kunmanggur but someone else—a woman—or, if it were Kunmanggur, then 'he' may have been bi-sexual. A pristine female, often called Kulaitj Mutjingga (literally, The Oldest Woman), was associated with sea-mist. The darkest band of the rainbow was sometimes referred to as Kulaitj, or Kirindilyin, and was then identified with the wife of

Kunmanggur and the mother of Kanamgek. Even those who asserted the maleness of Kunmanggur said that he had large breasts, like a woman's. I found it impossible to reconcile the differences.

(*b*) There was a fairly persistent suggestion that Kunmanggur and Kanamgek were not identical. One informant (on whom I found I could not rely) insisted there were two brothers Kunmanggur. I also heard of Kanamgek as the son of Kunmanggur, and of their having died in different places. It was a matter of common agreement that Kunmanggur was married, but opinion varied about the number and names of his wives. The name Kirindilyin was used less commonly than that of Ngamur.[15] There was a consensus that there were two wives, one of whom was Ngamur. The name of the other was suggested many times as Walumuma, The Blue-tongued Lizard. But it was about as common to have Walumuma suggested as Kunmanggur's daughter and Tjinimin's sister. I made many efforts to reconcile the statements, both by wide inquisition and by using sketches of the rainbow drawn by the Aborigines themselves. Little success attended the attempts.

All manifestations of the rainbow were represented primarily as *signs* left or made by Kunmanggur. I could not induce informants to go much beyond saying that any manifestation of a rainbow is 'his spit,' 'his tongue,' or 'water spat through his drone-pipe' (*maluk*). The last statement was usually accompanied by an explanation that the water contains flying-foxes and spirit-children (*ŋaritŋarit*).

The spectrum of colours in a rainbow is divided by the Murinbata into three bands (violet-blue, green-yellow, orange-red). The darkest band was variably identified as Kunmanggur, Kirindilyin, Ngamur, or Kulaitj. Or the top band might be identified as Kunmanggur, the middle as his drone pipe, and the lowest as Kanamgek. It was commonly suggested that Ngamur was older (*kulaitj*) than Kunmanggur, and may have been married—to someone nameless—before marrying him. She was represented as a black snake in the sea, the sea (*laliŋgin*) being The Child of River (*ŋipilin*) and sea-noises being the crying of the child for its mother. I attempted to follow through all the hints but found that to

15 Ngamur is also the name of a particular black snake.

do so was soon to become lost in deeps beyond an inchoate deep. In the end, I had to conclude that the difficulties were irreconcilable. They may arise from the fact that the rainbow, the chief sign, being visibly and variably differentiated in numbers, is a stimulus to imagination. The differentiations may invite imaginative speculation and, on the evidence, appear to receive it.

(*c*) Kunmanggur was always represented as having been in life a huge person, likened to a baobab tree in size, and of great strength and superhuman powers. It was implied that he was mild and beneficent. After the transformation, he 'came back' as a prodigious serpent, with sharp protuberances on his spine and a long tail that curves scorpion-like over his back. The tail ends in a hook (*kandinin*). Evidently, there was a change of temper too. In the transmogrified form he was reputed to be fierce (*mulak*). It was said that, using his hooked tail, he lies in wait for people in deep waters, with some ill-disposition towards them, and may 'sting' or 'bite' or 'pull' them unless restrained by Ngamur. The two sit back-to-back, especially at river-crossings. Ngamur, seeing the approach of travellers, and wishing to help them, changes her position (hence causing the swirl of whirlpools) so as to face and guard those who use the crossings. Both Kunmanggur and Ngamur were said to 'bite' evil-doers, especially warlocks.[16]

(*d*) Kunmanggur was represented visually in five different fashions: (i) as a scorpion-like creature in which there is no human suggestion (Pl. I, A); (ii) in a somewhat stylised human form, with a spear piercing his side and arms conventionalised so as to merge with a fish-net forming a kind of aureola around his head (Pl. I, B); (iii) as a head only drawn in a sparse but brilliant geometric style, a circle with radial lines (Pl. I, C);

16 I recorded many instances of Aborigines drowned in rivers or in the open sea, all the deaths being attributed to Kunmanggur. The general surmise was that they had been punished by Kunmanggur, who 'cannot bite for nothing.' Snakes and crocodiles which attack humans are also supposed to do so as agents, occasionally of Kunmanggur, but of warlocks as well. I have no reason to suppose that the theory of retribution by Kunmanggur is due to the influence of European beliefs.

(iv) as a complete figure (D) drawn somewhat in the style of (C); and (v) as a complete figure drawn in an elongate geometric style (Pl. I, E).

(*e*) There were mutually contradictory views about Kunmanggur's ætiology. He was spoken of as (i) *kadu baŋambitj*, a 'self-finding' person (i.e. self-creating and self-subsistent), an important division that runs through all the beings of the Murinbata theophany; (ii) as *kadu mundak*, 'man-before' or 'man-ancient,' a true man though possessing powers that men no longer have; (iii) as *kulaitj*, the first and oldest man; and (iv) as possibly having parents.

(*f*) I concluded from discussions that his relations with, and position *vis-à-vis*, certain other mythological beings, was surrounded by irresoluble doubt. He was said to be 'bigger' (i.e. in power and authority) than Mutjungga, The Old Woman, the central figure of the cult of Punj. But no one would say confidently that he is 'bigger' than Kukpi, The Snake Woman, the great song-maker and giver of spring-waters. Nor would anyone affirm his relationship and position in respect of Nogamain, another self-subsistent spirit reputed to be the sender of honey and beautiful children, and the only being to whom the Murinbata address something like an invocation. At the same time it is often said: '*Kanamgek manyiwata da mundak*' (lit. 'Kanamgek,' 'made us all,' 'anciently'). He was also commonly reputed to be the mystical source of spirit-children, flowers, rain, fish, flying-foxes, and the general increase of nature, as well as the maker of deep pools of fresh water found along his sacred path.

In this situation I came to think of the myth, however told, as *itself* being an attempt to systematise a throng of visionary shapes set up by mythopoeic thought over an unknown period, so that in any version at any time only some of the many possibilities are used. How many may have been used or neglected by different narrators at different times, and whether the core-story has remained constant, it seemed impossible to say.

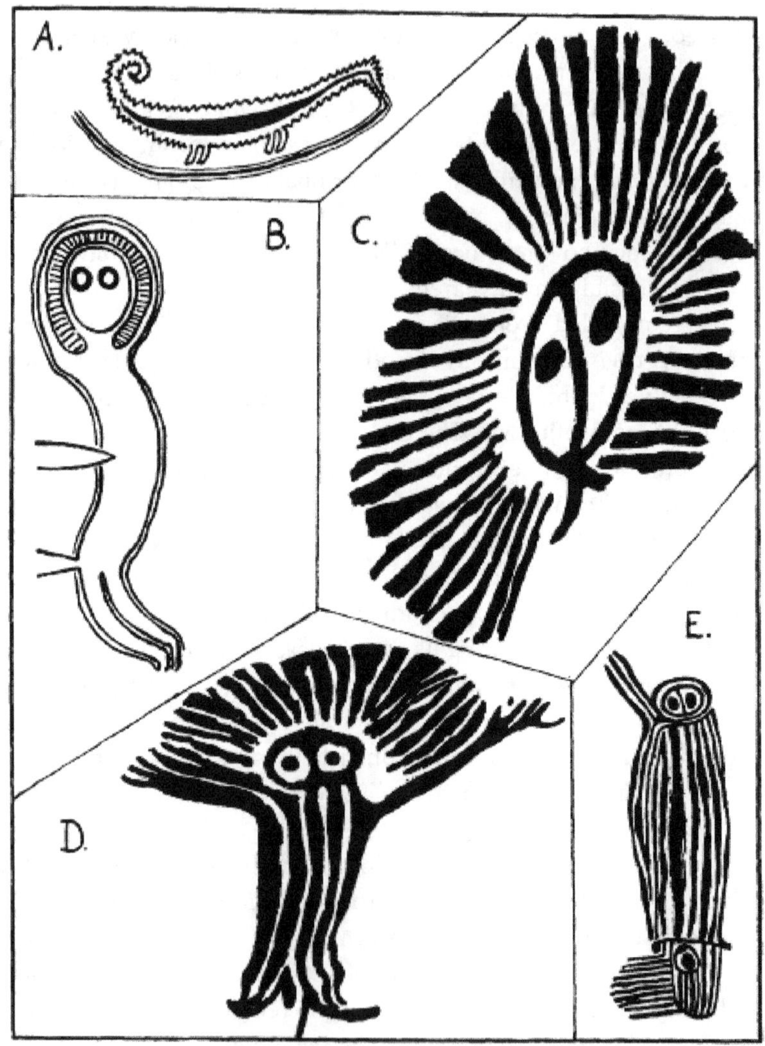

Figure 5. Five Visions of the Rainbow Serpent

If the myth is an attempt to systematise tenuously-connected visions, what is the principle or method of the system? My thesis is that myths of the kind are best understandable as allegory and, ultimately, as a sort of poesy. The criteria of selection from the stock of possibilities must have been, in the broadest sense, artistic, not intellectualistic. The discovery by an external observer that the myths are full of ambiguity, paradox, antinomy and other such obscurities is the product of an intellectual—and therefore misguided—criticism of the artistic-poetic process. If there is a principle then it is one of artistic appositeness, not one of conceptual rationality.

The evidence of method is *the fact of arrangement into a story.* But the problem of study then puts a conventional anthropology under strain. The task may be stated as follows: to study the use of archaic and current language, in a religious situation, to tell a drama in story-form in a manner consistent artistically with allegory and poesy. A 'scientific' approach is, plainly, as inappropriate as a 'science' of poetry. The necessary methods—analytic abstraction, an empirical concern, and an indicative language—are simply left transcended. To say so is not to put mythology 'above' or 'beyond' study, or to question the possibility or usefulness of studying the historical setting of myths, their particular uses of language, their reflections of social structure, their functions in social life, and the like. But such studies take as given the human experiences about which the myths make allegorical statements. The light that results does not fall on the stratum of the experiences. To reach the experiences one has to penetrate below the stratum on which expressed mythopoeic thought deals with them. The experiences are on one stratum; the perceptions of them, and the judgments about them, which are given symbolical expression—whether in speech, gesture, stance, dance, mime or song—are on another. The symbolical expressions are not the quiddity of the experiences.

Thus myths, like poetry, are doubtless efforts *at* self-understanding, but they may not be studied as works *of* understanding which have been thought up and perfected by conscious means under the control of intellectual canons. Where there is a demonstrable connection, or an organic relation, between a myth and a rite, so that one can speak of *the* myth *of* a rite, and where the rite can be analysed to the shapely constituents which (in the case of Punj) are identifiable as 'operations,' then one has a design-plan, exhibited by things one can see, to use to test the design-plan of the myth. There is no such aid at hand with the myth of Kunmanggur. One has to take a leap in the dark.

For here is a myth standing alone as though it were a monument to something forgotten but vaguely familiar, and rife with suggestive silences. Tjinimin's crime against his sisters is simply postulated, and left at that. But were the sisters truly innocents? They knew the rule on incest but did not comprehend his sexuality! Did Tjinimin, awakening as from a sleep, forget what he had done and suffered? From what motive did he go on to heal, mutilate and again heal himself? And then seek his father's death? Why did not Kunmanggur rebuke him? And did Kunmanggur condone his own death? Was it for this reason that Tjinimin was allowed to go unmolested? The questions, let alone the answers, are not formulated. The myth scarcely ventures beyond externals. But the silences are heavy, and a sense of obscure paradox obtrudes, especially in the climax-events. At last, Tjinimin alienates himself wholly from kin and kith, flees into the night, and looks back wonderingly—we are not told sorrowfully—at a world on that instant being transformed by the founding-mystery of things ... Kunmanggur, tenderly used by those who stay, puts all the world's fire upon his head and seeks to take it away, according to one version to try to keep it for himself forever and, according to another, with a promise to bring it back ... It can scarcely be doubted that propositional and moral truths are being stated, but what are they? The kerygma of the myth lies obscurely within the paradoxes. One has the sense that antinomies have been stated that would lose their import if their parts could be separated. The son's animus towards the father, and the father's intent towards the son, are left dark. Kunmanggur's intent towards the world he is about to quit is left quite fathomless. There is a hint of suicide for, although mortally hurt, he walked purposefully into the sea. Yet his death was not a death for, transmogrified into The Rainbow Serpent, he 'comes back' to make his mark on the sky as a sign that he 'looks after' people. The place of his last earthly struggle is commemorated by a symbol of femaleness! Not even the firm outlines of unconditioned evil or positive goodwill can be made out. It is as though paradox and antinomy were the marrow in the story's bones. And, among the Aborigines who are alive, Tjinimin is not execrated and Kunmanggur not mourned: all one can detect is a certain amusement about the memory of one and a certain warmth about the memory of the other.

In earlier papers it was suggested that the rite of Punj Was wrapped around a kind of affective and cognitive *pre*vision of continuing tragedy in human affairs, the myth of The Old Woman being its allegory, almost, one might say, its intellectual *after*vision. The two visions were shown to have congruent plan-structures. The 'leap in the dark' one must take towards the myth of Kunmanggur may be put as an hypothesis: the same congruence of structure extends also to it.

6. Analysis of a Riteless Myth

The design-plan of the whole drama is perhaps best shown by a contraction and restatement of the sequence of incidents, which fall into eight natural phases. Certain structural patterns then become visible.

Table 5. Structural Plans Of Three Dramas

A. Phase.		I	
B. Place.		Kunmanggur's home - camp at Kimul.	
C. The Main Incidents.		The Pilitman sisters hunger. They ask and receive Kunmanggur's permission to go far from home to find food. He gives them an added task—to plant trees* on the island of Nganangur.	Tjinimin lusts secretly after his sisters. He asks and receives Kunmanggur's permission to go far from home to visit kinsmen.† He does not mention any place. Kunmanggur leaves him free of his purpose.
D. Structural Parallels in the Development of Three Dramas.	**1. Myth of Kunmanggur.**	Children lack things of life; they seek to go away from camp; father imposes a task on daughters but leaves son free; daughters acquiesce, and son conceals evil private motive.	
	2. Myth of Punj.	Parents lack food; they decide publicly to hunt; they entrust their children to Mutjingga's care; the children acquiesce voicelessly; Mutjingga makes a secret act of ill will.	
	3. Rite of Punj.	Growing youths lack understanding; older men decide secretly to initiate them, and entrust them to initiators who keep the intent secret; the youths acquiesce in duties of silence and submission.	

A. Phase.		II	
B. Place.		Beyond Kimul.	
C. The Main Incidents.		The sisters leave in trust, amity and duty. They go unescorted by familiar places to a known and distant destination. They hunt and work together and make a camp co-operatively. They then go on to hunt flesh-food but leave the untended camp ritually dangerous with their blood.	Tjinimin follows the sisters with evil intent. He hunts and works alone. He finds their path, loses it, finds it once more, and then discovers their camp. He conceals his flesh-food. The blood excites him sexually.‡ He destroys their work and, sleeping and waking, hides in wait.
D. Structural Parallels in the Development of Three Dramas.	**1. Myth of Kunmanggur.**	The children go away from camp, the sisters to familiar places on agreed tasks, the brother to an unknown destination on a falsified task. The evil purpose shows itself away from the eyes of the trusting father, who stays behind.	
	2. Myth of Punj.	The children are left in a safe, known place with a guardian who, intent on evil, acts with duplicity as soon as the trusting parents leave camp to follow out their declared and necessary task.	
	3. Rite of Punj.	Growing youths lack understanding; older men decide secretly to initiate them, and entrust them to initiators who keep the intent secret; the youths acquiesce in duties of silence and submission.	

A. Phase.	III	
B. Place.	At a spoiled and dangerous camp.	
C. The Main Incidents.	The sisters return with flesh-food to find their camp in chaos. Innocently, they mistake the cause, and restore the former order. Their effort uncovers Tjinimin.	
		He leaps to view, laughing evilly. He lies about their father's wishes and conceals his own intent, but he exhibits excitement and attains orgasm.
	The frightened sisters disbelieve what he says and are confused by his sexuality.	He tells them to fetch and share the flesh-food he has concealed.
	They decline his flesh-food and say that they prefer their own first. They plead with him not to force them into incest. Under cruel usage, they cry unavailingly for help.	Tjinimin says they will eat his flesh-food later. He then goes apart in the twilight and uses non-human means to excite himself. He makes his sexual demand on them and arranges the fires as though for a married man's camp. † He dismisses the sisters' fears and pleas with cynicism, and by a threat of song-sorcery terrifies them into submission.
	They plead with him not to force them into incest.	

A. Phase.		III				
D. Structural Parallels in the Development of Three Dramas.	**1. Myth of Kunmanggur.**	The unprotected sisters find careful order now turned to chaos. They try to restore the camp to its former planned order.	A trusted brother suddenly offers them shame and evil.	He brushes aside their moral plea and uses a threat of song-sorcery to terrorise them.	He uses fires to mark out a false marriage-bed.	He forces them into incest while they cry unavailingly for help.
	2. Myth of Punj.	Mutjingga cossets the children she plans to destroy. She shows them good places to bathe, dry and then sleep.	She offers to search them for lice (i.e. to make them shameless).**	She draws the children to her with sweet-sounding words.	She caresses the children who lie in her arms without fear.	She swallows them one by one, until they are wholly within her body.
	3. Rite of Punj.	The youths are made into 'wild flesh' and are put outside society. Each night they are led privily to sleep unseen in their parents' camp.	The mime of Tjirmumuk sets at nought the conventions of mundane life.	The youths are put in terror by the sounding bullroarer.	They wait, fearfully, in expectation of being swallowed.	They are anointed with blood and, in token, destroyed.

<table>
<tr><td colspan="2">A. Phase.</td><td colspan="4">IV</td></tr>
<tr><td colspan="2">B. Place.</td><td colspan="4">Between the corrupted camp and the wilderness.</td></tr>
<tr><td colspan="2" rowspan="2">C. The Main Incidents.</td><td colspan="2">With the new day there is a conflict of wills. The sisters wish to leave the camp.</td><td colspan="2">Tjinimin wishes to stay but submits to their will.</td></tr>
<tr><td colspan="2">Their will prevails. They now plan their brother's downfall but they conceal their intent from him. Going ahead to show the way, they use song-magic to summon hornets to sting him and the tide to overwhelm him. Then they disappear.</td><td colspan="2">He follows their path. The hornets sting him grievously and the tide sweeps him away. He comes ashore at a rocky place, alive, but naked, fireless, possessionless and alone.</td></tr>
<tr><td rowspan="3">D. Structural Parallels imn the Development of Three Dramas.</td><td>1 Myth of Kunmanggur.</td><td>Tjinimin is ensnared by the sisters.</td><td colspan="2">He is injured and swept away by the tide.</td><td>He is left at last a bereft isolate.</td></tr>
<tr><td>2 Myth of Punj.</td><td>Mutjingga enters a river that winds and deepens.</td><td colspan="2">She is lost to sight and the camp left deserted.</td><td>They leave behind the last signs of uninitiated youth.</td></tr>
<tr><td>3 Rite of Punj.</td><td>The anointings go on as the youths are taken deeper into the cult.</td><td colspan="2">The parents discover the loss of the children.</td><td>They learn the true identity of The Mother.</td></tr>
</table>

<table>
<tr><td colspan="2">A. Phase.</td><td colspan="4">V</td></tr>
<tr><td colspan="2">B. Place.</td><td colspan="4">In the wilderness.</td></tr>
<tr><td colspan="2" rowspan="2">C. The Main Incidents.</td><td colspan="2"></td><td colspan="2">The autonomous Tjinimin restores his possessions and pursues his purpose in a new direction. After a long journey towards a distant sign he sees the sisters high on a cliff above him.
He asks their guidance and help to reach them.</td></tr>
<tr><td colspan="2">The sisters point out the steepest way and let down the rope for which he has asked. As he nears the top they cut the rope. Then they return to Kunmanggur.</td><td colspan="2">Tjinimin climbs the rope but is dashed on the rocks below.</td></tr>
<tr><td rowspan="3">D. Structural Parallels imn the Development of Three Dramas.</td><td>1 Myth of Kunmanggur.</td><td>Restored by his own magic, Tjinimin pursues the sisters.</td><td colspan="2">He sees their fire after a long journey.</td><td>The sisters entrap and destroy him.</td></tr>
<tr><td>2 Myth of Punj.</td><td>They send Left Hand and Right Hand in pursuit of Mutjingga.</td><td colspan="2">They discover her sign after a long search.</td><td>They entrap and kill Mutjingga.</td></tr>
<tr><td>3 Rite of Punj.</td><td></td><td colspan="2">The full secrets of the older men are revealed over many weeks.</td><td>The blood-covered youths receive the sign of those who 'understand.'</td></tr>
</table>

A. Phase.	VI	
B. Place.	From the wilderness to Kimul.	
C. The Main Incidents.		By secret knowledge Tjinimin mends his broken bones and acts as a man awakening from a deep sleep. Whole and refreshed, he seeks a sharp stone. After two failures, he severs his nose and then heals the wound.§ Then he returns to Kimul.
	Kunmanggur hails him as ***Kadu Punj***, an initiated man and 'one who understands.'	Tjinimin again misleads Kunmanggur and, after a day, departs on a falsified mission.
	An affine offers sympathy and help.	But his bones ache. He seeks comfort from an affine, attributing fault to women who allowed him to fall. He deceives the affine by saying that his own spear is really Kunmanggur's. He then musters all the world's people to come to dance at his father's camp at Kimul.

A. Phase.		VI			
D. Structural Parallels imn the Development of Three Dramas.	**1 Myth of Kunmanggur.**	Made whole again by his own magic, Tjinimin hurts and heals himself.	He makes a brief and deceitful return to Kimul.	He goes again to the outer world to continue his deception.	As though in amity and love, he brings kith and kin to where he intends to kill Kunmanggur.
	2 Myth of Punj.	They see Mutjingga's moving stomach, cut her open, and find the children alive in her womb.	They take the children from the dead womb.	They cleanse the children of their stains.	They deck the children brightly before taking them to their mothers.
	3 Rite of Punj.	As new men of secret knowledge, they swing and carry the emblem of The Mother.	The silent, unnoticed visits at night to the parents' camp continue.	The last mime of ***Tjirmumuk*** is celebrated.	The youths are prepared for formal presentation to their mothers.

A. Phase.	VII	
B. Place.	Again at Kimul.	
C. The Main Incidents.		As a sign, Tjinimin burns the hilltops during his return to Kimul.
	Kunmanggur greets his son and asks for news.	Hiding the spear, he shows his father only spear-thrower and fire-stick, thus mixing truth with falsehood.
	Maminmanga sings, Kunmanggur pipes, and all dance.	Tjinimin dances so as to make women desire him.
	Walumuma brings him water three times.	Three times, in a foreign tongue, he proclaims that he will kill Kunmangurr and, when asked what he said, replies that he thirsts for water, Each time the water is brought to him he spills it and draws the hidden spear nearer. Then he calls for the last dance.
	Maminmanga suddenly stops singing.	Tjinimin throws the spear at Kunmanggur. It flies true, and hits.
	Kunmanggur hurls his pipe into the deep water of Maiyiwa. A son pulls out the spear and throws it afar. The world undergoes the transformation of ***demnginoi.*** People become birds and fly away, spreading out.	Tjinimin flees unmolested into the dark and, from afar, looks back, wondering what people will do.

A. Phase.		VII				
D. Structural Parallels in the Development of Three Dramas.	1 **Myth of Kunmanggur.**	Tjinimin uses fire as a sign.	He deceives his father again, and hides the spear.	With double-deceit he prepares for parricide.	He spears his father.	He flees the scene and the world is transformed.
	2 **Myth of Punj.**	The men call from a distance.	The mothers weep for joy over the children.			The children are fondled lovingly as miraculously alive and now ***Kadu Punj.***
	3 **Rite of Punj.**	The men put a screen between the youths and the camp.	The mothers wail but do not touch their sons.	They return again to the secrecy of Ngudanu.		They are presented with food by their mothers and female kin and are welcomed to a new status and locus of life.

A. Phase.	VIII	
B. Place.	Again beyond Kimul.	
C. The Main Incidents.	In agony, Kunmanggur leaps to Purmi, and wanders far searching for a soft-lying place. He goes on and on. At each momentary halt marvels occur. He leaves signs of his passing at many places.	His people try to heal his wound by heated stones, but always fail. Each time, water comes through the fire to mix with the blood. The water and his signs remain perennially.
	At last he turns towards the sea and at the final place of rest sends Pilirin to hunt flesh-food.	Pilirin hunts and kills a kangaroo.
	But hungry, weary and in pain Kunmanggur does not wait for Pilirin's return. He puts all the fire upon his head and wades into the sea.	Kadpur summons Pilirin to rescue the fire. But come as swiftly as he may he is able to pluck only the last dead brand.
	The water puts out the fire, and Kunmanggur performs his last marvels at the place ***da lurutj Kalegale ya Kalegale.***	From his own knowledge he makes new fire, burns the grass, and brings the fire to the waiting people.

A. Phase.		VIII				
D. **Structural Parallels in the Development of Three Dramas.**	1 **Myth of Kunmanggur.**		Kunmanggur looks vainly for a place of heal-ing rest beyond Kimul.		In extremity, and foodless, he takes all men's fire and quenches it in the sea.	One man alone brings new fire to the world.
	2 **Myth of Punj.**	*No information.*				[? They join those who in turn will suffer from duty and trust.]
	3 **Rite of Punj.**	*No information.* [? The new initiates slowly sustain the privileges, duties and tensions of adult life.]				[? They join those who in turn must make youth 'understand.']

* Baobab trees are said to be 'Kunmanggur's children.'

† Classificatory affines.

‡ A double enormity by Tjinimin, to have been excited by female blood and by his sister's blood.

** A shameless person is colloquially called ***kadu managga mimbi***, 'one without head-lice.'

In Table 1 the development of the drama of Kunmanggur is shown in the eight phases (Col. A, I–VIII) which are made more or less distinct by the myth. Each phase is associated with a place or region (Col. B) and with a set of events (Col. C). Those events are divided into two groups in order to bring out more clearly the curious yet characteristic oppositeness that, almost throughout, marks the conduct of the principals. The entries in Col. C are a virtual summary of the myth. In Col. D, separated by double lines, a further contraction and construction of the myth is set alongside comparable reductions of the myth and rite of Punj, which were analysed in earlier papers. A few rearrangements and constructions were found necessary, but I hope to have avoided any serious interference with the material.

On the evidence of the table, there is not much room for doubt, while making allowance for possibly unconscious selections on my part, that there is a significant measure of congruence between the design-plans of the two myths and the rite. It is not by any means a complete congruence, and it is stronger at the beginning than at the end, but the common elements are too many, and the articulations too similar, to be dismissed lightly. The structures are homomorphic.

(*a*) The sequence of phases and places (Columns A, B) are strikingly like those found in the other myth and its rite. The transitions correspond quite closely.

Someone is sent or withdraws from a safe, habited place to a place of solitude. In the second place—the place of removal, or in the place deserted—wildness or terror, and a sort of corruption, become ascendant. Something—trust, young life, innocence—is destroyed there. Then, after a pause, there is a return to the first place. But it is now not the same as before; there has been a change; the old is not quite annulled and the new not altogether unfamiliar.

In terms of phases and places, without reference to incidents, the structure of the transitions from Kimul to Kimul-and-beyond (Col. D, 1) appears identical with that from the camp with The Mother to the camp from which she has gone (Col. D, 2) and from the camp of circumcised youths to the camp of men who 'understand' (Col. D, 3). A comparison of incidents strengthens that conclusion.

(*b*) All three design-plans begin with common situations of life: a felt need of food, materials, or mundane things of life; a desire to nurture or develop life; the demands made on life by, and by life on, young males. The metaphor of expression varies but the expressions appear equivalent, indeed interchangeable.

However phrased, the situations are depicted as tense, flawed by ambiguity or duplicity or duality, and issuing in acts of necessary trust to which duty is added. Tension, flaw, trust and duty develop together so as to make for a disaster. But the disaster is consummated by a good outcome. The outcome in its turn has something dual or duplex or ambiguous about it. In other words, the good is conditioned. Fire, that which serves and burns, stays with men only by The Father's death; young life is conserved only by the death of The Mother; understanding is attained only by fear and disciplined suffering under authority. And fire, life and understanding all need renewal from time to time.

(*c*) Each drama develops by its own internal dynamism, without dependence on externals. The stories in each case are of what men do to men and to themselves, not of what gods or suprahuman agencies do to them. The unfolding is from within, by a dialectic within which people are caught by the nature of their own condition and character.

(*d*) In each case the principals fall into three groups. There are (i) those who suffer, (ii) those who inflict suffering, and (iii) those who so to speak stand and wait, suffering vicariously.

The sufferers live to see the downfall of the inflictors and, in turn, become inflictors. It is suggested, in a shadowy way, that persons in one category pass into the other categories in the course of time. Thus, the ill-used sisters bring hurt and desolation to Tjinimin, and then sit silently while he encompasses Kunmanggur's death. Tjinimin, having been both sufferer and inflictor, stays alive—to watch the development of the marvels and grief he has brought to others? The suffering Kunmanggur tries to inflict loss on the guiltless, and then passes from ordinary life to keep watch over all. Mutjingga inflicts harm on the young, suffers death, and then becomes a real—and sorrowing?—presence at Ngudanu. The transitions are not stated with complete or explicit clarity, but the background suggestions are quite strong.

Thus, in four fundamentals—the sequences of transition, the development of common situations, the internal dynamism of the plots, and the relationships between principals—there are distinct resonances between the dramas. A consideration of incident suggests the virtual equivalence of each drama as a whole. In principle, and in most of the major details, the myth of Kunmanggur evidently could stand to the rite of Punj in approximately the same relation as the myth of Mutjingga.

The question arises: *three* dramas or *one*? But the same question, overturned, may be asked of the myth of Kunmanggur: one drama or several? It is noticeable that the story of IV is almost a reversal of the story of I–III, but with Tjinimin in the position of sufferer and the sisters dominant. Then V seems to tell, in short, bold strokes, very much the same story as I–III, but now arranged after the fashion of IV. In VI, it is as though the story of I–III were being told all over again in changed metaphors. The last phase, VIII, then develops the whole drama in a way for which a listener is rather unprepared until a familiar pattern emerges: here too is the story of a man, with a mortal defect of life, who acts ambiguously towards his nearest kin, though with an evident intent to hurt, and at the last quits their world. And, from being sufferer, Kunmanggur becomes—at least in intent—the inflictor of suffering until he passes from the world of living men. To become, then, the vicarious sufferer?

One is left with a strong impression that a single, unitary story runs through all three dramas, and that the core-plot would emerge clearly if one could but grasp the principle of commutation between the elements.

The myth of Kunmanggur extends to an eighth phase, but the myth of Mutjingga and the rite of Punj stop at the seventh. One is tempted to conjecture about possible equivalences, in the other myth and the rite, to the 'again beyond Kimul' phase of the drama of Kunmanggur. The entries made in Col. D, 2–3, VIII, with that intent, are conjectural and tentative. The 'beyond' in those cases can only be the futurity to which

Kadu Punj return. But the entries suggest what seems the import of the religion: that much of human social life is a flow or movement between coordinate species of experience; that a life of conditional good is one in which people in their turn suffer, inflict suffering, and watch others suffer.

When the three dramas, one acted and two spoken, are set side by side, they suggest that whatever be the historical standing of the myth of Kunmanggur, and whatever its past associations, its kerygma is somehow the most profound. May one not suggest that Aboriginal society is one in which insights can be lost as well as found? Lost, perhaps, in the fervour of new cults? The possibility can hardly be admitted—perhaps even suggest itself—in a viewpoint that would insist on the static and stationary character of Aboriginal culture, society and thought. But there is at least some evidence to suggest that Murinbata religion has been one of dynamism. The strong evidence of a succession of cults in the past has been mentioned. The myth of Kunmanggur, with its poignant complexity, and the splendour of the associated paintings at Purmi and Kirindjingin, are evidential peaks of attainment unmatched by any others in the regional culture of the recent past. We are entitled to look on them as works of passion and imagination, not contrived *for* effect, but having effect nevertheless.

Perhaps the myth said in words what was speakable about a rite that, dealing—as all rites do—with the unspeakable, had to do so by gesture and movement. Perhaps the paintings, by visual imagery, dealt with what could not be spoken or acted out, but still called on a few minds for expression. If there ever were such a rite, then it may well have had to do with that dialectic of life with which Aboriginal religion is concerned. One may suggest that rite, myth and paintings, each in its own way, brought to equipoise of form the understanding of that time about the transiences that were unavoidable within its permanencies. They are essays in expression, each subject to the limitations of its own kind, but each seizing on the fundamental theme of change within stability.

We have found no reason so far to differ from, and much reason to agree with, Sir James Frazer's view that a 'central mystery of primitive society' is associated with initiatory rites. But we have tried to show that analysis can go beyond the idea of a 'drama of death and resurrection.' That is simply one symbolical expression which is given to the dialectical ritual form. Having found the form in a riteless myth, we shall try next to see if it exists within a mythless rite.

V

The Design-Plans of Mythless Rites

1. Introduction

In my analysis of the rite of the bullroarer among the Murinbata it was possible to describe the myth of Mutjingga, The Old Woman, as the myth *of* that rite because of the demonstrable connection between them. The present article will deal with two important rites—those of circumcision and burial—which are not and, as far as I could discover, were not in the past associated with myths in that way. All that can be said is that they have a certain 'support' from the general system of beliefs, but are not arranged into a story-form, that is, systematically. The object of the article is to extract and analyse the structures of the rites to discover the extent to which their design-plans resemble or differ from those dealt with in the previous articles in this series. I propose at the same time to look for a possible congruence with the design-plan of yet another myth—that of Kukpi, The Snake Woman—which resembles that of the myth of The Rainbow Serpent in having no apparent connection with any rite. By those means I hope to be able to show that there is substantial support for my view that the ritual culture of the Murinbata is built to a paradigm persisting through great external differences, and between things in no apparent connection.

The study of Aboriginal religion inevitably has been much affected by theories *about* religion. Much that has been written reads as though the leading motive had been to vindicate, even to expand, some general formula, e.g. that of Tylor, Frazer, Durkheim or Freud. My approach has been to try, as far as possible, to let Murinbata religion exhibit itself. That is not to say I make a pretence of letting the facts 'speak for themselves.' Without construction and interpretation they would not be meaningful. But I have sought to keep as close as I could to the principle stated by Durkheim, although in another connection: 'to know what the division of labour is objectively it is not enough to develop the contents of the idea we have of it, but we must treat it as an objective fact, observe, compare; and we shall see that the result of these observations often differs from the one its intimate meaning suggests to us.[1] One of my objects has been to show that the objective facts of Aboriginal religion can be observed and compared from a fresh point of view, and that to do so reveals many unappreciated facts and similarities which, on the one hand, make imperative a revision of the 'intimate meaning' we have held of Aboriginal religion and, on the other, provide an empirical basis on which to do so.

2. Circumcision at Puberty

The Murinbata tradition recognised three distinctive styles in which a boy might be initiated by circumcision at puberty. He was referred to by the name of the style followed at his initiation, so that he might be called *ŋi-waŋga, ŋi-manbaŋgoi*, or *ŋi-naitpan (ŋi* = penis).[2] The particular name-style was determined by the region to which he was taken for

1 *The Division of Labour in Society*, p. 46 (1947 ed.).

2 In Murinbata usage the word *wangga* is the name of the initiatory style as well as the name of the associated dance and song. It has no other determinable meaning, but is somehow linked with the Daly River region. No doubt it may be connected with the name of the Ngolok-Wanggar (Mulluk-Mulluk, Malak-Malak) tribe on that river. On the other hand, *manbanggoi* is probably a contraction of *maiyen panggoi*, lit. 'road,' 'long,' but the song and dance that go with it are named *lirga*. The name *naitpan* is probably a variant of the adjective *naitpar*, 'distant.' That style of initiation goes with the *mindirrini* song and dance, which are identical with the *dingiri* of the Nangiomeri (Nangiwumiri) and the *kudjingga* of the Djamindjung (Murinyuwen).

isolation during the preliminary phase of the rite; if in a northerly direction, the *waŋga* style was followed; east or north-east, the *manbaŋgoi* style; south or south-east, the *naitpan* style. The differences between *waŋga* and *manbaŋgoi* amounted to little more than a few minor variations of songs, dances and ritual patterns: the fundamental plans of the rites were the same. The *naitpan* was the most elaborate and, as spectacle, the most impressive. It had four distinctive features. (i) On the night before his circumcision, a neophyte's escorts—'those with the penis'—performed a fire dance (*mindir̃r̃ini*) which (ii) females and young boys were forbidden to see. (iii) The dancers were covered with feathers or down stuck to their bodies by blood drawn from left-handed men (*kadu ṭakunbe*). (iv) The only musical instruments used were boomerangs, brought into play as tapping-sticks. I could see no other important differences.

If, as sometimes happened, relations with neighbouring tribes were too strained and the dangers of a boy's being abroad too great, or if his escorts were unable to persuade other tribesmen to return with them, a very truncated ceremony might be held, and boys—a very small minority—circumcised under those conditions were referred to as *ŋi-mulun* (lit. 'person,' 'leaves' or 'shadow'). The *mulun* could scarcely be called a style, but the three others are reputed to be very ancient and to have been 'level'—of equal importance—in the tradition. Of 23 instances of which I was able to obtain information for the decade 1935–45, 4 had been in the *waŋga* style, 7 *manbaŋgoi*, 10 *naitpan* and 2 *mulun*.

Murinbata men professed that the rite of circumcision was of small importance in comparison with that of the bullroarer. The occasions on which I saw performances of the rite seemed to me to belie them. The numbers of people concerned, the public excitement, and the conjunction with trade and fighting all made for a notable occasion. A comparison is, in one sense, mistaken in that the circumcision and bullroarer rites belonged to different families. At the first, the highest secular values were expressed; at the second, the highest religious values; the two scales were incommensurable. As I put the matter in an earlier article, one rite 'made a man'; the other made 'a man of mystical understanding.'

The traditional circumcisions ceased at Port Keats about the middle 1940s. The local missionary, alarmed by a supposed risk to life or well-being from loss of blood and septicæmia,[3] persuaded the elders to let him perform the operation on several boys. Soon afterwards, a hospital was established at the mission. It then became customary to have infant males circumcised by a trained sister. The traditional institution lapsed. The elders put up no great resistance and the youths, one need scarcely add, were in favour of the change.

Effects on the social personality of young adult males began to be noticeable within a decade. Many older men spoke feelingly about the indiscipline of the new generation, the disrespect shown towards authority—European as well as Aboriginal—and the lack of interest in old custom, arguing that all were due to the same cause. I heard many discussions on the desirability of starting the institution anew, but all foundered on the fact that there were no longer any young uncircumcised males! The mission was held to have 'spoiled everything,' but, in fact, for a good many years increasing difficulty had been experienced in organising the ceremonies. Many circumstances were involved. A brief explanation may be offered.[4]

After the 1870s all the tribes in the region bounded by the Daly and Victoria Rivers began to be upset in manifold ways by the arrival and spread of European settlement. Distance from the centres of development in itself gave no protection. The external structure of every tribe—its *necessary* dependence on others, often at several removes, in

---

3 As far as I could discover no fatalities attributable to circumcision had occurred, but Aboriginal testimony on the matter is unreliable since the death of a boy in such circumstances would probably be attributed to a breach of taboo or to sorcery.

4 For other comments, see my Presidential Address to Section F, ANZAAS, 1958 ('Continuity and Change Among the Aborigines'), *The Australian Journal of Science*, Vol. 21, No. 5A, and 'Durmugam: A Nangiomeri,' in *In The Company of Man*, ed. Joseph B. Casegrande, 1960.

matters of marriage, trade and ceremony—ensured that contact with aliens anywhere would have quick repercussions everywhere in the region over which equities *in rem, in personam* and *in animum* were connected. Since, in practice, in spite of reports to the contrary, those equities *always* had an inter-tribal aspect, the network of relations was disturbed hundreds of miles away from the nearest European. There were of course spiritual and psychological correlates of the social upsets. They all disposed far-outlying clans and tribes to move into the cattle stations, mining camps and mission settlements to protect their interests, to obtain European goods, and to seek adventure. Before long disease, conflict with Europeans, and murderous intercourse with other tribes that hitherto had been kept at a certain distance, led to heavy depopulation. Many men and women took casual or semipermanent jobs. Others, with claims on those at work, stayed close by to share the earnings. As the several causes compounded, there was a slow falling away from the old ritual calendar. The numbers free and willing to go to distant ceremonies dwindled. The impulse to hold ceremonies near at hand weakened with the scarcity of foreign visitors. Some rites simply lapsed, especially those connected with the bullroarer and with the burial of notable men, both of which required all the segments of ceremonial importance to be well represented. Others were shortened or held in token. A process that began first amongst the depopulated tribes and those drawn far from home eventually spread to those less disturbed and more numerous. A special effort seems to have been made to conserve the circumcision ceremonies, especially where any considerable number of Aborigines survived or tribal remnants made common cause. The close relation between those ceremonies and inter-clan and inter-tribal trade may have had much to do with that fact. At Port Keats, over the decade preceding the establishment of the mission in 1935, there was undoubtedly a considerable disturbance of the ritual calendar, even when the nearest Europeans were more than 100 miles away. For several reasons—in part perhaps because of the decimation of tribes to the north but mainly, I think, because of the higher appeal of the culture of tribes to the south—the Murinbata had come increasingly under the influence of tribes then congregating on the Victoria River. Hence the greater frequency of the *naitpan* style. But there too an analysis showed case after case of truncation or defect of procedure. An indication of the growing difficulty of following out any style in a fully-fledged way could be found in the nicknames of a number of men. There were several called Kadu Kungini ('people of the evening') because circumstances had required the rite to be held after working hours. Two were called Ngurugun ('darkness, without fire') to signify that no one had bothered to instruct them to hold fire-sticks under each arm after circumcision. Another was called Wuma, a contraction of *wungumaŋi*, to signify that he had been *manaŋga malakumbara*, without a party of escorts on his return from isolation before circumcision. There were several *Ngi-Mulun*. And I met one called Peme after the name of a sharp-edged leaf on which he had accidentally cut his prepuce; his father had fully circumcised him without further ado, and had withheld him from the rite.

The primary features of the pubic rite may now be stated briefly. Except for the statements contained in square brackets the facts set out are matters of my own direct observation.

(1) When a boy reached puberty, and began to show the sexuality, waywardness and egotism of that state, the initiative to 'make him a man' might be taken by one or more of several classes of men: a senior agnate such as his own father, one of his father's clan brothers, or a father's father, or a more distant relation of that class; or one of the class of mother's brothers; or a male affine, especially one standing in the relation of wife's brother. Evidently no particular importance attached to the matter, but of course only an older and fully initiated man could appropriately put his opinion forward. Importance lay, rather, in being given by a boy's father the function of becoming *malakumbara*,[56] he who was to 'pull' or 'lead by the arm'; that is, take a boy away from his clan prior to circumcision. That function was thought to belong most properly to a *naŋgun* (wife's brother); if possible he should be a brother of the girl to whom a boy was already betrothed but, failing him, one of

5 *Kumbara* is an ordinal adjective meaning 'first' or 'leader.'

that class. Up to a point, the choice lay with a boy's father or, failing him, with one or more of his patrikin; but the range of choice was restricted. That, as Durkheim said, was 'withdrawn from individual discretion.' In most cases the decision would have been made years before; and it might have become well known, or kept a private matter. The actual rite was very much a public affair; the preliminaries were thought of—within the limits mentioned—as a father's own concern. He might say as much or as little about them as he pleased. But I recorded cases of men suggesting themselves as *malakumbara* only to be told by a father: 'this boy does not belong to you; his man is there'—pointing in the direction of another clan—'and he will come up for him.'

There was a certain advantage, material and social, in being *malakumbara*, but it scarcely compensated for the time, effort and outlay involved; I seriously doubt if it were a leading, even an important motive. The function has to be interpreted in the light of two contexts—men's æsthetic enjoyment of ceremony, and their mature sense of social responsibility. To be fully understandable, both need detailed reference to the place in Murinbata life of the patrilineal moieties, Kartjin and Tiwunggu. But that discussion would take me too far from the subject of this paper. It will perhaps suffice to say that the dual organisation was the anatomy on which the æsthetic life came to its best flower and on which the social ethos found shape. The moieties made a context in which duty and right, command and deference, hostility and support, were correlative; according to situation, now one, now the other, would be stressed. Thus, a man could prepare his son for manhood—*social* manhood—and might take as his own affair the right to decide on the time and circumstance of the boy's public transition; but he could not confer that manhood; only men of the opposite moiety could do that; and to do so was both their duty and their right. The duality, even the ambivalence, of the relation often showed through the actuality of the event. For example, a boy's male kin were permitted by convention to show hostility towards those who were putting him to the knife. A clan father or brother might threaten them with a spear, or actually throw it. Lasting ill-feeling among the *malakumbara* party would follow from any failure by the boy's kin to provide enough food for a memorable feast—the *miŋi*, or 'food of the penis'—after the circumcision. Likewise, the refusal by a notable singer, dancer, or drone-pipe player to form part of the boy's escort would so affront the hosts at a ceremony that bloodshed might follow. The underlying duality and ambivalence meant that every initiation was in a very unstable equilibrium: the most trifling incident could precipitate uproar and violence. The management of the ceremonies called for watchful care, perfect manners, and diplomatic skill. Every effort was made to settle outstanding trouble before the ceremony took place, or—if challenges to formal duels had already been arranged—to have them held after the boy had been circumcised. But the plans often miscarried.[6]

(2) The choice of *malakumbara* having been made, and the task accepted, preparations were set in train—quietly rather than secretly—to entertain visitors at *Mununuk*, the father's camp, on a given day. All the boy's cognates—his *darikadu*—had to be warned to be there; not to let them know, or to do so too late, was to give serious affront, and might lead to violence. Many other men would also be invited to come as *Kadu mambana*—'outside people' or spectators unrelated to the boy, all of them being at the same time *Kadu ŋulain*—'free people,' that is, people without obligation on the occasion, and 'finished people' in the sense of having completed all the ritual business of life. Food was gathered and prepared in generous amount, the pretext being that a big dance was to be held.

---

6 The Murinbata still talk about an occasion, more than half a century ago, that required an initiation to be postponed for a day while blood-kin of the boy fought a pitched battle. It took place at Madinga when Nama, a boy of the Kurangaliwe clan, was about to be circumcised. One Djabakung, a classificatory father of Nama, threw a spear that wounded a kinsman, Madjera, a notable fighter—a *kadu tunbitj* (lit. 'person,' 'spear-thrower'). Madjera retaliated with a spear that hit Kalinyin, a classificatory father. Eight men, all of the same moiety, were soon exchanging spears. Three were badly wounded in the course of a struggle that lasted all afternoon. The men of all other clans of that moiety, and of the opposite moiety, stood aside.

When the appointed day came, the men painted themselves gaily in one of the secular styles. The boy to be initiated was painted too, a fact in open conflict with the convention that he was not 'supposed' to know what was afoot, though the convention was maintained for all that.[7] When at last all the company were present and fed, events proceeded as though for an ordinary festivity. One man—usually but not necessarily a visitor—played the drone-pipe (*maluk*); a few kept time with the tapping-sticks; others (including the women) sang; and the remainder (the visitors predominating) went time after time through the steps of an exhilarating dance. Some hours were thus spent. Outwardly, everything was on a plane of jollity and fellowship. The boy sat near his father, who might fling an arm affectionately and protectively around him. But gradually the cognatic kin, now become *kadu pirimku*—'they with the flesh'—ranged themselves so as to sit just behind and on both sides of the father, thus forming a 'little Mununuk,' the arcuate cluster commonly used on occasions of ceremony.

At a prearranged time the dancing and music died abruptly. The *malakumbara* rose from his place and, in complete silence, walked to the boy and put a hand on his shoulder. No words were needed; as the Aborigines say, 'everybody knows that thing'; but, if he wished, he might speak in a kindly but grave manner: 'now I take you to make

7 Aboriginal life abounds in such conventions. They couple with a clever art of putting a good face on things a realistic applied psychology. The ordeal facing boys is of course very painful; they vary in physique, temperament and personality about as much as those of any other race; and they mature as unevenly. Those facts are taken into account, very perceptively, in judging the readiness for circumcision. Much credit accrues to a boy who faces the rite manfully. The credit is the greater if, having been given broad hints and allowed to steel himself, he can still be 'supposed' not to know what is coming. Many men, recalling their own experiences, said that they were not told outright but had no difficulty in putting two and two together. I would not say dogmatically that all boys know. I listed many cases of those who ran away. I dare say that most of them were due to a collapse of courage, but a few suggest a sudden suspicion or discovery of what lay ahead.

you a man.' On that signal the people of Mununuk broke into formal wailing.[8] It was the due part of the close kin to express the deepest grief. Both men and women so wounded themselves that their blood flowed freely. While the wailing proceeded the boy was led off to be lost to view in the darkness. He was not permitted to look back; his name could no longer be mentioned; from now on he was *kuwere*, a 'wild dog'; *kadu ŋi*, 'person of the penis'; and—when his 'road' became known—either *ŋi-waŋga, ŋi-manbaŋgoi*, or *ŋi-naitpan* (sometimes also called *ŋi-meraŋgan*). The first camp—for that night only—was but a short distance off. The purpose was to allow the *malakumbara* to slip back unobtrusively next day to talk over with the father the details of the plan—the boy's 'road' (the direction and region of travel), the choice of song-man and drone-pipe player, the whereabouts of affines who might give gifts, and the time and manner of return. By the next night the party had to be far away.

(3) The rift with his kin and clan made, and his childish status ended, the *kuwere* was now wholly in the power of his escorts. But he was safer than at perhaps any other time in his life. He was considered to be beyond human injury because of his status; there is no Murinbata word meaning 'sacred,' but he was treated as if sacred.[9] Everything he did was under the protective eyes of his *naŋgun*. His guardians' duty was to nurture him—as the Aborigines put it, to 'make him fat'—and to instruct him in all the things a man should know while doing all in

8 I am referring to the manner or style of wailing, not implying that there was no genuine grief. On several occasions I saw close kin, especially but not only women, appear to develop hysteria. They inflicted wounds—with digging-sticks, sharp stones, axes and spear-points—that incapacitated them. But there was also a good deal of simulation, more so among the men than the women. I heard men sobbing in a heart-rending way but noticed that not a tear fell; on one occasion I heard two men trying to wail *in harmony*; and, quite often, someone who appeared to be in a paroxysm of grief, would switch in an instant to dry-eyed normality.

9 I have never heard of a boy's coming to harm during that period. My informants always insisted that not even the worst of men could feel ill-will towards him at such a time.

their power to win material gifts for him from his class of affines, and to attract a large gathering to return with them as *wungumaŋi*—'they having the penis.' A period of from six weeks to two or more months might elapse while that duty was completed satisfactorily. Over that time he was put under a severe if kindly discipline: a scrupulous observance of many food taboos, a sparing use of water, a modest demeanour, and a deferential attention to his instructors. Usually, his 'road' took him into unfamiliar country among *kadu kamalik*, 'strangers.' He had to learn and remember a host of new places and names, and many identities and categories of kin and kith. He also saw new dances, heard new songs, and was told new tales and myths. Thus, novelty and excitement went with obedience and discipline. He was among strangers, but he had with him at all times a boon mate, for it was the custom to include in the party one of his *pugali* or cross-cousins, in all probability his own father's sister's son or mother's brother's son, a 'dear acquaintance' with whom he was to have a lifelong intimacy as joking-companion. In this way he passed the time until the whole party, now known as *wungumaŋi*, left—without ceremony—for the return to Mununuk.

(4) When at last they came near his clan-country two or three men went ahead, carrying a ceremonial spear known as *nandji mada*.[10] They took precautions to stay unobserved but by prearrangement or artifice made their presence known to the older men of Mununuk, so that the day and hour of their coming were known. The last phase of their approach was left until after sundown, at the time when the Wangga dance was at its height. The men of Mununuk contrived an incident or diversion—usually connected with the dance—to ensure that everyone was intent on the festivity. The *wuŋgumani* men were thus able to make

10 It had this name only in initiations of the *manbanggoi* and *wangga* styles. In the *naitpan* style it was called *nandji tjinggin*, which could mean 'thing,' 'fingernail' (*tjingin* = fingernail). The other name cannot, evidently, be given an English equivalent. In both cases the spear is short, coloured red with ochre, and is tufted with the yellow-and-white feathers of the 'white' cockatoo. The prefix *nandji* distinguishes it from hunting and fighting spears, which have the prefix *tjo*.

a stealthy approach and, in spite of the darkness, to throw the spear with accuracy into the centre of the circle of fires. It appeared there, suddenly, quivering in the ground, its white tuft visible in the firelight. At that well-understood signal all the *darikadu*, the boy's cognates, burst into their formal wailing as before. The demonstration—again accompanied by self-injury—lasted well into the night. The others there—the 'outside' or 'free people'—comported themselves quietly and respectfully, moving in now and again to restrain the cognates from lacerating themselves too seriously.

In the *naitpan* style the preliminaries were much more spectacular. A full day elapsed between the throwing of the *nandji tjiŋgin* and the actual circumcision. On the intervening night the magnificent *mindiřřini* dance took place. The main features of difference, which I do not propose to describe in detail on this occasion, were as follows: (*a*) the neophyte, covered by a blanket, was brought near the dancing-ring; (*b*) the dancers, blooded and feathered, having hidden themselves in the outer darkness, sprang suddenly into view and ran along a path of blazing grass made clockwise around the boy's position; (*c*) he was then uncovered and allowed to watch the ceremonial drama.

(5) The next day was one of high spectacle and sustained emotion. Throughout the morning rumours and alarms swept through Mununuk. The *wungumaŋi* were coming! No, they were not. There was to be trouble; everyone would fight! No, it was only a tale. By early afternoon the excitement was intense. Eventually, without warning, a long serpentine of painted men came into view a quarter of a mile away. Thence they sent a far-carrying hail towards Mununuk. *Waaaaaa! Eeeeee! Rrrrrr!* At the sound, the boy's cognates, weeping and shedding their blood, took up the arcuate form, and sat with bowed heads, the 'outside' and 'free people' behind them and on their flanks. The rite then developed in three phases.

In the first phase, the boy stayed hidden behind a screen of trees. The *wungumaŋi* men, keeping in sinuous serpentine, ran towards Mununuk, in short bursts, shouting and brandishing their spears. With them were a drone-pipe player and singing men. After each burst the formation paused and clustered to dance the *waŋga*. The final burst brought them to a halt a short distance from 'the senders of the flesh.' Again they danced the *waŋga*. Then with a tumultuous shout and a flourish of spears, they changed from line to mass and came almost to the threshold of Mununuk. From that point they pranced forward within the span of the arc of bowed heads, and danced again, pounding the ground so that the dust rose in swirls. Within a few minutes they broke away and ran back to the shelter of the trees. The lamentation continued among the cognates until exhaustion brought silence. Then followed a pause of several hours. At Mununuk, the people ate or slept. In the hidden place in the timber, the *wungumaŋi* men painted the boy with the design proper to his status—forearms and lower legs reddened with ochre; torso and upper arms reddened and over-marked with vertical white stripes separated by white dots; shoulders and upper trunk crossed by double lateral lines of white so as to form a 'collar' resembling the ruff of a bird; and face contoured by white bands. A whitened band (*wařkuř*) was placed taut around his brow and head. Valuables (*nandji ŋi*, 'things of the penis') were put upon him as the traditional gifts of all his *naŋgun*. Thus adorned, he was ready to become a man.

(*b*) By now it was late afternoon. Taking the neophyte with them, the *wungumaŋi* again appeared at a distance—Mununuk thereupon starting to wail anew—and moved forward in the slow, stately manoeuvre of mass which is like a horned new moon, moving with pipe and song. At intervals they halted, and the dancing-men moved from flanks to centre to perform the *waŋga*. With repeated shouts—*Waaaaaa! Eeeeeee! Rrrrrrr!*—and with much fondling of the boy, they made a progress to within perhaps fifty paces of the waiting kin. From that point they took the boy twice forward and twice back. On the third occasion, the *malakumbara*, holding the boy by the hand, led him first to one flank of the arc (i.e. to the more distant cognates), then transversely to the other, in so doing avoiding the primary kin at the centre. All semblance of order then disappeared. Female kin, who had been sitting or standing behind the men of Mununuk, rose to their feet and sought to break through the line; male kin tried to wrest the boy from the throng of *wungumaŋi*; child-siblings threw stones and dirt at 'those with the flesh.' All the boy's kin wept uninhibitedly. The hotheads ran to take spears and boomerangs; the cool heads sought to restrain them; heavy struggles went on in the midst of the broil where father and mother were clasping and weeping over their son.

(*c*) The rite now reached its climax. All the men—*wungumaŋi, darikadu* and *mambara-ŋulain*—rushed to interpose themselves between the boy and his mother, who was shouldered aside. They formed themselves into a dense screen through which nothing could be seen by the women and children. Four of the boy's class of *naŋgun* sat on the ground and interlaced their legs so as to form a platform. An elderly man grasped him from behind and laid him back down on the bed of legs. A second sat across his chest. Others pinioned his arms and legs firmly, but at the same time with fondling and reassurances. A surgeon—*kadu ŋimar*—circumcised him swiftly. At each cut all the men shouted lustily—*Waaaaaa!*—so that no chance cry of pain might be held heard.[11] A slip of twine was bound around the organ to stop the flow of blood. The boy was then lifted upright. Acclaimed by all the men, and handled with tender affection, he was taken a few steps aside to where, in a hole in the ground, a small fire of wood-coals was burning. Under instruction, he micturated into the fire and squatted over it so that the heat and steam would help to staunch the flow of blood and ease the wound. A fire-stick (*minga*) was thrust under each arm.

(6) Then followed the ceremonial feast upon the *miŋi*, 'the food of the penis,' which had been prepared by the people of Mununuk for the *wungumaŋi* and all visitors other than the boy's cognates. Neither they

11 It is at this instant that spear-throwing is most likely. On one occasion Ngunima, a particularly fierce man of the Kultjil clan, beside himself with sorrow and anger about the suffering of Dapan, his adopted son, killed the boy's mother with one spear and with another pierced the surgeon through both legs. A third spear wounded another woman. True to his craft, the surgeon went on to complete the operation. Ngunima was later called to account but survived the battle.

nor the boy himself might partake. At its conclusion, the visitors might leave unless—as was usually the case—there were further dances that night, or other matters—especially trade-exchanges and formal duels—to settle next day.

(7) The initiated boy did not at once return to the life of the camp. While his wound was healing he stayed a little outside, still under the care of his *naŋgun*. Food was brought to him by his mother and other female kin, but neither his sisters nor any other young females might go near him. The healing took one or two weeks, and over that period his disciplines continued. They were relaxed—and then slowly—only after the last part of the rite, the ritual washing.

(8) The object of that part of the rite was to make him *taraŋga*. The precise meaning of that word presents difficulty. The Aborigines give it the English meaning 'clear.' That translation will serve—I cannot find a better one—but the word is probably best thought of as having a range of connotations in different situations. In everyday speech, water is *taraŋga* if it is limpid and translucent; so is a place if it is free of obstructions; and a situation in which grievances have been adjusted satisfactorily may so be described. However, there is no general or specific antonym to describe the state preceding or opposite to *taraŋga*. But there is no strain on Aboriginal intention to say that the word connotes 'ritually clear' in the context of initiation, even if there is no verbalised concept of the opposite state—ritual 'unclearness' or 'uncleanness.' However, much evidence points to an implicit idea that *because* of what has happened during the rite a boy, after being circumcised, is in a state or situation of great danger—from Kanamgek, The Rainbow Serpent, and from magical causes—if certain measures are not taken to make him 'clear.'

He cannot take them himself; he must be 'helped' by others; and the helpers must be 'old people' (i.e. his seniors) and, pre-eminently, from his class of wife's brothers. The Aborigines say: '*naŋgun* have to do all the jobs of work.'

[There were three essential measures. (*a*) After the wound had healed, a boy was escorted by male kin and affines to a deep pool of fresh water, or to a flowing stream. Some of the escorts sang (actually, chanted) and one played the drone-pipe.[12] All except the boy entered the water, about thigh or waist-deep, the drone-pipe player continuing to play. (*b*) One or more *naŋgun* filled their mouths with water and, as a privilege and duty, spat it on to four parts of the boy's body—the region of the navel (*tjirimeme*), forehead (*wulumu*), and shoulders (*lamala*)—which symbolised classes of kin: in the order given, mother, paternal grandfather, father and father's sister.[13] That done, there was a display of gaiety and fellowship, and the boy was taken into the water so that—helped by the others—he could wash away all traces of his physical ordeal. That done, he now played the drone-pipe and, having played his fill, he was rubbed all over with red ochre and painted—again by his *naŋgun*—with the bright, gay design that signified his new status. (Some Murinbata told me that the playing of the drone-pipe quietened Kanamgek; others, that the washing gave the boy a new skin (*dar̊ipi*) of such a kind (untainted?) that Kanamgek did not (could not?) smell it from afar). He could now safely go near or enter known deep waters, though the same precaution—the spraying by *naŋgun*—had still to be taken with unfamiliar waters. There was a deep conviction that if the spraying were left undone a boy, even though *taraŋga*, would court death.

(*c*) A last task remained. He must be helped to become *taraŋga* in relation to the discipline of forbidden foods—a list so extensive that weeks or months might elapse before all risk of sickness from magical

12 The symbol and emblem of Kanamgek. See 'On Aboriginal Religion. IV. The Design-Plan of a Riteless Myth,' *Oceania*, Vol. XXXI, No. 4.

13 The spraying always began with the abdominal region. Some old men said that the proper order was abdomen, head, left shoulder, right shoulder. Others, that it did not matter. I could not determine the order. The partial resemblance to the Christian sign of the cross has not escaped the Aborigines' attention, but they scoff at a suggestion that they may have imitated that sign, or that there is any connection. Their conviction is that the custom was *mange detemam*—as they put it in English, 'a hard law'—long before Europeans were known to exist. I have heard them cite it as one of several matters in which 'blackfellows just missed,' meaning 'came close to the Christian fashion.'

causes was removed. The relaxation of the ban was slow, orderly, and strictly enforced; the sequence of foods was prescribed[14]; and the ritual form in each case was the same: each food-species must be given, with formality, by one of the class of wife's brothers. The ancient custom was to rub the entrails and/or fat of each animal species on the boy's body, and to paint him with the totemic sign associated with it. But the practice had all but disappeared by the time I reached the region. Only the first few foods were being given in that manner. After that he was now a man—*kadu tjambitj*—and bore proudly on his body, for all to see, the blazon of that status.]

3. The Mortuary Rite

In the Murinbata tradition the mortuary rite was made up of perhaps six phases. The cycle took several years to complete. In the last phase men of many clans and both moieties gathered in large numbers to bury a man's ashes within his clan-estate. Men from several neighbouring tribes invariably took part as well, for not only were some border-clans thought of as being part of both tribes—'half-half,' as the Aborigines say—but the plan of the ultimate ceremony required two opposed regional clusters of clans—quite distinct from the moieties—to perform a coordinated dance with the object of pressing the ashes of the dead into his ancestral soil. That part of the cycle began to wither long before there were any Europeans in the area. It was perhaps the first Murinbata custom (and probably of all tribes in the region) to be affected by the two conditions mentioned earlier—the heavy mortality from disease and fighting, and the instability that broke up the external structure of tribal life. The long drawn-out course of the rite and the complexity of its final phase, encountering those two conditions, made the bringing together of sufficient numbers of men from the due segments less and

14 It proceeded from the common to the rare foodstuffs. The responsibility to see that the foods were eaten in the required order was put upon *nanggun*.

less practicable as time went on. The preliminary phases could be, and were, followed through for a long time but the culminating act soon began to lapse. There were just too many deaths in rapid succession; everyone became just too scattered. Finally, Christian burial in the Mission cemetery became the rule. Only fragments of the traditional rite now survive. There was no attempt at, nor any need for, dissuasion by any European agency (as with the rite of circumcision), or prohibition (as with the rite of the bullroarer). I could detect no great feeling, even among older people, that any significant loss had resulted. On the contrary, there was every indication of solace and gratification in the prospect of Christian burial.

As far as I was able to discover, the last full celebrations of the old rite took place about twenty years ago, some time after my first contact with the Murinbata (in 1935). To my lasting regret, I was unable to see any of them. The possibility of anyone's doing so has now gone forever. But my experiences in 1935 persuaded me that only the most fortunate circumstances would have allowed one to do so for some years before that. There had been so many deaths and so much turmoil—including pitched battles in which a few Aborigines used shot-guns—that the full rite could have been carried out only on rare occasions of transient peace or truce. My luck was simply out: I met the Murinbata at the wrong time for unobstructed research. The following account, therefore, is not an eye-witness account as in the case of the rites already described in the articles. It contains a number of fragmentary observations but should be regarded as a reconstruction at second-hand, based on accounts by men who were drawing on their memories. Except for incidental references, the discussion deals only with the deaths of mature men, for whom of course the rite was best elaborated. The distinguishable phases were as follows: (1) Isolation of the body outside the camp of death; its exposure on a platform to await decay; a ban on any mention of the personal name(s) of the dead; and abandonment of the locality. (2) Breaking-up of a dead man's chattels preparatory to their later destruction by fire. (3) Sending away his hair and stone-axe. (4) Dismemberment and cremation of the dried corpse. (5) Celebration of a funerary feast (*magindit*) over a fire in which the broken chattels were burned at the same time as cognates gave food to affines against a counter-gift of valuables. (6) Final interment of the body-ashes at a ceremony (*mulunu*) held in a dead man's clan-estate.

In discussing the rite the Aborigines tend to fix on the two main features: *magindit*, the ceremony dealing with 'things' (the material valuables known as *nandji merkat*), and *mulunu*, the ceremony dealing with 'bones' (*munu*). But the cycle was really a co-operative effort by the living to help a human spirit (*ŋjapan*) make the transition from the here-and-now to after-life. By a series of measures the once-bound spirit was severed from all ties for disembodied existence as a free spirit. The tie with a particular identity—the social person—was broken by the ban on the name (1). The body or flesh (*ŋen*) which housed it was put outside the company of the living (1). Its visible or material form—its *ŋinipun*—was destroyed by fire (4). Its material extensions, the personal chattels, were destroyed (2, 5) in the same way. Symbols of its vitality, masculinity, and shame were sent away (3). Its wordly accounts were settled with justice (5). And its last physical traces, by the action of all, were made at one (6) with the earth (*putek*) on which, at birth, it had 'made a mark' and so become a named social identity.

The main elements of all this are reasonably clear. Some matters of detail are open to doubt and my inquiries, which still continue, will perhaps clear them up eventually. For the present I shall give only a summary account of those things on which I think my information is reliable.

(1) The disposal of the bodies of children and women did not call for high ceremony. The dominant ethos was that the young were scarcely social persons, and that women were far less important than men. From those facts no inference can be drawn concerning the human feelings. At any death from any cause there was immediate lamentation; the expression of grief at the loss of near-kin commonly led to self-injury and often to violence because of suspicion of neglect or malpractice; the emotions were certainly slow to die—one of the most commonplace experiences among Aborigines is to hear a sudden outburst of wailing,

months or years after a death has taken place, as some incident or thought calls the dead to mind. But simply because human affection is what it is—variably felt and variably expressed—no rigid canon covers Aboriginal conduct concerning deaths outside the range for which formal ritual measures were prescribed by a tradition. The bodies of young infants might be thrown away in the bush or, wrapped in paper-bark, carried about for years by one or other parent, most commonly by the mother, to be left finally in a tree, in a shelter or cave, or simply abandoned, when grief had had its day. The same practice was followed with older children: the strength of attachment and a very practical circumstance—the weight of the burden—determined the matter.

In the case of more mature persons, both male and female; immediate disposal was by exposure on a platform outside but at no great distance from the place of death. Four forked stakes (*ḍLaranin* or *pandaṙuma*) were fixed firmly in the ground, and a solid platform made by means of crossed sticks on strong bearers at a height (5–6 ft.) sufficient to give protection against wild dogs. The body, swathed in sheets of paper-bark, and bound by strands of fibre or twine, was left lying face-up on the platform on a bed of leafy bushes. (In this region no importance is attached to the direction in which head or feet pointed.) There the bodies of women were left to rot; those of men, to await the next phase.

Immediate duties towards the dead were not parcelled out in a rigid or definitive way. There were, however, some clear dispensations. The primary kin—the 'close people' (*Kadu manda*)—were spared the more painful tasks. A special set of mourning terms denoted five such categories—*kuli* (father and father's sister), *ŋuṙyiṙ* (mother and mother's brother), *mikmunuṙ* (spouse of either sex), *minartji* (children of both sexes), and *ḍaiguda* (siblings). Within that group a previous relation of restraint was now intensified, that between people 'from the same mother,' siblings. No brother or sister who had become *ḍaiguda* because of a sibling's death could imaginably touch the body or possessions. But that avoidance—called *lagarin*, the word being a reciprocal used both for persons and their possessions—was evidently felt, from all accounts, to be as much a matter of sorrow—with—shame as of possible corruption by the dead.[15] With that exception, the dispensations were probably due to an ordinary human sympathy with those who, from the nearness of tie, felt—or were supposed to feel—the most grief. The more painful tasks were thought of as falling properly upon secondary and thus less-affected relatives; on kith or 'outside people' if there were any present; and in any case on older persons—for youth too had to be spared needless pain. The close kin daubed themselves white with paint as a mourning-sign. But, as far as my observation and information go, there was no other solemn ceremony at that stage.

Before the bark casket was closed around a mature man someone—father, son, or other close agnate who was not *lagarin*—cut the hair from the head. The symbolism of that act is not completely clear. Possession of the hair was essential for divination; some or all of it was also sent abroad for a purpose to be mentioned; but, as well, it was thought to be somehow intrinsically connected with the being, the *social* personality, of the living. The hair of the head betokened life and vitality; it was likened to grass on fertile ground; warriors once used to wear it, from pride, piled cone-like on top of their heads. But lice (*mimbi*) in the hair betokened a person with proper feelings of shame (*yidiwe*) about shameful things, or able to have such feelings—the point is not clear. A person without lice was one without—unable to feel?—shame; whether the connotation was innocence or shamelessness, or both, is hard to determine. Taking the hair from a corpse was evidently a complex and compound symbolism: perhaps it signified several things at once—that,

15 In ordinary life, brothers from the one womb did not like to make close physical contact. Brothers and sisters felt there was something deeply contaminating in the blood, sweat, urine and fæces of the other sex. A whole set of resultant cautions, restraints and avoidances lay between them, and were extended to classificatory siblings, but with diminishing force according to distance. 'Distant sisters are good sweethearts.' I think that death dramatised rather than changed the character of the sibling-relations. Death as such had about it little 'ritual horror,' whatever the phrase means. I recall seeing one man lying with his head pillowed on, and an arm around the body of his wife, who had been dead for a day.

being beyond life, a man was now beyond shame; but that some shamefulness still endured; that if the hair, a symbol of his life, were sent away then the actuality of his shamefulness went with it too; and shame then lay with others. But here one touches the most cryptic layer of Aboriginal symbolism.

From the moment of death, the personal names of the dead might not be spoken for years by anyone. If the dead had to be mentioned, there were seemly ways of doing so—'the brother of X,' 'the father of Y.' If a name were also (as was often the case) the name of a place or thing, then a substitute or circumlocution was used. And the place of death was abandoned, not to be used again for a long time.

(2) It was the task of a dead man's close cognates—a task which one, such as a father or son or mother's brother, might perform for all—to gather together his chattels and break them to small pieces. That duty could be carried out either before or after the platform-burial. Two articles only were left intact. One thing (any article might serve, but in more recent years, usually a blanket) was kept for final destruction by fire at the funerary feast. The other was his stone-axe, a primary symbol of the male. The axe was given to one of his class of *naŋgun*, probably someone with whom there had been special intimacy or friendship. There was thought to be ritual danger to any close kin who 'ate from the axe'; for example, by eating honey from a tree on which the axe was used. So it was sent away to remove that risk. But it could not pass to the husband of a dead man's sister, since that would bring her children into danger. Even food that a man had collected before death was dangerous to his near-kin, so it was set aside for the class of affines. (After the introduction of European goods, some other articles were exempted from destruction: the irreplaceable iron axes and spear-blades could be kept by close relatives, though the handles or shafts were destroyed and new ones fitted.) The pieces of the destroyed articles were then bundled together, wrapped in paper-bark, and preserved as *nandji magindit*[16]

16 The word *magindit*, which connotes 'burning at the funerary feast,' is in inter-tribal use throughout the region. I could not discover the dialect or language from which it came, but I suspect that it came from the north.

against the time when they would be burned at the funerary feast.

(3) The right of disposal of hair lay with agnates. But as in other such situations (e.g. the selection of *malakumbara* at circumcisions) there were many men with a right of claim. Any man, however 'distant' (*naitpar*) in spatial-genealogical terms, if yet still within the class of classificatory affines (*kamalik*, or 'strangers') might press his claim, but the most effective claims lay with those *naŋgun* (wife's brothers) who were known as *kamalik ŋala* ('big' or 'great strangers'); *kaka* (mother's brothers and thus wife's fathers); or *ŋaguluk* (fathers and thus wife's mother's brothers). To gain the hair was a privilege that stemmed from right; but it meant also the acceptance of a cost that lay with duty: a counter-gift of prized valuables (see (5)). In more recent years no formalities attended the transfer of the hair; I doubt if there were any in olden times. The first phase of developed ceremonial was yet to come.

(4) Many months might elapse between the exposure of a corpse on its platform and its destruction by fire. The choice of time depended on two things: the body had to be dried out sufficiently to allow older female cognates—but no one who was *lagarin*—to take out, as memorials, both bones of each forearm[17]; and a due number of cognates and affines had to be present to perform the two main tasks—the extracting of some bones and the smashing of the others to pieces, and the burning of the remains so that only ashes and charcoal were left. The first task was for female cognates, the second for male affines.

The occasion was a dangerous one, especially when the solemn duties were being performed for someone who had been a great notability. Emotion ran high; the closest agnates stood by, watchfully

---

In 1935 some old men told me that the whole custom of 'dancing-burning' had been introduced from that direction.

17 In crannies within a rock-shelter in Murinbata country I saw numerous human bones, cleaned of all flesh, and evidently of some age. I did not disturb them, but thought they were mainly femurs and ribs. My informants—while insisting that the 'true' Murinbata practice was to keep the forearm-bones—thought that I may have found evidence of other custom of an older time.

alert—so it is said—for possible misdemeanour or insult, or sign of malpractice; evidently, it was then that accusations of poison or warlockry were most likely to be made and lead to fighting. But when the fire had done its work—a week might be needed—the ashes and charcoal were then bundled in paper-bark and taken by one of the class of mothers—the actual mother if she were alive—father's mothers, or mother's mothers, to be used as a pillow until the final interment. The preserved bones went to close agnatic kin, or those stemming from the *ḍamun* (mother's father). Then those who had done the work washed and painted themselves brightly. The bier was sometimes made the pyre, or left intact for a time. There was an old belief that the spirit of the dead sat or perched upon it, 'to look after his own bones,' until his remains were pounded into the earth at the *mulunu* rite. In that case, some time between cremation and last interment, someone set fire to the bier.

(5) The fifth phase centred on *magindit*, a ceremony that took place a considerable time—as much as two or more years—after cremation. Its main feature was the confrontation of affines by agnates and cognates at a feast prepared by the second for the first, accompanied by a gift of valuables (*nandji mimbi*, lit. 'things,' 'lice') in the reverse order. It was a solemn occasion but not one for singing and dancing.

The whole emphasis among the bereaved was on giving affines their due from the dead—'working from our own people' by 'cooking for *naŋgun*.' The term for wife's brother (sister's husband) was used in this context to typify the whole affinal class. The *magindit* was often described to me as 'different from any other thing; that is the way he (the dead) wants it; it is a thing not anyone is allowed to do.' It was not thought of as being like the confrontation at Mununuk during circumcision, perhaps because it was the terminal of a worldly life, and not a mere point of transition to a more valued status.

Only vegetable food was appropriate to the feast. By tradition, the daily staple (*milala*, the nut of the zamia palm) was chosen, but many years ago European flour began to be substituted in whole or part. The collection of the raw food was the strict preserve and duty of the closest cognates; so too was its preparation; and it had to be cooked by them on the same fire on which the broken chattels and last whole possessions of the dead were burned. Under the *lagarin* avoidance, siblings could not partake of the food (though they might prepare it), and it was thought improper, but not actually forbidden, for a widow and primary kin to do so. If 'free people' were there they could have no share in either the cooking or the eating. It was not their affair: 'they see, they know; they don't come up looking.'

The gifts brought by affines were all valuables (*meṙkat*) of the kind that entered into intertribal trade. They passed into, and through, the hands of the primary classes of bereaved people in very much the fashion followed in that system of trade.[18]The way was then clear for the final phase.

(6) The Murinbata who remember the *mulunu* rite—all those in middle and older life—told me that it was 'bigger than Punj,' meaning in both importance and scale. They cited, as proof of their statement that 'people came from everywhere,' the numbers who used to attend, listing names of persons, clans and tribes, remembered as having gone to places still identifiable as Da-Mulunu. I was able to some extent to confirm what they said by careful if indirect tests to work out actual attendances when men were buried at places I visited, and about whom

18 The following is a typical instance. A man N of the Nangor clan died. His own immediate *nanggun* were themselves long dead, but the *magindit* obligation was accepted by P, who had married N's daughter L. That is, a son-in-law acted as surrogate for wife's brother. Several other classes of affines could have done so quite satisfactorily in Aboriginal conventions. N's hair had been sent to affines in another tribe, but the *nandji mimbi* eventually reached P. From P it passed to L, and successively to her brother J, to N's widow Ng, to J's three half-brothers, S, M and F, to the two half-sisters of N's widow, and thence into the hands of two half-brothers of N. After that the articles went, in the fashion that Murinbata call *lingu* or 'straight,' into the system of trade. The complete sequence was thus from *kamalik* ('strangers'? to *kamalik ngala* ('heavy' or 'big' strangers), that is, P, and from him to *minartji* (L), to *mikmunuṙ* (Ng), to other *minartji* (S, M, F), to two further *mikmunuṙ* (the half-sisters of Ng), and finally to two *daiguda* (the half-brothers of N).

I had full genealogical information. Evidently, it was not exceptional for as many as twenty clans to send members. Even on the last regional occasion of celebration, eleven clans were represented.[19] The idiom of valuation of rites is interesting. Whereas Punj is *nandji ŋala ŋala*, a 'heavy' or 'big thing,' Mulunu is *nandji kalegale*, a 'mother-mother thing.' But it was not a rite kept secret by men. Women too attended, taking their children with them, though men only performed the dance that was the main feature.

The male *kuli* or *minartji*—that is, the class of bereaved fathers or sons—of the man whose ashes (*lunbum*, a word used for any finely-divided stuff), were to be buried, took the initiative to summon kin, kith and strangers to the place known as *da mulunu* (there were one or more in each clan estate). Those who came ranged themselves by countries or clan-estates into two great formations which I propose to call The Butt of Spears (*Lumbu Damul*) and The Rump of Birds (*Lumbu'iltji*).[20] The first indicated broadly all clans coming from the north and east, the second those from the south and south-east, reckoned with reference to the clan-country of the dead. They were thus primarily the names of directions, and were only *ad hoc* regional formations. (The same names applied in the system of trade to the directions—and *a fortiori* to the people—to and from which valuables moved.) At Mulunu, a clan that was Lumbu Damul on one occasion might on another be Lumbu'iltji if it were then attending the rite for a man belonging to a clan to the north or east of its own estate. On any occasion both patrilineal moieties were

---

19 The occasion referred to in Casagrande, *loc, cit.*

20 The word *lumbu* means 'butt,' 'rump,' 'seat' and perhaps connotes 'base' and 'foundation' too; *damul* is the generic term for 'spear.' The name Lumbu Damul is used interchangeably with Lumbu Wargat, *wargat* being a name applied to the region inhabited by the tribe referred to in the literature as Worgait. I think, but am not sure, that Lumbu'iltji is *lumbu+tjiltji* (originally perhaps *tjeltjel*); while I was never able to determine the meaning of *tjiltji*, since it is apparently not a Murinbata word, some old men told me that it made them 'think about birds.'

intermixed in each formation, thus obliterating the cardinal segments of the social organiation.

The proceedings began at Da-Mulunu in late afternoon when the heat of the day was over. The men painted themselves with a simple but striking design (upper chest and face reddened with fatted ochre; a white line from shoulder-cap to shoulder-cap on both sides of the body; and a narrow vertical bar, edged with white, from sternum to navel). The 'close people' had brought with them the container of ashes and charcoal and the saved bones. They cleared a ring perhaps twenty feet in diameter and at its centre made a shallow hole in which they put the remains. They filled in the hole with earth and marked it with charcoal from the cremation-fire. On top they put *nandji meřkat*—gifts of high worth, such as spears, boomerangs, pearl-shell and hair-belts—which all who came could see. The affines who had gone to *magindit* did the same. Now all was ready for the rite to begin.

At a distance from the clearing The Butt of Spears and The Rump of Birds gathered into formation. Someone set fire to the grass so that it would burn outwards from the grave in a widening circle. The 'close people' and affines removed the valuables, each taking the articles the others had brought. One of the formations stood by while the other—evidently it did not signify which—moved towards the clearing. Each man carried a spear-thrower and spear, (?) with its point towards the ground and its shaft held under the left arm. As the formation came near the clearing, the men in it formed a line and began to chant. *Pe! Pe! Pe! Pe! Pe!* The line passed through the smoke and burning grass, and moved in an anti-clockwise spiral round the open space, the point circling so as to come nearer the grave with each round. Every man kept rhythmic step in time with the chant. *Pe! Pe! Pe! Pe! Pe!* When the leader reached the charcoal on the grave, all in the formation gave a triumphal cry, turned inward, and thronged to the centre. Each man pounded his right foot on the grave. The leader gave a long-drawn, pulsating cry (made by flapping a hand rapidly against the mouth so as to block and release the flow of sound). *A-a-a-a-a-a! A-a-a-a-a-a!* (Some say it is the sign by which things are made secret or kept hidden.) The others responded in chorus. *Waaaaaa!* (The sound of waves breaking on the beach.) *Eeeeee!* (The sound of the receding wash, or of water running in the river.) *Rrrrrr!* (The sound of wind in the trees, or of flying foxes in flight.) Then they broke formation and moved outwards from the grave, repeating the whole evolution two or three times. It was now the turn of the other formation to do the same. The two thus alternated throughout the afternoon, vying with each other to vivify the rite, until all were tired. There was no musical accompaniment, neither drone-pipe nor tapping-sticks; only a solitary singer (*tjanbanai*), who stood at a distance, singing a song that he had 'found' by his own mystical power; its words and meaning were known only to him.

At sundown there was a halt while everyone rested and fed. Then the alternating dance continued until a late hour. At intervals throughout the night the singer would rise, go out into the darkness, and continue his song.

Next morning each formation carried out the spiral dance once again. That brought the rite to an end. There was nothing more to do. The *ŋjapan* was entirely free of ties with the living, who had nothing now to fear from it. The people returned to their own countries unless there were—as after the other initiatory rites—other matters (trade, duels, fighting) to be settled.

4. Kukpi, The Black Snake-Woman

I shall turn now to an account of the myth of Kukpi,[21] The Black Snake-Woman, whose position in the tradition is comparable with that of Kunmanggur, The Rainbow Serpent. Indeed, according to the Murinbata, Kukpi and Kunmanggur would have been 'level' but for Tjinimin's crime against his father—'level' meaning, I think, two things: coeval, and of equal force and importance. Kukpi is said to have been *tiduk* ('behind' = later in time) in relation to Kunmanggur. No other

21 The pronunciation varies. Some say the name almost as *Kookpi* or *Korkpi*.

connection between them is known or asserted. Nor was there any connection between Kukpi and Mutjingga, although implicit suggestions to that effect are many. Taken in their extant forms, the myths about these three eminent personages stand out like peaks from a hidden mountain range. One cannot see the range, though one knows it is there. But the Kukpi myth, on closer scrutiny, seems to dissolve into a vague cluster.

The story of Kukpi, like that of Mutjingga, deals with a mysteriously-motivated destruction of males by a female. There is no univocal version. That given below represents the best judgment I could make of the version one is likely to hear most often. In that form it narrates how she deceived and destroyed three men. But different versions of the myth mention from two to five men, and some narrators go on to include the killing—by a wise man or warlock—of two women who had acquired a knowledge of Kukpi's secret song. I have reason to suppose that the many versions are probably attempts to fuse several myths which are perhaps best regarded as originally separate entities.

The figure of Kukpi is a baffling and mysterious one. It moves in and out of focus almost, though not quite, as much as that of Kunmanggur. The background information that may be collected does little to steady the image. It leaves one with a feeling that the narrative breaks off before its time: it trails away so as to suggest that there *ought* to be something more. In that respect it lacks the sort of completeness that one finds, in spite of other kinds of vagueness, in the myths of Kunmanggur and Mutjingga.

There is another unusual feature. Kukpi, like Kunmanggur, was a restless wanderer. She made a long journey looking for a good place to rest—a warm, well-watered place compared with Kunmanggur's soft-lying place. But the places from which she started, and at which she completed her wanderings, are unnamed and evidently unknown. That fact, though not conclusive in itself, inclines one to suspect either an incomplete borrowing or a lack—or loss—of secondary development. An added weight is perhaps given to the first suspicion by the fact that a tenuous connection can be made out between the Kukpi myth and part of the bullroarer rite. During the secret phase of Punj, at least one song is explicitly attributed to Kukpi. The song is made up from a repetition of three phrases—(1) *pambara badinya*, (2) *dilwarawara*, (3) *yelyayemene*—in an unknown language. All that I could discover about them was that they 'came from Kukpi.' On the last occasion on which I heard the song, six distinct totemic designs were worn by the dancers for whom it was sung. One of the six was of the *lakumin* (pine) tree mentioned in the myth. None of the others was in any way connectable with the myth, or with the background information given about Kukpi. There are two other fragments to take into account. When a young man is escorted from the secret bullroarer-ground to sleep at night in the open camp, his escorts pause outside the camp to sing a song in which there could be a reference to a place (Mariwan) at which Kukpi turned to retrace part of her journey. And at night in the open camp, while the rest of the people sleep or pretend to, older men sing over the youth a song in which the name of Kukpi's main song—*Wangguwala*—is clearly mentioned. I did not find it possible to make the connections any more clear. The best judgment I could form was that in the rite as it had been constituted for some time past Kukpi was but a minor figure off stage. At the centre of the stage was Mutjingga. In that context she and Kukpi were utterly distinct. For that reason I felt that I could take the myth of Kukpi, like that of Kunmanggur, as being to all intents and purposes unrelated to any extant or recent rite. But my knowledge remains unsatisfactory in many respects, and much might yet be done to clarify the matter by inquiry among the Aborigines in the region between the lower Victoria and middle Katherine Rivers.

The following statements express the consensus of Murinbata opinion about Kukpi. (1) Her sex was female, but at the same time she is freely identified with *both* sexes of the black snake. (2) She was half-woman, half-snake. Drawings sometimes give all four limbs a human shape, but the legs may be reduced to notional bumps. From between the legs a long tail protrudes. It is described as having an 'inside' uterus or womb but I could not find out exactly what was meant by that statement. (3) She went on her journey carrying a digging-stick (*kiniŋga*), a primary symbol of the female. (4) There is uncertainty whether she was truly human. The myth seems to contrast her status with that of her victims, who are referred to as *kadu ḍaitpir* ('person,' 'lips' =true, truth). But she was clearly a person (*kadu*). I also heard her referred to as *kadu ŋamenga*, which connotes 'someone from a mysterious far place,' a dangerous foreigner with, in this instance, according to my informants, power to make children. But I also heard her referred to as *kadu baŋambitj*, which connotes someone who was 'self-finding, self-subsistent.' That description puts her outside the human order. Perhaps the descriptions, taken together, may best be interpreted as meaning 'human-but-more-than-human.' (5) Her repute is dual and ambivalent: a wonder-working sea-being, a restless wanderer, a danger to men; a beneficent songstress, a great water-maker, especially of deep pools and springs, and a law-giver. There is a somewhat secondary, but still strong, emphasis on her child-making power: she 'made' or 'put' a multitude of spirit-children in all the waters linked with her name. A poisonous snake (*ŋunbalin*) is referred to as her 'child.' In discussions *about* the myth the main emphasis seems to fall on her song-making; in the narrative itself, on her water-making (apart, that is, from her destruction of men). I was told that she made a song about every place at which she stopped on her long journey, and also about the morning and evening stars; that she sings perennially; and that, should she ever stop, everyone would die. The only song I was able to record was given in several versions in unknown language(s). The Murinbata thought the song had to do with the sea, but could not be sure. On many evidences I had to conclude that there was some intrinsic connection between her and the sea. (6) There is also some intrinsic connection between her and the system of subsections (*ŋinipun*). She is reputed by some to have given men five out of the eight 'skins' and to have told them to 'work out' the system for themselves, which they did. Her own 'skin' was Nanagu or Namij; that is, she belonged to the opposite moiety (Tiwunggu) from that of Kunmanggur (Kartjin), and to the classes of women eligible to be his wives. (7) Her road (*maiyen*) went from north to south and is thought of as distinct from that of Kunmanggur, though the two evidently crossed and may have had one or two resting-places in common. (8) There is a background suggestion, particularly among the southern Murinbata, that she was connected with poison, but a poison that did not kill.

In the following account I have included (in single square brackets) important variations from the version of the narrative that seems to me most representative. The doubled square brackets contain other information that may be helpful.

(I) Kukpi started. She came from somewhere (unknown northern place). Her road (went by) open sea (past) here. Hence she went on, went on ... to Marai. She sat down (rested, stayed) at a place there. She tried (tested) that place, Marai. No, it was not good. She poked—stirred (the ground), and water (was) there; that water (since, continuously) is there. She went on to Lili. She put a big water there. She rested there. She said: 'this place is not good,' so she left it. She stirred—poked, made a hole. That water is still there. She went on towards Dapan. 'I shall try this place.' She said: 'this place is not good.' She left it. Water still (exists) there. Thence she left for the place called Nimati. There she rested. Water is still there: She (dug a hole) poking—stirring with a stick. She left that place (went towards) Karinggawulkul.[22] She (did the same thing) poking-stirring with a stick. That water (exists) still there. She moved on to Kanung. There, she poked—stirred; water (came out). She rested there. She said: 'No, this place is too small, too cold.' She left it and moved to Ngaiyilu. 'I shall try this place' (tasting), the water. 'No, not good.' She stirred and the water came out. She moved to Karinmem. She put there the bamboo-grass that still exists. The water is still there. Then she went on, went on ... She kept going a long way ... she went, rested

22 There is a suggestion in some accounts that after Karinggawulkul she 'went round' (turned) towards Kimul, making waters and naming places as she went. That course would have taken her across Kunmanggur's road. At one such place (Yambanyi or Yambermin) I found a rock-shelter with a vivid painting of a female figure alongside another painting with features in common with those of a painting of Kunmanggur a few miles away. The region is one where the territories of four tribes—Murinbata, Djamindjung, Nangiomeri and Wagaman—march together. It is at such places that a commutation between elements of myths seems most likely to have occurred.

at Nganangur. She stirred with a stick; water came out; bamboo-grass is still there. She did not stop long. She went past that place, went on ... and rested at Purgala (Purgaiyala). She looked back over her shoulder. 'Ah, that is the road on which I came.' Resting there, she made a song. She sang that song!

She sang:

Ah, Purgala wura nyenyi
Lawa nyenyi, wura nyenyi ...
Lardpanga lardpanga
Waŋguwala karalak pindji pindji.

[A second version of the song is:

Kara nyinyi binyi binyi
Toitpayaŋga toitpaŋara
Waŋguwala waŋguwala.

Neither is in the Murinbata language. But everyone agrees that Kukpi was singing about her journey on the sea, and that she was 'sorry' (thought with sad affection) about her journey.]

'Ah, this place is good. It is warm. I shall stop there.' She stayed—rested there (forever).

[There is some obscurity about Kukpi's movements after Purgala. One version holds that she turned aside, went along a small creek, made a large water-hole, and reached the hills at Mariwan after a journey in an anti-clockwise direction. At Mariwan she turned and retraced her steps to Purgala. Then she went on to the unnamed place of final rest. There is mention of two intermediate places—Kiningga and Ngananggi—between Purgala and the final unnamed resting-place, at which she is said to have made a 'nest' (*diri*). I should point out that the circular excavation in which the dancers throng at the rite of Punj is also sometimes described as a nest.]

(2) A true man (was) there (who) did not see—know. He said: ('I shall go to catch a rock-wallaby.' He took spear-thrower and spear and went hunting. A wallaby went jumping towards that place (where Kukpi was). She saw it. She said *Kidjirudup!* That sufficed! The wallaby fell

down (dead) at once. That man was still running after it ... ah! close now (to Kukpi). She called out to him *Yau!* He (startled) said: 'Who is that?' Kukpi said: 'The wallaby is lying there!' The man said: 'That is well.'

[Kukpi said: 'You are very afraid; you should not be afraid.']

Kukpi said: 'You should sit down here where there is deep shade from the *lakumin* tree; you should make fire with fire-sticks.' Slowly the man tracked the kangaroo, put it on his shoulder, carried it to a tree, left it there. Kukpi said: 'There, close to me, there ! You should sit down in the shade.' He made fire with fire-sticks (*minga*). [The fire came with one twirl of the sticks!] He put the wallaby in the smoke to singe the hair. He cut open its belly. He waited; the fire was now all charcoal. He began to make a place in the charcoal to roast the wallaby. He offered some to Kukpi. 'Do you want some of this flesh?' 'No,' she said. 'You put it on your shoulder.' The man said: 'Where shall I go?' Kukpi said: 'You should go straight to that place there, where there is a cleft; there is a clear place there.' Carrying that wallaby, he went (where she had said); he went ... close to Palarngga, where you can look down (from a high place). Kukpi said: *Kidjiridup!* That sufficed. He was no more. He fell down (that steep place) and was broken to pieces.

[The man had lost his way; he could not find the road he had come by. Kukpi said: 'You should not go back on the same road; if you want to go back you should go that way,' pointing towards the cleft. He carried the wallaby there, up a steep place. Looking down, he thought he saw the road. Then he could not see it any more. No road was there! He could not find a way down the steep place. Kukpi said: *'Kigiritup!'* At once that man fell down to the bottom dead.]

(3) His people (in camp were) waiting-watching. They were talking (among themselves). *Yau!* 'What (unknown) thing did he see?' Another man went (to see, look). He followed the track, followed the track ... to that place. *Yau!* (Kukpi spoke). 'That man has gone back; I sent him back.' (He spoke to himself.) 'Who is (unknown) person here?' Then (seeing Kukpi): 'O, there is a person here, of a yellow colour.' Kukpi said to him: 'I saw him roasting (a wallaby) there, right there,' pointing. 'Yes,' she said, 'there. You track (him) from there, where the road (goes) to

the cleft over at that place.' He went, following the track, to where you can look down (from a steep place). Kukpi said again, *'Kidjiridup!'* He was no more. He fell down and was broken to pieces. She did (said) that thing to him at that same place.

(4) His people (were) watching-waiting fruitlessly. Another man got up to go. He followed that track ... to that place. *Yau!* Kukpi said: 'One man came to me.' The man was frightened. He looked back-sideways (across his shoulder), thinking: who is this differently-coloured one? Kukpi said: 'That is where he went, over there. Yes, there. Do you see? I sent him on that road over there. He went on that road. You go too.' The man went on that same road. He looked down from that high place at Palarngga. *'Kidjiridup!'* Kukpi said it again. He was no more. He fell down and was broken to pieces.

(5) Those people (were) watching-waiting. (Now) they began to think-from-the-belly, differently. There was something strange-different yonder. What (unknown) thing had destroyed three men there? They said (to one man): 'You go (try to find out).' One old wise-man went. [That man was Padurutj, the first *wanaŋgal* =wise man.] He was strong and big, bearded down to his chest. The north-west wind blew from that place. Kukpi was singing. The wise man heard her singing. *Kong! Kong! Kong! Kong!* The sound of the tapping sticks! She went on singing. [Kukpi was singing Ningga Ningga (the 'sweetheart' song). Padurutj said: 'Something is there, where those three were destroyed.' He crept up, looked at Kukpi, and went back to camp. He told no one what he had seen. He was sick, and then got better. He went again to that place, by a different road, upwind. Kukpi was still singing. Padurutj listened.] 'Ah,' he said, 'that is the woman who destroyed those three.' He went upwind to that place. 'Ah,' that wise man said (to himself), 'what is this (unknown) thing?' He listened-learned that song, the Kurangara song from Kukpi. [Kukpi sang: *'Pingarala milpirin paŋu waragadji mala.'* (We do not know that language.) He listened to that song. He understood it at once. Kukpi sang: 'I am sitting here at Purgala.' She sang in Murinyuwen: *'Waŋguwala kara ninyi binyibinyi toitpaŋgu.'* He

got up now (went back).] He listened-learned ... then he went back to the camp.

(6) He spoke to all the people. *Yau!* 'She has destroyed-finished them, that unknown person who is there. There is a little island. It is a place where there are trees.' That is what he said. Everyone wept. They were weeping.

I am reasonably satisfied that the core-story of the Murinbata myth ends at that point. But one may sometimes hear an extension which, in my opinion, is an accretion from the Djamindjung to the south. It fuses with the story of Kukpi an account of the origin of the bullroarer which, in the real Murinbata tradition, is attributed to Kudapun, The Apostle Bird.[2324] In the accretion, the fourth man to try to solve the mystery of the successive deaths of the hunters at Kukpi's hands is identified as Padurutj, who is said to have been the first *kiṙman* or *wanaŋgal* (in that context implying both 'wise man' and 'warlock'). On the first visit he is said to have heard Kukpi singing both Karwadi and Dingiri songs. He knew that such songs belonged only to men, and not to women or children. On the second visit he recognised, on flat stones near where Kukpi was sitting, secret marks that are put only on bullroarers. Kukpi's son was there, and he told Padurutj that the marks and songs were both *Karwadi* (in that context implying 'sacred and secret'). He gave two stone bullroarers to Padurutj, who took them back to camp and showed them to other men, who then made bullroarers of wood. Two women now went to that place and picked up stone bullroarers. They took them back to camp and showed the men. By that time everyone knew what bullroarers were, and knew their significance. The men made a pretext of changing camp, and during the move killed the two women with stone-axes.

---

23 'On Aboriginal Religion. II. Sacramentalism, Rite and Myth,' *Oceania*, Vol. XXX, No. 4, footnote, p 263.

Table 6. Structural Parallels in Two Mythless Rites and a Riteless Myth

I. Phases.	II. The Rite of Circumcision.	III. The Mortuary Rite.	IV. The Myth of Kukpi.
A	Onset of puberty.	Death supervenes.	Kukpi is restless and discontented.
B	Open-secret agreement to circumcise youth as duty to the living.	Sorrowful public acceptance of painful duties to the dead.	She decides to find a good, warm place of rest at the cost of effort.
C	Removal of youth from camp by token show of force.	Removal of body from camp; exposure on solitary bier.	She abandons many places but endows them with water.
D	Youth made into a nameless wild beast.	Ban on name of dead; abandonment of death-camp. Chattels broken.	She finds a solitary, nameless place.
E	Youth isolated in a safe, distant place with friends and under a guardian.	Hair and axe sent away from clan to well-disposed affines; body cremated.	She decides to stay there forever.
F	Token return to camp to be wailed over by sorrowing cognates.	Bones and ashes brought to camp and kept lovingly by cognates.	She looks back and sings sorrowfully; she deceitfully overcomes men's fears by false sociality.
G	Old ties with childhood and kin ended; youth circumcised within a male screen.	Social ties of/with the dead ended at *Magindit*; physical remains returned to earth at *Mulunu*.	She destroys men by magic but the first wise man triumphs over her.

I. Phases.	II. **The Rite of Circumcision.**	III. **The Mortuary Rite.**	IV. **The Myth of Kukpi.**
H	Ritual washing to make youth 'clear'; presentation of valuables and insignia; relaxation of taboos; gradual return to social life as adult.	Exchange of valuables between the living; spirit of dead freed to make a a new entry into the cycle of life.	He returns taking her secret with him to the sorrowing people. Kukpi stays unmolested forever.

5. Common Elements of Design

In Table 6 the two rites and the myth are set out so as to allow three things to be compared: the sets of primary elements, their assembly into structures, and their development towards ends by temporal phases. The table should be read down and across. The effect is to bring out the same kind of two-way resonance found in other such comparisons in earlier papers.

I have no evidence, or reason to suppose, that the Murinbata see any resemblance or connection between the three components of the table. But that fact, in my opinion, increases the value of an anthropological comparison.

It is sometimes said that anthropologists are intent on trying to relate everything social, even things that are not related, and that the forcing of facts into assumed 'systems' results from that cause. The criticism is not justified if one is dealing with *relations of similarity*. The similarities listed in Table 1 are between structures of like elements that exist empirically in connected sequences which have, or appear to have, like patterns. The purpose of the table is to find the common elements of the design-patterns. The judgments about the basic similarities rest on observations of a kind that any anthropologist could make. My inquiries were as careful as circumstances allowed; I have given as much as possible of the evidence for them; but, although the accounts probably contain mistakes, I feel that the similarities, not unimpressive even now, might have shown themselves to be more impressive still had I seen all the possibilities from the beginning and been able to obtain finer detail.

Certainly, II, III and IV co-exist (or co-existed) within the one regional form of life, and were 'related' in being practised by the same people. But, to the best of my belief, II and III were not thought of as being connected except as events that should have a due form in the life of individuals; they were, indeed, put into two different cognitive systems—II into a secular system, III into a religious system. And IV had no discernible connection with II, and only tenuous, partial and rather sidelong connections with III. I consider it to be an essential task of anthropology to deal abstractly with relations of similarity between things in apparent disconnection. In this respect I may point out that analysts of 'social structure' do not think it material that 'the people who live in any society may be unaware or only dimly aware' (Evans-Pritchard) of the existence of the classes of relations which the analysts are prepared to generalise into a holistic structure. But the 'enduring relations' of 'social structure' are not relations of observable similarity, and any general statement about them has much less empirical warrant than statements well-based on observed similarity. It is one matter to *postulate* an organic, holistic system embracing *all* of *many* different kinds of relations, and to search among particulars for illustrations or demonstrations or justifications of what has already been asserted to hold among the particulars: it is altogether another to begin the interpretative task by arranging for further study the empirical similarities.

In Table 1 the phase-developments from A to H (down each column) have a certain likeness, more markedly between II and III than between II-III and IV. The sets of elements compared each with each (across all columns) again have a certain likeness, also more markedly between II and III than between II-III and IV. There is thus a not unimpressive, though limited, measure of congruence between the design-plans in three respects: the sets of elements, their assemblies into articulated structures, and their temporal developments. Within each plan there is something very like the formula—setting aside, withdrawal, transformation, and changed return—that was found within the plans of the rites and myths analysed in earlier papers. And the description applied to the riteless myth of Kunmanggur and the rite and myth of Punj is not wholly inapplicable to the mythless rites of circumcision and burial and the myth of Kukpi. 'Someone is sent or withdraws from a safe, habited place to a place of solitude. In the second place—the place of removal, or in the place deserted—wildness or terror, and a sort of corruption, become ascendant. Something—trust, young life, innocence—is destroyed there. Then, after a pause, there is a return to the first place. But it is not now the same as before;

there has been a change; the old is not quite annulled and the new not altogether unfamiliar.' Some changes of words, and a more embracing generalisation, could reduce or eliminate the main differences.

It now becomes a question of trying to elucidate the human and social meaning of such a structure. What further can be said of the dynamism investing that anatomy of acts?

The rites and myths under study deal with events or happenings over time in social life. The entries in Table 5 are fairly straightforward descriptions of those events. But to call them 'primary elements' is scarcely exact; they are complex, compound and systemic resultants by no means resolved to their irreducible components. Hence my view[24] that if there can indeed be what Professor Firth has called a 'micro-sociology' then its task is to resolve such components. But the less exact usage suits my immediate purpose. The entries at least describe observable events.

Each column in the table exhibits the evidence of two things: an ordered arrangement of parts, a structure, which is transposable *between* columns; and, *within* the columns, three material manifestations of that structure. The structure is relatively invariant. The concrete manifestations are highly variable. Each column may be said to exhibit and define a field of social life. Two fields have in common the fact that, in each, a rite of initiation takes place. What can be said of the dynamism of both that holds true of the third, which has no empirical connection with either? With that problem in mind one may conceptualise initiation in a sufficiently abstract way to embrace all three.

Let us set up the conception of a field of life composed of entities—persons, things, and situations in relations subject to forces with a given distribution—which have been disturbed by change. The change may come about by the entry of a new dynamic entity or by a redistribution of the existing forces. The field then has to be transformed to accommodate the change. A new integration between the entities is necessitated. Initiation may be regarded as an instance of purposive transformation

24 I examined this matter in an unpublished article, Professor Firth's 'Conception of Social Organization.'

of that kind. I shall now apply these outline conceptions to Table 5, under the following assumptions: (1) The sequences of events set out in the table are serial events. (2) The serial aspect maps out a course or path along which entities are moved by forces acting in a direction. (3) The forces that effect the movements and their purposes are human acts or operations, some of which are transitive, some non-transitive, and some intransitive; the transitive acts demonstrably effect their purposes; the others can but symbolise efficacy. (4) Each event is modified by the one preceding it, so that the modifications are progressive. (5) The progressive character relates the events dynamically, that is, integrates the entities in respect of the dynamic change, and thus eventually constitutes the serial as a newly determinate structure, a system of relations, and a process towards an end. (6) In its most comprehensive aspect, the process transforms the field and its entities from one state to another, the states being connected but qualitatively distinct.

We may now reconstruct the table in the following way. The formulation is entirely provisional. It will be looked at again in the next article when all the materials are jointly reviewed. The present sketch is simply an indication of the approach that seems to me to be necessary if the dynamism of the ritualised structure of operations is to be understood.

Phase A. There is a field of social life (F) made up of a complex-compound situation (SI) defined by related entities in conditions of near-stationary equilibrium. The situation is disturbed by a new dynamic force (II, puberty; III, death; IV, discontent) which may be permanent (II, III) or transitory (IV), conditioned (II, IV) or unconditioned (III). The equilibrium can be restored only at a new level, and then only if something of positive value is conserved (II, a beloved person; III, a human spirit; IV, euphoric life) and if something of negative value (II, an outmoded status of youth; III, a dead body; IV, a place of discontent) is cast off. Measures of contrasted character (+) (–) are thus necessitated to restore equilibrium at a new level.

Phase B. The changed situation modifies (determines) the next temporal phase. A decision is formed (II, openly-secretly; III, lovingly-sorrowfully; VI, sadly-hopefully) to perform ambivalent purposes (II, to give youth a higher status at the cost of loss and pain; III, to destroy the loved-corrupting body and its social extensions and to conserve its spirit; IV, to wander in hope at the cost of effort).

Phases C, D, E. The decision determines the character of operative acts to effectuate the contrasted purposes. A progressive serial of operations followed (II, the beloved youth is forced away from a familiar, disturbed place to an unfamiliar, safe place, and the symbols of his former status are cast off; III, the body, its material extensions, and symbols of its social self are destroyed or sent away, but part of its substance is saved and its spirit is honoured; IV, dissatisfying places are abandoned but are endowed with life-sustaining waters).

Phases F and G. The things of negative value having in part been cast off, and the things of positive value in part conserved, the remainder of the serial of operative acts is thus determined. A residuum of good has now to be freed from, or integrated with, a residuum of ill. The operative acts must thus still be contrasted or ambivalent. (II, the beloved youth is brought home, wailed over, withheld from his kin and, by the painful suffering of circumcision, integrated with the new dynamic force—the permanent, conditioned, continuous maturation of life; III, the corporal and social extensions of the dead are brought home to be destroyed by fire and neutralised by gift-exchange, while the last ashes are merged with the ground of former being, and the spirit is freed to find a new life, so that the new dynamic force—permanent and unconditioned death—is integrated with proximate and ultimate life; IV, some men are destroyed by unexpected, gratuitous and deceitful evil; but one man of wisdom triumphs and takes back to the living—who sorrowfully weep over their new understanding—the supposed secret of Kukpi's power.)

Phase G. In the same field of social life, there is now a new situation (S2) defined by new relations between almost the same entities in changed conditions of equilibrium, the dynamic entity having been integrated at the cost of a changed distribution of power (II, the initiated youth is cleansed, freed from restraints, adorned with the symbols of a new positive value, and allowed to enter into a new, positive locus and station of life distinct from but connected with the old locus and station; III, the spirit of the dead is freed from all earthly ties, is accorded due honour, and is allowed to seek a new, positive locus and status of life on a new plane different from but connected with the old; IV, Kukpi is left unmolested, and living people have sad but positive knowledge of a negative power over life that is beyond their control).

It will be apparent that this course or sequence of serial happenings, progressive in a direction and having an integrative character, exemplifies—though in a rather strange idiom—a patterned structure or form that is very familiar to theorists of dynamic systems. For example, it accords very well with many abstract models of field-transformation, and with S→I→R models of conditioned responses, where S=a stimulated situation, I=the integration of stimuli by receptor and effector-structures, and R=the patterned response. I shall simply note the fact in passing. What is interesting—and challenging—from an anthropological point of view is that it seems to vindicate my contention that the study of Aboriginal religion has more possibilities than are explored if an inquiry is too rigidly limited to matters of social structure as conventionally understood. That approach, by analogy, limits inquiry to the receptor-effector structures of patterned responses. A religious system is a dynamic system, to be studied from dynamic concepts, not a stationary system to be studied—except as a provisional step—statically. I thus return to the impressionistic formula drawn from observable things, the ritualised dialectic of setting apart, withdrawal, transformation and return. I am profoundly persuaded that an understanding of Aboriginal religion depends on a growth of insight into that work of primitive intuition. It is like an essay on metamorphosis around a moving stability, a reconciliation of polarities that perennially condition men's being. But the tradition of study from Tylor to Durkheim, and the more recent *idée fixe* that religious things are but the dependent variables of social things, have scarcely allowed the possibilities to be explored.

Throughout these papers I have contended that one must bear constantly in mind the character of the material under study, and that its character imposes terms of approach. For such reasons I have felt forced to use impressionistic words like 'resonance.' The problem is: how to reduce the impressionism? The material of study belongs to those expressive orders of social fact—symbolism of many kinds—that in one way or another transcend controlled methods, at least as they are at present. One seems for the moment to have but two options: to take the view that the material, because of its character, is simply beyond further inquiry—a view I am reluctant to adopt since it seems to make a principle out of what may be only the failure of one's own imagination; or to experiment patiently with ways of deducing the assumptions and principles, used by the Aborigines, that allow the facts to be as they are. For the facts are certainly realities—even if some are unrealised or unperceived realities—within the ontology of Aboriginal life and thought. In the hope of further clarifying them, I shall turn in my next article—the last of the series—to the ruling conceptions of life and death under which the Murinbata used the same ritual form to celebrate the transitions as well as the terminal of their social being.

VI

Cosmos and Society Made Correlative

1. Introduction

I have three main tasks in this article, which is the sixth and last of the series. I will discuss the positive features of Murinbata religion, the dynamical or integrative aspect of the rites, and the underlying philosophy. In order to put those subjects in context I will first sketch the probable development of the religion over part of the nineteenth century so as to show the ascendancy of old symbolic forms over change, and will survey some of the circumstances in which the symbolisms lost their power when direct European influence made itself felt.

In many respects the Murinbata material is a remarkable confirmation of the worth of Arnold van Gennep's schema as set out in *Les Rites de Passage*. On a factual level there is much that fits his classifications as closely as if it had been collected with that intent. I found his work unsuitable only in some of its schematic and conceptual aspects. For example, his sixteen possible ways of classifying rites were far too complex, abstract and dependent on ideas that have proved mortal. More important, his conception of *three* major phases of *passage* did not fit the Murinbata material which, in my opinion, required at least *four*. It was not a matter of an additional minor phase but one decisive for studying Aboriginal religion *as* religion and not as something else, e.g. a symbolical extension of social relations. Between *séparation* and *agrégation* van Gennep allowed only for *marge*: but if I identified the Murinbata 'wild dog' phase with *séparation* and 'swallowing by Mutjingga' with *marge*, there was a third phase before *agrégation*; that is, the phase of token return before incorporation. But the identification of *marge* with symbolical destruction was at least doubtful. It seemed to me closer to van Gennep's thought to identify *séparation* with 'setting apart' and *marge* with 'wild dog.' What then of 'swallowing by Mutjingga,' which was the actual turning point of the main Murinbata rite and, if I am correct in my analysis, the symbolic equivalent of *demŋinoi*, the great transformation of The Dream Time? I had intended to examine the schema in detail in the last paper of this series but space will not now permit and my primary object here is to present original material. A discussion of the utility of van Gennep's whole approach, including its apparent (for 'apparent' see p. 273) dependence on Durkheim's empirically inadequate and logically defective categories, and the real suitability of terms like 'passage,' 'transition' and 'initiation,' must wait upon another occasion. Such an examination is long overdue in the context of Australian Aboriginal studies. But I should not fail to make clear here that my dependence on him though indirect is profound. I regret that I have not found it possible to enter on the bearing of the material on a number of important recent developments in the study of myth and ritual.

As to the positive features of Murinbata religion, I conceive them to have a special claim on careful statement and thought because in the past so much was made of the negative features of Aboriginal religion. The Murinbata in all essentials closely resembled the Central Australians whom Spencer and Gillen described as having 'nothing whatever in the way of a simple, pure religion.' Had they been studied at that time they probably would have been dismissed in the same terms: magic and totemism, yes; religion, no. Earlier in the nineteenth century the Rev. John Dunmore Lang might have said of them what he said of the whole Aboriginal race: that they had 'nothing whatever of the character of religion, or of religious observance, to distinguish them from the beasts that perish.' Such descriptions owed something to theistic conceptions of religion and to fashionable social theory. But primarily they were due, I suggest, to the conversion of negative facts into a supposed proof of the thesis that the Aborigines, being primitive, could not possibly therefore be religious.

I have described the Murinbata as a people who had no idea of a god or gods that called life into being. Life always had been and, in spite of a mediating catastrophe, continued. Earthly life was supposed to cycle between mystical source and mystical goal, but there was no first cause or final end. Many spirit-beings were supposed to exist and to intervene in men's lives for good and ill, but nobody worshipped any of them or, in any formal sense, prayed or made offerings to any of them, even though dispositions to do so were implicit. There was a belief in a shadowy after-life, but in that state no reward for this-life conduct was expected, or punishment feared. No institution existed that could be called a church, no functionaries rightly describable as priests. Nothing in the tradition suggested that anybody need be, or was, concerned over sin or salvation or felt the rack of conscience. Neither individual nor total life was supposed to move towards an end that would consummate history; indeed, there was no true sense of history at all. On such grounds they too could have been denied both religious capacity and attainment. Possibly they had a rather narrow escape: the naturalist Knut Dahl, who visited the Jesuit mission on the Daly River less than a hundred miles from Murinbata country, formed the view that the local Aborigines were 'without trace of real religious conceptions.' The Jesuits did not share that opinion. In a report to their superiors they criticised a prevailing estimate that the Aborigines were 'in a kind of transition stage between beasts and men,' and in particular, were 'deficient in the most elementary spiritual notions.' In that respect they were, with Ridley and Threlkeld, in the sparse company of nineteenth-century missionaries who fought against the current of their time.

The Murinbata rites were, at the most fundamental level, attempts to make social life correlative with the plan and rhythm of the cosmos. The appropriate occasions for rites, it is true, were 'socially defined' but the definitions were in terms of an inexorable cosmic cycle, to which the social situations were made correlative. The strongest symbolisms may be read to say that cosmic necessity was the datum of social necessity. It probably was the power of those symbolisms that led the Murinbata to fit change to the form of permanence, with the result that change resulted, not in the evolution of an open society, but in the further involution of a tradition-oriented society.

2. Tradition as Symbolised History

Like other Aborigines, the Murinbata believed that their tradition was old, continuous and true. On the evidence, I had to conclude that, historically speaking, it was shallow, selective, and neither true nor false; as Lauriston Sharp said neatly; 'somewhat adjusted to meet the exigencies and accidents of the inescapably real present'.[1]

My experience bore out Sharp's among the Yir-Yiront of Cape York. In 1933–35 he made intensive inquiries to find if there were any memory of a clash in 1864 between Europeans and Aborigines (in all probability the immediate ancestors of the Yir-Yiront) on the Mitchell River. He wrote: 'some 70 years later—in all the material of hundreds of free association interviews, in texts of hundreds of dreams and myths, in genealogies, and eventually in hundreds of answers to direct and indirect questioning on just this particular matter—there was nothing that could be interpreted as a reference to this shocking contact with Europeans,' an event in which about 30 Aborigines were killed and many more probably wounded. In 1935, hoping to find a datum for a chronology of changes of social organisation which I was then studying, I tried to discover if there were any memory of an attack made in 1839 by men of the Nangor clan on Captain J. L. Stokes R.N. when he landed at Pearce Point (Treachery Bay) from H.M.S. *Beagle*. I was less persistent than Sharp but I failed then, and on subsequent occasions, to find anyone who had heard of the affair. Many other inquiries about the past ended inconclusively but gave strong indications that important episodes had altogether dropped out of mind. A conclusion became inevitable: to conceive of *a* tradition was misleading if it implied a unitary body of attitudes, beliefs and customs persisting unaltered over

1 R. Lauriston Sharp, 'Steel Axes for Stone-Age Australians,' *Human Organization* Vol 11, No. 2.

time. If one could speak of Murinbata tradition at all it had to be as the product of a continuous art of making the past consistent with an idealised present. There had been 'history' in the sense of events of both change and development; one thing had led to another; but 'what really happened' must rapidly have ceased to signify in important respects. There had been a continuous compounding of history. Otherwise, the homomorphism between institutions which was still the case could not have developed and persisted. But under what principle had history been compounded? In whose interest? By what means? How far into the past could the process be found to have operated?

In the hope of finding at least the shadow, if not the substance of the past situation, I collected what information I could about Tjimburki, the oldest rite of which I had heard. Evidently it had last been performed before the end of the nineteenth century. The fact that it was celebrated was a matter of Murinbata testimony about a number of deep, circular earth-excavations which were clearly man-made. I discovered them by accident after I had learned a little about the rite. The Murinbata had not thought to point them out, having little interest in them. Evidently no one feared, avoided, or respected them although, from all accounts, they were sacred places in the past and were kept as secret and inviolate as the bullroarer grounds more recently. No one then or recently alive had taken part in the rite, but I was able to piece together some information given me by old men who as small boys, still uncircumcised, had been told a few things by their older male relatives.

Tjimburki was clearly a rite of initiation—'bigger than Punj,' I was told. But it was also a religious celebration, with other aims than initiation. Possibly, it was a productive rite either to bring and end the rainy season, or more likely, to end the rain and bring the dry season. A few men thought it started in the season known as *Tjäṙke* (late September-early October) and lasted until *Wiṙ* (late April-early May); the majority, that it started in *Wiṙ* and finished in *Tjäṙke*. But it lasted for many months. Circumstantial details inclined me to think that it probably began at 'burning grass time' (*Wiṙ*) and reached its climax, but not its end, at 'new grass time' (*Tjäřke*). Youths to be initiated were introduced into it just before the dry season was due.

It 'belonged' to the very old men, even more so than Punj, and was a more draconic rite. The celebrants had to avoid all intercourse with women and stay silent—except for singing—for the duration. A ritual leader (*kiřman*), showing himself at a distance from one camp, summoned all the mature men by a high-pitched hail. He smothered them with soft charcoal, after which the two disciplines became immutable. He then led them from camp to camp, at each one summoning and painting the men, until there was a large assembly. Coming at last to a secret place, they danced by clans, while the others sang, within the ring-shaped hollows. [My informants said that the rings were more than 6 ft. deep and 50–100 ft. in diameter but, as far as I could judge from the silted remains, the ring still to be seen at Ngadinitji may have been 30–50 ft. wide.] The outer edge was girdled by a fibre-rope buried in the piled earth, and on top of the earth leafy bushes were made into a screen blocking the vision of anyone outside. Little was known of the style of dancing but two features were agreed upon, the first being very reminiscent of the death-rite, the second of the bullroarer-rite.

The dancers went in spiral around a pole (painted red and white) which was fixed in the centre of the ring and, while they danced, the *kiřman* swung over their heads, in the manner of a bullroarer (which, however, was not used), a type of bag or basket (*muṭai*). For the bag to touch the dancers was thought to be extremely dangerous, so that they had to crouch as it passed overhead. The men wore no bodily decorations other than charcoal. 'My father told me: "all you could see were red eyes,"' one man remembered. The *kiřman* was thought to have had a great secret concerning the dry season, but no one knew what it was; possibly, it had to do with *pulupulu*, a hawk, and the poisonous sting-ray, which were celebrated in the dances. The rite followed the same plan each day. All men slept at the sacred ground. Women had the duty of providing food and a few men went daily to obtain it from them. When the time came to burn the grass the young men who were to be initiated were secreted at the dancing-ring. They were put to severe disciplines of an unknown kind. Several old men said they remembered how the rite ended. Celebrants and initiates came back, marked with paint, to the camp which, in welcome, formed the arcuate cluster known as Mununuk. Women, lacerating themselves until blood flowed, wailed formally. The adult men were at once freed from the rules against speech and cohabitation, but some time had to elapse before the youths could speak or enter into adult life. It was not known whether they were given a special name or title in their new status, but my informants could remember that food had to be presented ceremonially to them by women.

Although the information was slender it was sufficient to establish that there were important resemblances between Tjimburki and Punj, the rite that displaced it, if I interpret the facts correctly, three or more generations ago. But Tjimburki evidently required a much longer period than Punj, possibly more than twice as long. Its custodians were older. The rules about sex and speech were more severe, which suggests that its other disciplines were too. Its liturgy may have been less complex, and less rich aesthetically. [The encircling rope and the swung bag or basket had disappeared from Murinbata culture by 1935, but the central, painted pole was occasionally used in a secular dance known as Malgarin.] In the main, as far as the scanty facts would allow me to judge, the external differences from Punj were matters of style and emphasis. Unfortunately, I could learn nothing substantial about the content of ideas and purposes. There were no extant myths dealing in any but an incidental way with the two natural species mentioned. Tjimburki may have belonged to the class of mythless rites, but my knowledge of it is too thin for me to attempt a structural examination as with other rites of that class. At the same time, both Tjimburki and Punj clearly were religious celebrations as well as initiations, with at least some motifs and structural elements in common. But if Tjimburki was concerned with a mystery then no one remembered what it was.

There is no doubt that Tjimburki had one or more predecessors. In and around Murinbata territory I came unexpectedly on a number of stone-structures which were as clearly the work of men as the excavations. Hundreds of stones, in some cases thousands, were arranged in geometric shapes (circular, ovoid, arcuate and linear). No one had confident knowledge of their provenience and use. There was also the great puzzle of the many splendid rock-paintings—some reminiscent of skulls—in and around the region. I have already remarked on the fact that some were asserted most positively to be connected with Kunmanggur, The Rainbow Serpent, and some with Nunakangal and Kulumbin, two other mythical heroes associated with dysentery and death. It was tempting to see in all these remains further evidences that Murinbata religion over time had moved among a range of major emphases. I could see that the seasonal cycle, catastrophe by disease, puberty, maturity and death all had in common, from the Aboriginal viewpoint, the fact of inexorability. Could an hypothesis be shaped along those lines? I felt I had to cling to those aspects of Murinbata history which some could remember, or said they could remember, reasonably well. However, I was compelled to conclude from the purely physical evidences that the development of the religion had been much more complex, certainly more discontinuous, than they remembered, knew, or admitted. A brief account of two matters will make that fairly plain.

There was a time at which the Murinbata did not possess the bullroarer. In its stead the spear-thrower was used in the same fashion that is, swung from a cord so as to make a humming sound by vibrating in the air. The oldest men thought that custom may have come *after* the fall of Tjimburki, at which the bag or basket was swung, because they knew that the Djamindjung tribe had taught their fathers to abandon the ritual use of the spear-thrower in favour of the bullroarer. At first the bullroarers had plain, unincised surfaces. Those with incised patterns came later; indeed, they were new to the Murinbata when I first visited the region in 1935. But the oldest known to the Murinbata were coloured black, not red, which suggests a possible assimilation to the colour-style of Tjimburki. However, either Tjimburki was more ancient than I was led to believe or there were more co-existent rites in the second half of the nineteenth century than the Murinbata could remember clearly.

An accumulation of fragmentary facts inclined me to the second view. I could satisfactorily prove that five great decisions had been taken in series.

The Murinbata, situated on the frontier between two distinct cultural regions, were progressively imposed on by their southern neighbours, the Djamindjung and associated tribes, which were themselves under or coming under the influence of bullroarer cults and the highly segmented forms of social organisation of *their* southern and south-eastern neighbours. The religious influences preceded the social, which the Murinbata had comprehended very imperfectly even in 1935. Four elements—circumcision, the cult of the bullroarer, the abstract scheme of subsection organisation, and matrilineal totems (*ŋulu*)—all came to the Murinbata by Djamindjung pressure in couple with their own attractions. Each required some adaptation of the northern ritual complex, of which Tjimburki, allied in form and style with Mulunu, the death-rite, was the senior initiation. The fourth element (*ŋulu*) came to nothing, but the three others were adopted in the order named. (1) *Circumcision was taken over as a rite for mature men.* It probably displaced or compounded with one or both of two other rites, known as Ngangula and Jandurtji,[2] which were preliminary to Tjimburki. I presume, but am not certain, that the spear-thrower was used ritually in one or the other, perhaps both, of those rites. The Djamindjung continued to impress on the Murinbata that the spear-thrower should be replaced by the bullroarer which they themselves were now using in conjunction with subincision. That aspect of the rite appalled the Murinbata, who would have none of it. However, they took over the bullroarer and adapted parts of its ritual to a similitude of the form of Tjimburki. (2) *They gave the new rite the name of Manggawila and made it the senior initiation.* In that way Tjimburki dropped out of sight.

2 In 1935 I heard both these names, but unfortunately did not investigate what they implied. I knew that they referred to rites that were no longer practised, but concentrated most of my attention on the new social forms (subsections and matrilineal totems) with which the Murinbata were struggling.

In Manggawila the bullroarers were unincised, coloured black with charcoal, and decorated with tufts of kapok in simple linear designs. I am uncertain how long that phase continued but, from all accounts, the ritual calendar was now congested and made heavy demands on time and resources. At some stage the Murinbata took an important decision. (3) *They passed the rite of circumcision to boys at puberty* who, up to that time, had been initiated, within the northern ritual complex, at a rite known as Karamala, which did not require circumcision. (4) *Karamala became an initiation for boys not yet ready for circumcision.* But the cult of the bullroarer continued to grow in appeal. A substantially new style of rite—known as Punj—appeared, characterised by red instead of black bullroarers and with incised patterns rather than tufted decorations, and new secret songs and dances. Another important decision followed. (5) *Punj was kept exclusively for mature men, and Manggawila, the former senior rite, under the name of Djaban was 'given'—that is, forced on—small boys in place of Karamala, which dropped out of use.* In that way the northern ritual complex survived only in covert ways within the initiatory series, mainly in two of the three styles of circumcision rite described in an earlier paper. When I arrived at Port Keats in 1935 memories were still fresh of a time when 'men with beards' had been circumcised. It was possible positively to identify Djaban, the then pre-pubic rite, as Manggawila under another name, and to talk to men who, as boys not yet circumcised, had taken part in Karamala. And, as among the Nangiomeri, the cult of Karwadi (Punj) was at its height.

The process that I have reviewed appears as one in which 'history' was both accepted and yet defeated by being made captive to symbolic forms. Diffusion brought exciting new motifs and styles of religious activity. But to be acceptable the new apparently had to be compounded with the old. The unfamiliar had to be put in symbolic continuity with the familiar. In the upshot neither the past was disowned nor change made impossible. But to combine change with a rational conservation of the sacred forms and values already existing led to an involution of development, not to an evolution.

A summary of the facts about Karamala and Djaban will be relevant at this point.

Karamala was intended to prepare young boys for the ordeal of circumcision. Like that rite itself, it was supposed to speed a boy's physical growth to manhood. It must also have been a powerful psychic, mental, emotional and social stimulus. Furthermore, since in effect it rehearsed every feature of the next rite except the act of circumcision itself, it must have done much to dispel childishness by revealing the rewards, excitements and power of the world of men.

When boys were within two or three years of puberty men of the class of wife's brothers (*naŋgum*) took them away, with parental consent, to a distant place. Entirely safe from human harm, they were kept under kindly but firm guardianship, and instructed in male knowledge. After a lapse of weeks or months, clansmen from the host country mustered to take them home, with many gifts. Later proceedings were, in principle, a simplification of the circumcision to come. No warning spear was flung into the home-camp to announce the boys' imminent return. Instead, one of the escorts approached the camp just before dawn and blew a long drawn-out note on a drone-pipe. The boys' relatives at once started formal wailing and self-wounding, and when daylight came formed themselves into the welcoming arc, Mununuk. The escorts then came out of concealment and, accompanied by musicians and singing-men, all being brightly painted, brought the boys forward laden with gifts. As in the circumcision rite, they were taken to be wailed over and fondled by close kin. Dancers repeatedly performed the goose (*ŋalmuŋgiṙ*) dance while the boys sat embraced by their fathers' arms. A break came then in the proceedings while the visitors and boys retired to eat food prepared by the hosts. In late afternoon the ceremony started on a second phase. Freshly painted (black and white were the only colours used) the visitors brought the boys to Mununuk but, a short distance from the waiting kin, covered them with leafy bushes and stood clustered around them. A set of 'nests' (*diṙi*) had been made along a wide arc fronting and flanking Mununuk and the leaf-hidden boys. Painted dancers, at first singly, then in pairs, sprang from the nests and performed the goose-dance to the musical accompaniment of drone-pipe and tapping-sticks. When the dance had been repeated many times the bushes were removed and the dancing visitors went a short distance away while the musician piped the boys close to their kin. While the assembly listened to the piping, the main guardian explained to the boys the food taboos they must observe for a long time to come. That task over, the visitors formed mass and rushed at Mununuk as though to thrust the boys home. Halting a few feet away, they danced while the boys were again being fondled by their joyful kin. At sundown the celebration ended. The boys were now free to sleep with young friends within the circled fires of the camp. Each gave to his father the gifts brought from distant places. The fathers passed the articles into the *kulu* exchange system, in which each boy had now earned a place. They were ready for the greater challenge of circumcision.

The resemblance between Karamala and the circumcision ceremonies[3] practised until recently is plain. I could obtain no other explanation of its abandonment in favour of Djaban than that there was 'too much business,' and the probable truth of that may be accepted. Possibly there were other pragmatic considerations. From all accounts the nineteenth century circumcisions were exceptionally painful affairs; perhaps the surgeons were less skilful; at all events there was a rationalisation that the operation was too severe for grown men ('the skin is too tough') and that it would be better done at puberty. But I have no doubt that it was the attraction of Punj that really explained the change. Consequently Karamala, now the least important secular rite, was given up; the age of circumcision was lowered; Manggawila, in the name of Djaban, but still a secret, religious rite, replaced Karamala; and Punj, in successive stages of complexity, wholly replaced Manggawila as the main religious celebration and higher initiation for mature men. All appear to have had, in spite of difference of content and style, much the same structural plan.

3 See 'On Aboriginal Religion. V. The Design-Plans of Mythless Rites,' *Oceania*, Vol. XXXII, No. 2, December 1961, pp. 80–89.

I will now deal briefly with Djaban. In the early dry season a recognised *pule* ('boss' or leader) talked quietly with the fathers of uncircumcised boys (*lamitiŋi*) to get their consent for a secret meeting to arrange the place and time of initiation. Invariably groups of boys were initiated together, since the ceremony was complex, lengthy, and sometimes a burden on resources, and the ritual calendar was usually very full. At a time when several clans were at one place, the *pule* flattered the boys by inviting them to go hunting with him and with other mature men and circumcised youths. To allay suspicion, the party often hunted for a while, but the *pule* soon led them to a prearranged place where, perhaps pleading fatigue, or a wish to eat, he halted. All then sang until sundown. The party returned to camp, where the boys were required to sleep between fires in the centre of the camp-circle. By that sign the women knew, supposedly for the first time, what was afoot. But there was no wailing; nor was there any next morning when the *pule* took the boys away—now as *ku were*, 'wild dogs'—to yesterday's place, now called Ngudanu Nandji Djaban.

At Ngudanu the boys were made to sit down, with older classificatory wives' brothers (*naŋgun*) as their mentors. It was conventional to pillow their heads on the mentors' thighs or loins. The older men for some time sang from a large repertory of songs. Later in the day it became necessary to conceal from the boys preparations for the first revelations. Some pretext was seized upon (often quarrels were simulated and fighting postures taken up) to send them off to Da Mambana, an isolated and secret place, out of eyeshot but within hailing distance. They were put under a guardian to ensure that none attempted to spy on Ngudanu. While they were absent dancers painted themselves with kaolin and put on decorations of white kapok, then hid themselves in a thicket.

When all was ready the *pule* went half-way to Da Mambana and hailed the guardian, who brought the boys to Ngudanu, forcing them as they came to bow their heads and to keep their gaze fixed on the ground. Simultaneously, all the grown men other than the hidden dancers and a handful of singers burst into the wild horseplay known as Tjirmumuk.[4]

4 See 'On Aboriginal Religion. I. The Lineaments of Sacrifice,' *Oceania*,

The boys were told to stand facing the singers and then, quite suddenly, were ordered to look to one flank, where the painted dancers sprang to view from concealment. Thence they ran behind the singers to perform a dance which was repeated frequently throughout the afternoon.

At sundown the party returned to camp. The boys were now required to wait in the bush, with the guardian, until dark. They ate food brought to them by affinal relatives. In the distance they could hear the uproar of Tjirmumuk being performed in camp, but were much too far off to see. Then, with full darkness, men came out to escort them to their sleeping positions of last night. They might not speak to anyone, nor anyone to them, not even their brothers or parents, though fathers might give sons titbits of food without speech. Late at night, older men stood over them and sang one of the public songs of Djaban. Then they slept.

Next day a sterner and darker aspect appeared. Boys who were thought too hard-spirited (in Murinbata, 'bad headed,' 'hard eared') were put to sit in the sun, or to lie face-up with eyes open to the sky. But only the most recalcitrant had to do so alone; the others might have at the same time the comfort of the arms or lap of *naŋgun*. That lasted throughout the phase of singing. Then the ritual pattern of the previous day was repeated, and so on for many days. The boys heard splendid songs and saw spectacular dances, each linked with culture-heroes and with Dream Time exploits. On the seventh day two disguised men, carrying spears, sprang from the thickets to simulate Kumaijen, The Flesh of the Road, the warlocks who at times put the region under a reign of terror.

Towards the end of the dancing-phase, the tension fell markedly. The last dance of a long cycle was performed by only a handful of men. Most of the others had taken the opportunity of the boys' absence at Da Mambana to paint themselves grotesquely in such a way as to put on a frightening aspect. With faces plastered and heads masked by bark, no one's identity could be recognised. Some put a stick through their pierced nasal septum and drew it up and back, tying the stick tightly with string knotted behind the head, so that the face took on a brutish

Vol. XXX, No. 2, December 1959, pp. 112–115.

cast. Thus disguised, they had vanished before the boys' return. The dance petered out in a desultory way and the guardian, playing on the boys' fears, told them that all the men had gone to prepare for a fight. He urged them to go with him to camp, the one place of safety. The road back became one of fear as the guardian, looking this way and that in well-simulated anxiety, spurred his charges on. When they came near the camp they saw that there were fires burning close to the path. Under the guardian's order, one boy was sent to pluck a brand. Instantly, from behind the fire, a masked figure sprang from hiding, and threw a spear so as to miss the boy by the narrowest margin. The terrified boys ran this way and that but, turn where they may, another monstrous figure appeared, out of nowhere, and a spear, an axe, or a heavy stick was thrown, to the accompaniment of a grunting imprecation. Only one path was clear—the path back to Ngudanu. They ran there, led by their guardian and, as they reached it—'those boys, their hearts thumping always,' one man told me, recalling his own feelings—the dancers came again before them, together with men disguised as Flesh of the Road. At that stage each boy was given fire-sticks (*minga*) by his *naŋgun*.

That night Tjirmumuk in camp reached an exceptional pitch. Burning sticks were flung without regard for where they fell, and licence of speech and conduct were at a peak. But the play was confined to men. The women, mere spectators, sat holding their children. The Djaban initiates as usual stayed out in the darkness at fires from their own fire-sticks.

Next day the whole character of the assembly at Ngudanu changed. There was singing but no dancing. The boys were painted with red and white colours and festooned with gifts from *naŋgun* and other affines. That done, they were escorted to camp for formal presentation to their female kin. As in Punj, each boy crawled on hands and knees to Mununuk between the straddled legs of a line of men of the opposite moiety from his own. Briefly wailed over by the women, who lacerated themselves (mothers cutting their thighs, sisters their calves, other women their scalps), they crawled back through the lines of men, and all the male participants ran back shouting to Ngudanu. There, having been washed, the boys were painted on chest and legs with the sign of the bullroarer, though only the older men were supposed to know its secret significance. They were now Kadu Djaban, but still must be isolated and watched by guardians, who had the special task of seeing that they used only their own fires, made with their own fire-sticks, and that no one else used the fires by accident or intent. A month elapsed before they might speak to close female kin, and then only after the women had presented food formally to them. They continued to wear the sign of the bullroarer, not knowing its import. In a few months the time came to repay and reward their *naŋgun* and others who had helped them through the rite. That was done by a feast of food cooked on a fire lighted from the boys' own fire-sticks, which were destroyed in the fire at the same time.

Even so brief a description makes clear that Djaban or Manggawila was very much the same rite as Punj; at the least, the chrysalis from which the senior rite developed. There were considerable differences of content, and also of mood and tone, but they both had the same plan and configuration. The resemblance to Karamala is also clear. Thus, as far back as it seems possible to go, there is evidence of a certain continuity of ritualised form and symbolic content in two important fields—the secular field of circumcision, and the religious field of celebration, both being fields of 'initiation' but at the same time a good deal more. It is a reasonable hypothesis that the homomorphism between changing rites, between variable myths, and between rites and myths, over a period in which sacra and sacred values were themselves in change, was due to the suzerainty of symbols. But not, one would think, to their sovereignty, since the symbols pointed beyond themselves.

The absence of a time-datum is a real embarrassment in such a study. On several occasions I thought I had found one, only to have it slip away under other inquiries. I had to conclude that even in matters of genealogy I was dealing with testimony that allowed judgments about presumptive fact, but not very much more. A hard fact—one beyond the polite collusion of memories—was hard to obtain. It is a painful wrench for a European mind to have to deal with so shallow a perspective on time, and with mentalities that are ahistorical in outlook while asserting the contrary. Fortunately, although—as someone has said—variation is the law of oral tradition, constancy appears to be one of the laws of ritual tradition. One may even suppose that in a society affected by change it is the inertial property of ritual concerning sacred things that countervails what Professor Firth has called 'the plasticity of myth.'

3. The Collapse of a Tradition

Since I began writing these papers, I have been made aware that some anthropologists still treat with reserve reports of the Aborigines' intense preoccupation with sacred rites. Evidently they suspect subjectivism in the accounts or perhaps a mere convention of description. I can only say that the evidence that the old Murinbata were fascinated by their rites seemed to me plain and credible. But gratuitous doubts are notably hard to dispel.

The ritual calendar evidently had already been substantially curtailed when I first met members of the Murinbata tribe in 1932. That had come about because of two things. There had been heavy depopulation by dispersal, disease, and fighting between clans. The external or inter-tribal structure had eroded. But the clans were as interdependent in ritual as they were in marriage, trade, and the settlement of serious disputes. The only really important field of life in which a clan was independent was that of domestic economy and even there autonomy was limited by consideration for kin, affines and friends in other clans. In 1935 12 clans of three weakening tribes around Port Keats could muster only 150 souls, but all the major rites—with the exception of the main mortuary rite—though truncated were still being practised. The evidence that the Murinbata in particular had gone to pains to keep them alive was substantial. Anything from three to six months of every year were spent mainly on the various ceremonies. Visitors came from long distances in spite of the fact that the adjacent regions were almost depopulated. There was a jealous insistence on prescribed forms, rights and duties. Painstaking care was lavished on preparations, and participants entered into the rites with every appearance of zeal. Both men and women had been killed for real or supposed offences against sacred places and things. The development of the mission station was much hindered by the sudden disappearance of men and boys in order to practise one or other of the rites, and by attempts to block the use of areas with sacred associations. While it is true that the ritual activities were enforced by the power of older men, and that younger men and women conformed, the facts cited are not intelligible except as the outward signs of deep attachment to the work in hand.

The collapse of the old ritual life came about by a conjunction of three things: persistent pressure by the missionaries to put an end to all pagan ceremonies, the decay of the external structure of tribal life, and the onset of a general sophistication. But the process was a slow one. The older Murinbata condoned it, in the first place, from motives of expediency, not from loss of enthusiasm, although a decline of interest set in once the impairment of the external and internal structures—a progressive trend—had reached a certain stage. The pressures to bend before a new, single authority, against which there was no appeal, were too insistent to be resisted except by a common front for which the men had no genius. The value placed on European goods—of which there was no other source—weakened everyone's will. The flow of candidates for initiation dried up when all infant males were circumcised at the mission hospital and, as they came to a right age, were withheld from the other rites. The number of visitors fell off when, because of their interference with the work of the mission, they were made to feel unwelcome, and because the shrunken ceremonies were a disappointment. But, in my judgment, it would have been possible to revive the entire ritual complex as late as the early 1950s, since there were still alive a sufficient number of older men possessing both the secrets and the interest. After that time, many deaths occurred among the ritual leaders, and a new set of influences became ascendant. The general inflation then affecting the whole of Australia had impact even in the remote bush. All the Murinbata, irrespective of age, became intensely interested in making money, which became more plentiful. Wage-labour, travel, producing goods to sell, and gambling absorbed everyone's attention. But on my last visit (1962) I found in one clan efforts to keep the old mystical culture alive.

So much for the foreground. There was a background, entirely Aboriginal, which suggests that a certain corruption of the cults had set in as the product of religious conservatism and politics. By extending the displaced rite of Manggawila to immature boys the Murinbata set in train a number of consequences. Hitherto, perhaps only a secular sanction—at least on the conscious level—had dictated the sexual rift between growing boys and females, especially their mothers and sisters. Now it had a specifically religious sanction. That intensified the psychological and social disabilities of women. Their loss of status was reflected in an attempt by the men to force a kind of initiation on them. During the 1920s—precisely when I could not establish—older men took a number of girls, at or after puberty, into the bush for several weeks under the pretext of making a Djaban for them. They used the girls sexually but, for reasons I could not discover, the attempted innovation did not prosper, and no systematic custom developed. The attempted extension of men's political power, under religious sanction, suggests that there was some religious deterioration in Djaban compared with Manggawila. Probably some of the mystical content of the parent-rite was lost, or withheld. The details of the rite, as practised in the 1930s, inclined me to that view. It was clear that the central experience through which the initiates had to pass was one of force and terror. In spite of solicitous care and days of brilliant theatre and social pomp, they were made conscious of duress by men who must have seemed to them half in league with powers of darkness. The Flesh of the Road did not appear at Punj, nor was there anything like the attack by—as far as the boys knew—the brutish demons of the bush. The instructors said that the rite was 'to make boys understand,' and spoke of it as an essential preparation for Punj, but—judging by what I saw and by what initiates said—they remembered the rite most strongly in after years for the mortal fear it caused them. There was of course a positive content. They learned something of the religious culture and became familiar with ceremonial patterns. The new status to which they attained brought satisfaction. But all that was within a repressive conditioning of mind, outlook and personality. It was an integrative experience that left a mark for life. Theirs were the generations that tried to defeat the efforts of the missionaries, who arrived in 1935, to interest them in Christianity. The Jesuit missionaries among neighbouring tribes on the Daly River had found that 'once a young black has been initiated at one of these corroborees he becomes quite impervious to the religious instruction of the missioners.' That was found to be the case at Port Keats also, and, because of it, Djaban was suppressed.

Within a decade Murinbata elders had noted and spoken unfavourably to me about a great change of social personality among boys and young men. The suppression of the rite of Punj during the same decade, and the inanition of the second puberty rite because of infant circumcision, had produced a generation as much at odds with their own elders as with the missionaries. It seemed ironical that the fully initiated Aborigines then gave the mission more loyal support than those to whom the pagan rites had been forbidden. The explanation was not far to seek. The initiated men, unshaken in attachment to their own rites and beliefs, and already possessing all the power and status that an Aboriginal culture could give them, had worked out an expedient *modus vivendi* with the mission. The younger men were between two worlds in neither of which they had confidence, unambiguous status, acknowledged power, nor—in their judgment—sufficient reward. They were insouciant, impatient, and given over to an aimless activism. The older Murinbata, perhaps characteristically, said of them that they 'did not understand.' In a sense that is as good a description as might be given. Their grasp of the European world was negligible, and of the Aboriginal traditions very poor. Many complained to me that their own old people could, or would, tell them little or nothing. The old people, in turn, said that they had 'let go' the big things. But I think they may be interpreted also as saying, in effect, that the 'big things' must be done to bring understanding; talking about them was not enough. That was perhaps their rationalisation. But I also felt that they had compensated themselves for a loss of power and privilege by withholding secrets from a generation that had slipped away.

At about the same time as the attempted Djaban for girls, an effort was made to couple with Punj a custom named Wilili which, by repute, was common among the Victoria River tribes, probably as part—more likely a political extension—of a distinctly different bullroarer cult. As it was practised for a short time by the Murinbata, Wilili was associated with the use of a tiny bullroarer (known as *karait pule*—'dead friend,' 'ghost leader') which, when swung, gave out a high-pitched, shrill sound that, according to some men, made women overcome with sexual desire. The ritual leader (*kiřman*, itself like Wilili a Djamindjung word) stood at a distance from camp at night, and swung the *karait pule*. At this signal all men who were Kadu Punj, that is, fully initiated, and all adult women, went out into the darkness to have intercourse according to their appropriate *ŋinipun* (subsections). Each man, that is, coupled with women from the two subsections into which he might marry. I could discover little else that was significant. The attitude of my informants was somewhere between shame and amusement. They would not admit to having taken part themselves but hinted that others, who roundly denied the charge, had done so. All agreed that Wilili was not true Murinbata custom. I felt fairly sure that that was so. I judged that a comparatively small group of men, enthused by their experience among the southern tribes, from which they were learning the new subsection system of social organisation, had tried to impose on their own people as part of Punj a custom that was possibly not a religious feature of the southern cult but a political extension of it. Be that as it may, Wilili was clearly incremental, not integral, to the bullroarer rite of the Murinbata. I suspect an attempt to give a religious sanction to the new system of social organisation, which was then causing upset because it challenged too many vested interests. Other episodes came to my notice—the mass sexual abuse of women for real or fancied threats to the men's secret life, and the killing of several men for supposed profanations of Karwadi—which showed plainly enough the interplay between religion, politics and private motive. The facts must weigh in the balance of judgment about the religion or, rather, the manipulation of it. It would be a pity if Aboriginal religion, once denied as a possibility, should be judged by its excesses or abuses. But it would also be a pity if total disbelief should be replaced by a sentimental estimate.

4. The Positive Features of Murinbata Religion

I propose now to state and discuss a number of propositions about the religious complex that in part summarise the main fields covered in earlier articles and in part depend on new material. The facts are local, but each proposition appears to bear out in a broad way conclusions which have been reached by many anthropologists who have studied other Aborigines. In some cases the facts of other regions have been left either as uninterpreted 'custom' or dealt with from viewpoints which I do not share. The extent to which my propositions hold true of those regions can therefore well wait on occasion and criticism. For the moment I put them forward as applying to one region only. They are not tied to any particular definition of 'religion,' and are drawn rather to illustrate what it meant 'to be religious' in the former context of Murinbata life.

(*a*) The religion incorporated a view that the structure of the world and life was fixed once-for-all at a remote time in the past. There was no creation *ex nihilo* but a culmination and transformation of things and conditions already existing. What then happened prefigured what could and did happen afterwards. The possibilities for men's life were determined. All significant things took on their distinctive structures and tendencies, so that existing things were types or symbols of ancient things.

(*b*) Myths depicted the structuring past as a set of dramas, each of which moved to a climax in which a particular set of things became determinate. Persons and animals diverged from a unitary stock. Each went to its appropriate domain of present life, with powers and limitations as they now are. The main institutions of mankind began. The great features of the physical environment took shape. Thus, although some of the content of the myths was cosmogonical, they were on the whole cosmological, giving a pattern of relevances between things, a moral order between structures of existence, such that the totality of life was a cosmological structure.

(*c*) Certain myths, principally but not only those closely associated with religious rites, dealt with divisive things, dualities or opposites, that somehow were reconciled or brought to a term, though only momentarily, and with effects that were both unitive and disunitive and continued as concomitants of existence thereafter. The whole set of definitive, institutive dramas gave the process of life a kind of dualistic ontology.

(*d*) The Murinbata thought the dramas of the past a very great mystery, but one that their forefathers had understood and that they too could understand, at least in part, by depending on a received tradition, which in fact was not questioned. There was no class of detached questioners nor evidently any growth of facts *seen* as problematical. Instead, there was a strong emotional and rational impulse to conserve and act on a received tradition that had supposedly proved its truth by continuity from the storied past.

(*e*) The Murinbata considered the countryside filled with plain evidences that the dramas had occurred. The places of climax were known and named, and each one contained proof—a shape, or form, or pattern—of a great event. Even when not well understood, the presence of such evidence was taken to be a sign betokening old intent and present significance. The forces expressed in the dramas were thought to be immanent in all such places and to be dynamically available for men to use. The whole environment, though charged with numinous import, was still a ground of confidence since it had been continuously occupied by their own people.

(*f*) Living persons were thought to be connected intimately—as individuals, sexes, genetic stocks, groups and categories—with personages, places and events of the dramas. The connections were thought of as historical, mystical, substantial and essential. They were expressed mainly through the device of totems. Totems, as signs, stood for the identity of and unity between persons known to possess them by proper or mythical title, and proclaimed the possessors as the true custodians of rights *in rem, in personam* and *in animum* over such benefits and limitations of life as were instituted by the dramas. As symbols, entering into a large number of systems, the totems mediated to Aboriginal imagination the things made determinate in the dramas, and guided the Aborigines in appropriate conduct towards them.

(*g*) It was thought that during the dramas two domains of life became distinct but remained co-existent and interdependent. There were then, and are now, an incorporeal (but not necessarily invisible) domain, and a corporeal (but not necessarily visible) domain. The former has the greater power. The Murinbata believed that daily life gave continuous proof that spiritual force intervened in men's affairs of its own accord and, to some extent, at the behest of men with mystical power over it. They supposed that many classes of beings existed in the spiritual domain, two having particular importance: eternal beings which resembled human persons but had not lived as such, and beings that once had been human though possessing powers beyond those of ordinary humans. The most elaborate myths and, in some cases, rites developed about the second class.

(*h*) The main rites simulated events of the founding dramas, though in covert ways often difficult to perceive through the complex and crescive symbolisms. The rites followed a set liturgical formulary, and had the character of great celebrations, being made the repository of the highest products of imaginative, theatrical and material art. Each ritual occasion vivified in the minds of celebrants the first instituting of the culture, deepened the sense of continuity with men's beginnings, and reaffirmed the structures of existence. Inevitably they produced an archaist outlook, a reactionary temper, and a conservative impulse.

(*i*) The ruling stratum, the older men, enforced a general assent to the terms of life which they, as the last receivers of tradition, had adopted at pain and cost. In part to conserve their own investment in ultimate values, they coupled religious celebration with disciplinary ordeals for youths, the next receivers. Thus, openly as well as covertly, they used the rites to sustain the paramountcy of male interests. By ritualising the biological and social development of males they put a higher worth on their own sex, both as flesh and as spirit, than on females. But although the rites exemplified and the myths rationalised that relative valuation they also tacitly acknowledged the fleshly and spiritual worth of women. In this respect political force may have dominated the religion in the interest of men, but it did so only in their secular interest; it did not, and could not, deny women their place—in some respects a leading place—in the structure and ontology of the life-process.

(*j*) Within the rites the initiated men used kindly, but often severe, methods and condign sanctions to attain two purposes: to subdue youthful egotism so as to accord with modes approved for men, and to bring some understanding of traditional mysteries. The mysteries evidently were obscure but powerful intuitions of men's life and condition. Being so complex, they could only be adumbrated by means of symbolisms couched in familiar idioms, e.g. sexuality, the conflict and trust between kin, parricide, family relations, and so on. But the symbolic idioms were mediating, not ultimate, expressions. Their significations were the structures and transactions which were instituted for men by the transformative marvels of The Dream Time. The design-plans of the main myths and rites were symbolic affirmations of those events.

(*k*) To pass through the ritualised ordeals put a mark on the psychological, emotional, mental and social character of the initiates. It probably heightened their sense of ambient mystery and may have deepened their interior life. It certainly put them in fear of authority and taught them the value of social fellowship. The instructive artifices were extremely skilful. Throughout the ordeals fear was in some sense countered by security, isolation by comradeship, privation by sustenance, and pain by reward. A discovery of the dependency of life was eased by the revelation of things that could be celebrated joyfully.

The dangers to life were relieved by a gift of the ritual means to assure its confident continuance. The end of the ordeal was the seal of manhood and the key to a man's privilege. All this was done in a context of high excitement, secrecy and beauty. Every man who came to full manhood did so, not only with no man's hand against him, but covered by the freely-given blood of a class of men who, though inherently opposed to him, depended on him as he did on them.

(*l*) Until very recent years the weight of the past, pressed by the hand of authority, lay heavily on the Murinbata present. But evidently it was not a dead weight. In spite of archaism, reaction and conservatism, a dynamic of life found and used a potential for change and development. There is evidence that several cults followed one another in a sequence. Some of the myths suggest a certain growth of cognitive discovery. Some facts can also be interpreted as an abuse or corruption of the religious cults.

The sum of evidence sustains three conclusions. (i) If any Australian Aborigines lived, as used to be suggested, in a stationary state of society with a static culture, the Murinbata were certainly not among them over any period which it is possible for inquiry to touch. (ii) To identify their religion with totemic phenomena would be a mistake. (iii) The society was not the real source and object of the religion.

These conclusions seem particularly important in view of much that has been written concerning the Australian Aborigines. Few anthropologists would now uphold the nineteenth century idea that the native Australians had settled on a dead plane of uniform changelessness, although some may still underweight the dynamism within their institutional life. But it is not seen clearly enough that totems and social situations simply provided familiar, convenient symbols by which to adumbrate what could not be designated more sharply or succinctly; that is, the things of ultimate religious concern. To regard totems as the essential content of the religion would be to say that symbols are more important than what is symbolised. To make Murinbata society religion's source and object would be to treat as ultimate what is only proximate, and to deny a patent fact: that in their rites the Aborigines had *some* objects beyond themselves, beyond egotism, and beyond social gain. The great symbols, and not just the totemic symbols, were valued for their own sakes; in some sense they may even have obscured what they stood for; but they were never of ultimate concern, that is, empty of further reference. Social and selfish objects were pursued within the religion, and to some extent it may have been a religion of functionaries; of the elders, that is, who controlled its administration; but that part was not the whole. Both the rites and myths, when analysed, suggested that the religious objects were the intuited dualisms supposed to compose the life-process. The rites did so obscurely and only in part; the myths much more vividly and fully. The stories of founding dramas that transformed the archetypal past into an ontological process in which every Now could be justified or judged by Then, were surely nothing if not cognitive essays to justify high concerns of life and to guide conduct towards them.

5. The Context of Understanding

In the space of a few pages I will do what I can to substantiate these statements by illustrations and comments referred when possible to 5 (*a*)–(*l*). They will also outline the context of understanding I have used.

In earlier articles I suggested that the key to the mentality set out in (*a*), (*b*) and (*c*) was an idea that not only the structure and process of life were settled by the drama but man's whole lot, including the possibilities for his life. Different myths dealt variably with that theme. The myth of Old Crow and Old Crab is particularly interesting. The version given in brackets is an alternative.

Crab (*bali*) was *mutjiŋga* (very old woman). She was very sick. Everyone thought she was dead. They buried her in a hole. But she was not dead. She stayed there about five days. She made a new shell and left the old one in the ground.

[Crow (*wa'k*) and Crab argued. Crow said to Crab: 'What are you going to do (in order to die the right way)?' Crab said: 'You wait here.

This is what we people should do (in order to die the right way).' She went into a hole. She stayed there changing her shell. She made a new shell. She threw the old one away.]

Crow was there waiting. The people were crying. *Yau!* Crab was there! The *mutjiŋga* came back. Everyone was happy. Crow was angry. He said to Crab: 'That way takes too long. This is what we people must do.' He plucked Crab's eyes out. Then he died immediately.

[Crow was there waiting. He went to search for Crab. He looked in the hole. He said: 'This way takes too long. It takes too long to get strong this way.' He went back to the waiting-place. Crab stayed in the hole until her shell was thick and strong. Then she came back. She said to Crow: 'That is what we should do.' Crow said: 'No, it takes too long. Someone might come and kill (hurt) us. There is an easier way to die. This is what we should do.' He rolled his eyes, fell down backwards, and died at once.

Crab took water and poured it on him. 'O, he is dead.']

The two versions illustrate the difficulty of obtaining univocal versions of myths, but both exemplify the point under discussion. The Murinbata maintained that crabs did not die if left unmolested. When they grew old they changed their shells and renewed their youth and strength. The same possibility existed once for men, but was spoiled by Crow.[5] The myth was the standard answer to questions about the ultimate why and wherefore of death: Crow's decision determined all men's fate thereafter.

The idea of death in a life that otherwise might have gone on renewing itself is a vivid particular image of the fundamental trauma that had so many expressions in Murinbata culture.[6] Life, the process

---

5 Was it a true option? The Murinbata likened the question put by Crow to Crab to the question put by one dancer to another in a rite if there were a choice between a man's being, say, Turtle or Kangaroo for the next dance. Each man decided on a dance he *knew* how to do. Crab's decision rested then on special, possibly secret, knowledge? No, the Murinbata said. Crow could have followed Crab's example if he had wanted to.

6 [6] It may be noted, incidentally, that in a broad sense the story-structure

of existence, was determined and thus limited—death being the great limit—by its structure. Its structure set all the possibilities within life. The myth seems to have overtones: a hope of immortality and a fear of its possible risk and cost, or at least of attaining it. The significance of the second remains obscure. But the Murinbata of the past gave themselves a certain assurance of the first through their beliefs about life.

There was evidently no myth about life's genesis, but the *fact* of life was posited for the heroes of The Dream Time. Nor was there any myth, as far as I could discover, concerning the first manifestation of spirit-children (*ŋaritŋarit*), except insofar as Kunmanggur or Kukpi put them in spring-waters. But those heroes were doubtfully true begetters. The central idea was that life was natural but death was not; the proof: that men had to be shown how to die *without renewal.* But 'death' was corporeal only. The body (*ŋen*)[7] 'fell down,' the breath or 'wind' (*ŋitkit*) stopped, and the shadow (*wul*) became still but the spirit (*ŋjapan*) survived, and—less certainly—so did an image/double/reflection/counterpart (*ŋuluŋ*). But what happened thereafter to the spirit was far from certain. There was talk both of a double death—that a ghost eventually became a butterfly,[8] which acquired the colours of the ground in which burial had taken place—and of a transition in which the spirit either used an agent (*miṙ*) to take it to a new womb or transformed itself, or the woman, into that agent, so that it was both. Testimony on these points was divided. It also left a little uncertain whether it was the child-spirit itself or its guide that sought a woman of the opposite moiety. One notion was well established: that the *ŋjapan* went a long

of the myth follows the plan of the rites and myths analysed in earlier articles.

7 [7] The word *ngen* was used for both human and animal bodies, but *ku* ('flesh') could be used with reference to humans only after death, when their ghosts were called *ku-karait.* In all other contexts *ku* implied edible flesh.

8 [8] Some Murinbata, however, maintained that the word for butterfly (*manman*) had two meanings, but they had lost the exact significance of the second.

way away. Hence the number of Murinbata supposed to be incarnations of the dead of other tribes. Facial or bodily resemblances were taken as proof that a dead person's soul/spirit had found a new body and—of a sort—immortality.

The myths on which I have concentrated in the articles bear out that preoccupation with subjects of gravity suggested by (*a*), (*b*) and (*c*). But I learned also of many other myths that *prima facie* seemed to reflect only inconsequential interests. The tragic element scarcely appeared at all. Some conformed, in a very broad way, to the paradigmatic plan of the major myths. But (*d*) not all conformed, or did so evenly. The whole body of myth seemed made up of elements of different substance and weight. But the *fact* of the attachment of *some* myths to rites, and the probability that *all* rites could be ranged into historical series, made me consider seriously a possibility which, if it could be established, would be of much importance: *that the span of the total body of myth was the measure of the depth of ritual development.* In other words, cults may wax and wane, but the insights that men have once attained into their rituals of passion have a longer life, and perhaps too a life of their own. If the true function of myth is to rationalise the exalting of things to the status of cult objects and if myth has a longer life than cult, then two sets of facts are easier to understand. The symbolic correspondences within and between the religious and secular orders may be interpreted as proof of a constant preoccupation with a limited class of sacred things. And the myths not attached to any recent or extant rite are as much the memorials of old formations of cult as are the stone-structures and earth-excavations. That may be put as an hypothesis, although one that I could not prove conclusively. But all the evidence pointed to the probability that change—and decay—had been continuous in Murinbata ritual life for a very long time. The great problem of interpretation was not to account for that, since flux is the natural law of human affairs, but rather to account for two things: the recurrent stabilities of ritual form, and the apparent repetition of the one ritual theme. I was satisfied about the fact of both and saw in it the measure of the unimportance of many discrepancies in Murinbata culture which might otherwise have seemed of central and intrinsic interest. But I felt persuaded that to search for the system of Murinbata life was as mistaken as to search for the tradition. At the most there had been workings towards system and momentary captures of it.

In point of fact, the beliefs by which the Murinbata assured themselves of their human continuity were not at all well stitched together. The outline of the main ideas of life and death sketched above were a sort of general doctrine. But some clans at least seemed to consider that the spirits of apical ancestors stayed on near the 'big' (i.e. main) totem-centres.[9] Nothing seemed farther from the living clansmen's minds than that such spirits should go off for alien incarnation. Possibly the supposed presence of spirits explained the association (not a uniform one) between some totem centres (*ŋoigumiŋgi*) and 'poison countries' which were places of religious dread. Men would avoid such areas in the territories of other clans, and approach their own circumspectly. Each man called out his personal names in direct address to the spirits. No one knowingly ate food obtained in the immediate locality, since it was supposed to bring death or sickness. But the *ŋoigumiŋgi* as such were not places of danger or dread. I felt there were gaps between the world-drama as depicted in (*a*)–(*d*) and the more domestic aspects dealt within (*e*) and (*f*).

There was no difficulty in getting the Murinbata to agree that their traditions left much unclear, but the conflicts were evidently of little interest to them. I had many discussions of this order. So every person had a soul or spirit and after the obsequies—what? 'It comes back *ŋaritŋarit* (child-spirit).' How? '*Miṙ*.' What was *miṙ*? 'Anything—fish,

9 The persistence of this belief is illustrated by the following episode. In 1961 a young man whom I had known since his infancy dreamed that he was visited by two clan-spirits, who took him to the clan's main totem-centre. There they showed him beautiful visions, and two spirit-dancers taught him a song and a dance. On waking, he drew a striking picture of his visions, and taught his clan-fellows the song and dance. Picture, dance and song are now thought of as the clan's precious possessions, not least because of the young man's death a year later.

fat, food, bird, smoke, lightning.' Were *miṙ* and *ŋaritŋarit* the same? 'No. That *ŋaritŋarit* is a child (*wakal*); it is *ŋjapan*; it catches hold of *miṙ*.' How did it do that? 'It finds a good place; *miṙ* brings it to *dimbitj*.' What was *dimbitj?* 'Where a man's *ŋjapan* grows up.' Was *dimbitj* the same as *ŋoiguminŋgi* (totem-place)? 'No, *dimbitj* can be anywhere; wherever *ŋaritŋarit* finds a woman, that is *dimbitj*; *ŋoiguminŋgi* is father's country.' But the totem-place was also *ŋjapan*-place? 'Yes; it is different; *ŋoiguminŋgi* is *ŋakumal* ('dreaming'-place).' So *miṙ* and *ŋakumal* were different? 'Yes; that *miṙ* has nothing to do with *ŋakumal* and *ŋoiguminŋgi*.' So *miṙ* and *dimbitj* were the same and different, and *ŋakumal* and *ŋoiguminŋgi* were the same and different? 'Yes, one thing, one thing, one side, one side.' That did not seem very clear: let us talk more of *miṙ*. 'A man gets marks (*liṭai*) from *miṙ*.' What kind of marks? 'That child there; his *miṙ* was buffalo. There are marks on that child where the spears hit. Every time that child cries it sounds just like a buffalo.' So the buffalo was *ŋaritŋarit?* 'No, it was *miṙ*; it just stood there, waiting for the spear; that *ŋaritŋarit* made it deaf; it wasn't really a true buffalo: *it was that man's wife!*' That was hard to understand: how, the same? 'They were *ŋinipun numi* (of one kind).' Were they one *ŋjapan?* Laughter: 'woman is *kadu* (person); buffalo is *k* (animal flesh).' Were they *ŋakumal numi* (one totem)? Laughter: 'buffalo walks everywhere; he has no *ŋakumal*.' Were they *ŋuluŋ numi* (one image)? Laughter: 'buffalo has four legs, woman has two legs.' So; well, what does a man get from *ŋoiguminŋgi?* 'He gets marks (*liṭai*) from that.' What kind of marks? 'You look like your *ŋakumal*; you smell like it; *ŋakumal* is like you, yourself; like your father (brother, friend); it is just like you being there; it is pushing you; you can't let that place go.' What else from *ŋoiguminŋgi*: the *ŋuluŋ* (image)? 'Men do not know; the old men did not say.' The *ŋinipun?* 'No, a man's *ŋinipun* is from his mother.' Always? 'Some people like to follow up the father.' Had they heard that some blackfellows 'throw away' the father? 'Yes. Murinbata do not like that. We like father-son to be *kuṙjik numi* (one moiety).' So they got *kuṙjik* from *ŋoiguminŋgi?* 'No, it is different.' But every *ŋoiguminŋgi* was Kartjin moiety *or* Tiwunggu moiety; it could not be both? 'Yes, it cannot be both.' But what about X, where there was a Kartjin totem-place in Tiwunggu country? 'We don't know; maybe that place really belongs to Kartjin. That was before we were alive.' That seemed very mixed up; let us start again; perhaps a man *really* got *ŋinipun* from *ŋoigumiŋgi?* 'No.' Well, from *ŋakumal?* 'No.' Well, from *kuṙjik?* 'No; from mother, sometimes from father.' Let us start again: how did *ŋaritŋarit* find the right woman? 'The *miṙ* finds one.' How? 'Maybe it smells her; no one knows.' But *miṙ* is *nandji* (a thing); how could a thing smell? 'It isn't really a thing; people say it is like your wife; we don't know properly.' Well, it was all very hard to understand. 'Yes. That is what we think.' What was 'the hard hand' (*maŋe detemam*), the law, in all this? What were 'the words of the lips' (*murin ḍaitpiṙ*), the truth? 'That is all the old men said; we do not know any more.' What was 'the weighty, the big thing' (*nandji ŋala).* 'The big thing is *ŋakumal*; it is like you yourself; you yourself are there; something is pushing you.'

Inquiry, as a European understands it, could bring few such matters to clarity, as a European demands it. Intelligent and helpful Murinbata would point out that they had never thought of such questions. Some younger men, whom I had set to work to question their elders, told me they had been rounded on quite fiercely. *There*, they were told, is what is true: the dreaming-places, the dreamings; as I recorded it, each such place a nexus of four symbolisms: essential ('that *ŋoigumiŋgi* keeps you alive: you are strong from that'); substantial ('the *ku-karait* know you are the right man; they know the sweat from that *ŋakumal*'); mystical ('a thing we do not hold in the ear, but true'); and historical (agnatic links from living men to remembered ancestors). And *there* were the proofs: the groove cut in the rock by Tjinimin's spear; the cleft of rock pierced by Karak's beak to bring back water to the world; the place where Nginu chose fresh water as a domain rather than salt; the rocky bar where Wa'k and Bali debated how to die; as I recorded them, instances of faith transforming arbitrary signs into symbols of an assured provenience of life. Each sign was supposed to designate a source or ground of order *in* life, and each symbolism mediated that order into the constructions *of* life. In such circumstances Aboriginal fact and European category had precious little to do with each other. The Murinbata clung stoutly to what old repute as being true had. They seemed to say that, however remarkable, things were true because they had served trusted men well from the beginning, and I felt capped for an answer.

Selective tradition, plastic myth and exuberant symbolism are an awkward triad. I found it scarcely possible, even with parsimonious aims, to see more than broad shapes, and then only by disregarding the social aspects of symbols; not dismissing them as unimportant, but as peripheral or incidental to a study of religion. For example, the varieties of totemism (*f*) seemed to me of secondary interest in that sense. It is not necessary for me to defend that view here[10] beyond saying that I share Tylor's opinion that totemism has been 'exaggerated out of all proportion to its theological magnitude,' and Goldenweiser's that it is 'a conglomerate of essentially independent features'; but, within that general view, I thought it clearly more important to try to study the symbolised rather than the symbols. The essential aim was to find the significations of the content and structure of a particular life of devotion within and under the masks of symbolism, one of them being the exotic mask of totemism, which in that respect I saw as but a language of imagery and, as I judged, of little religious interest in itself.

It was not of course possible to follow that aim directly. Every turn in the study of Murinbata imagination, experience and effort threw new light on the structure of their life of devotion. Only those perhaps who have attempted such a study will grasp the difficulty of avoiding sidepaths. For example, the rich inventiveness of imagination (*g*) was the source of unending problems of choice. Drive through one strong inquiry, or several necessarily weaker? If one, then would there be more profit in clarifying the puzzling and perhaps crucial element known as *ŋuluŋ*[11] and if possible linking it (as the Murinbata did not) with the

10 I have stated it sufficiently in a paper 'Religion, Totemism and Symbolism' which will be published shortly.

11 I referred earlier to *ngulung* as 'image/double/counterpart' for want of a better description. I heard it used on different occasions in distinct though related senses. The painting of Kunmanggur at the cave at Kirindjingin was said to be The Rainbow Serpent's *ngulung*; the actors in

borrowed and much misunderstood *ŋulu*, the Djamindjung matrilineal totem, or in finding a possible link between the sharp-toothed women of Merkem, who still—so I was told—seduced and ate incautious men, and Mutjingga, who comforted and ate the trustful Dream Time children? Inevitably I left unexplored fields that may have been more fruitful than those I chose, and I cannot do more here than hint at the complexity of the imaginative culture. Except for incidental remarks I will omit topics on which my information—and in some cases the Murinbata's too—was notional (e.g. the hobgoblins supposed to people the sea-strand, hills, caves and jungles); those (e.g. magic and warlockry) which I would prefer to examine in a different context[12] and those which require a very detailed discussion (e.g. the particular and general scope of important symbols). The last is an unfortunate omission in that Aboriginal culture derived much of its aesthetic appeal from the symbolisms of water, fire, earth, wind, smoke, thunder, lightning, blood, the body's members and exuviae, hills and caves, earth and sky, sea and land, wet season and dry, animal kind, and all environing things that exhibited motion, vitality, distortion, striking form, or oppositeness. In the religious sphere such symbolisms play vivid parts. To write of 'exuberance' in that connection

---

cinema films were called *ngulung*; an abandoned camp was *ngulung*. The Murinbata said that it meant 'something like a trick' and tried to clarify that by the example of a camp from which, in fear or duplicity, people had gone away leaving things behind to suggest that they were still there. Yet *ngulung* is 'like *ngjapan*' but distinct from it. Perhaps its core-meaning is somewhere between 'illusion' and 'simulation.' Probably 'simulacrum' is the most apt word.

12 Aboriginal warlockry seems to me religious superstition used from political motive. It appears to consist of distorted elements standing over (*supersto*) from otiose cults and myths and used as a system of private menace within the contemporary social and religious orders. Its category is distinct from the abuses of contemporary religion, e.g. the submission of young women to Djaban for purposes of lust. To treat its co-existence with a religion as a ground for giving it equality with the religion seems to me unjustifiable unless in actuality it has that equality, or even dominance. In my opinion, neither was the case among the Murinbata.

is not an over-statement. I must depend on the descriptions of the rites to have suggested how a different study—say, of Aboriginal theatre as an art-form—would reveal the affinity of the Aboriginal mind for symbol—construction from commonplaces. The greater significance of the things to which the symbols point is my only reason for giving the symbols but passing note.

Perhaps the main matters in (*g*) on which comment will be helpful are the distinctions between spirit-beings. The personages mentioned by name or status-term in myths (Kunmanggur, Mutjingga, Kukpi, Kulumbin and Timandji being among them) were thought of as *kadu ŋjapan*, 'spirit/ghost persons.' The belief was quite clear: they had once lived as true persons, though possessing superhuman powers. They were described also as 'persons with fathers.' It was indeed that property that marked them off from another great class of spirits, who had no fathers and were thus *kadu baŋambitj*,[13] persons who came, or caused themselves to be, in some mysterious way, by their own power; as the Murinbata said, 'found themselves, without fathers.' They were supposed to be invisible (except to men known to be *tjämuŋ* or spirit-seers) and also insubstantial ('they have no *ŋen*') but at the same time to have a man-like appearance. Although 'not from blackfellows' they were sometimes spoken of as *kadu karait*, or 'dead persons,' in contradistinction from *ku karait*, actual known persons who had died. It may make for clarity if I refer to *kadu baŋambitj* as pure spirits and to *kadu ŋjapan* as clan-spirits or ghosts in order to mark them off from another genus, that of creature-spirits or hobgoblins, known as *ku baŋambitj*.

The Murinbata were terrified of hobgoblins, more so if that were possible than of ghosts. They feared the dark, and disliked jungles, thickets, caves and gorges. No one liked to walk alone. They were manifestly uneasy in some dank, solitary places I had reason to visit, and spoke much about hairy monsters with feathered arms, claws and

13 The verb was used only in the third person. The prefix *bangam* was used with a large class of transitive verbs (cut, drop, follow, cover, break, strike). The meaning of *bitj* is obscure. It seems to connote a life-source, as in *dimbitj*. It is probably at least cognate with *bit* in *ngembital* (semen).

teeth of huge size and red eyes. I heard the most circumstantial tales from men of a matter-of-fact type, whom I knew to be full of physical and moral courage, about their own and others' encounters and escapes. While they gave free rein to their imaginations, they nevertheless produced fairly standardised accounts and followed a more or less uniform convention in describing the classes of hobgoblins.[14] Even so, they left me less than sure that there were firm dividing lines between hobgoblins and ghosts on the one hand and ghosts and pure spirits on the other.

In the actual practise of the religion the special class of clan-spirits to which Kunmanggur, Mutjingga and Kukpi belonged were clearly ascendant. But the pure spirits should be noticed too if only because they had no positive place in the recent cult-life, and possibly had not at any time, though firmly established in the belief-system. These self-subsistent beings had as their realm the sea-strand, the land, and the sky. Evidently they shared it peaceably. People professed to have no fear of them although in fact parents used their names to frighten children, and there is no doubt that one member of a pair of *kadu baŋambitj* (see p. 264) aroused acute fear because of a supposed link through The Flesh of the Road, the warlocks, with a class of hobgoblins.

The most eminent of the pure spirits was known as Nogämain, a sky-dweller, who lived (according to some) *maŋe nukunu*—'of his own will' or 'in his own fashion'—and alone, except for a dog, with 'no father, no mother, no brother, no child'; but (according to others) with a wife and son, the son being symbolised by a hunting spear (*tjänba*). It was supposed to be Nogämain's influence, through his son, if a hunter killed a kangaroo or wallaby with one throw of a spear. Some people identified Nogämain with the man in the moon, and one of the smaller marks on the moon was often pointed out to me as the dog. Others were not so sure and, when asked about the spirit's abode, made a generous gesture towards the whole sky and said a single word—*kangal*, 'on high.' Now and then I heard thunder and lightning attributed to

14 Many of their sketches strongly resembled the hominid figurines painted by unknown artists in rock-shelters in the region.

'the people of Nogämain.' It was generally agreed that he was one of the spirits responsible for sending spirit-children: I heard the statement *wakal bata Nogämain manḍadai* many times—'Nogämain sends down good children.' But since I had heard the same of both Kunmanggur and Kukpi, and could find no myth about him or any evidence that he had a connection with the religious ritual, I thought him comparatively unimportant. I was therefore much surprised to be told by one of the oldest Murinbata men that as a child he remembered hearing *ŋalanḍar ŋalanḍar* (the oldest men) calling out to Nogämain at night when they lay in camp short of food or 'hungry in the tooth' (i.e. craving) for the special foods that the spirit was supposed to be skillful in finding. My informant told me that the men would begin with a cry *Kaṙ!*, follow it with a long trill *rrrrrrr!*, and then use the imperative *Ku wada tjiŋabup !* or *tjitai ḍuŋapak!*: 'flesh-for-eating+? waiting,? wanting+you leave (it) for me'; 'honey+you put it up (in tree) for me.' The petitioner would repeat the invocation at intervals throughout the night, using the same form each time, varying it only for the food of choice.

Because it was the only instance that came to my notice of a direct petition, in a form approaching that of prayer, to a spirit for a benefit of life, I was inclined to be incredulous. But when other old people told me the same I felt that I had no good reason to be gratuitously doubtful. The old people to whom I spoke were impatient with any suggestion that they had been influenced by the example of Christian prayer. As I pointed out earlier (p. 259) direct appeals to clan-spirits for protection in places that would otherwise be dangerous were routine. Appeal to a pure spirit for a material benefit would seem to be psychologically continuous. It is perhaps relevant to point out that Nogämain, alone—as far as I could discover—among *kadu baŋambitj*, was also supposed to be *kadu ḍaitpiṙ*, 'true man,' and thus distinct from Kunmanggur, Mutjingga and Kukpi, who were *kadu re*, which seems to have the sense of 'man as he was before man as he is now,' that is, man of The Dream Time, who was unified somehow with what is now the animal kingdom. One aspect of Nogämain that I found baffling, and could never disentangle satisfactorily, was the distinction between him and one of the pair of spirits mentioned (p. 263) as having some kind of relationship through warlocks with a class of hobgoblins. Some Murinbata insisted that Nogämain was also Kangalmau, though others denied it. Those who identified them said of Kangalmau what the others said of Nogämain.

But those who argued that Kangalmau was different were themselves divided in opinion whether there were one or two Kangalmau. I thought the tendency was to confound Nogamäin, under the name of Kangalmau, with a *pair* of *kadu baŋambitj* known as Tanggamau, both sky-spirits, one well-disposed towards humans and the other malign in the extreme. They were thought to be in strange alliance with warlocks, who were themselves some sort of embodiment both of humans and a predatory class of creature-spirits known as *ku tida*. I had reason to believe that the name Tanggamau was borrowed from the Djamindjung tribe to the south, and that what was taking place was yet another instance of the crescive growth of plastic myth which I had noted in the case of Kunmanggur. All the mythical personages seemed clear-cut figures in ordinary conversation but lost outline or became shadowed by ambiguity under closer study. It seemed to me precisely that property which allowed both their mythological and ritual development. Hence also, I concluded, the somewhat blurred dividing line between the three classes of spirits. At their centres the differences were clear, but their borders commingled like sky, sea and earth themselves. Eventually I saw the wisdom of not forcing the ideas to a precision that was not in them. And, further, of accepting in a hospitable way what the Murinbata also said: that in the bush all around them were still strange people, true living persons, who showed themselves from time to time—like the women of Merkem, on the other side of a creek or, like the wild-looking, bearded, unknown men who would stand for a moment on hilltops and then vanish.

With imagination so active, and danger so omnipresent, the Murinbata had the highest confidence of life within their own clan-estates. Beyond, they were *kamalik*—'strangers'—except in the mother's country (*kaŋatji*), the country of the mother's mother's brother (*kawu*), which was often identical with that of the father's father (*kaŋgul*), to a lesser extent in the father's mother's (*maŋga*) country, and in the *dimbitj*, where the *ŋaritŋarit* first appeared or came from: 'that is where my *ŋjapan* grew up'; 'the people there are calling for me.' The ghosts of such places were benign, or likely to be if one's name were known. Elsewhere, both human and mystical dangers were great, although cognates and close affines could be counted on for some protection. It was a measure of the enthusiasm for the rites that, at some peril, men went long distances and stayed for long periods in order to take part. In that respect (*h*) the religion had a civil and political function. However transiently, it muted the tension ruling between opposed groups. And, in every rite, the very principle of some main symbolisms was to express the power of trust over hostility. The social structure was not the only, but it was not the least, of the structures of existence brought at such times into relation with the plan and rhythm of ritualised life.

The darker side of the religion should be noted in connection with (*h*)–(*l*). I have mentioned the victimisation of women and the self-serving way in which the cult leaders used their power. There is no doubt also that real or fancied slights to Karwadi were made the excuse for frequent homicides. Something must be allowed of course for the approved modality of male personality, the anarchic secular polity, and the diffuse ethical sanctions but, even so, the religion plainly was one that lent itself as easily to private as to political use. But other facts set out in (*k*) and (*l*) may be thought to have a certain dignity. That a people who (if one accepts the evidence of the myths) saw themselves as the heirs of a cracked estate should have been so enthusiastic (if one accepts the facts of observation) in the pursuit of ever-new values of actuality argues for a revision of one's view of 'primitive' man and religion in Aboriginal Australia.

6. A Philosophical Speculation

The Murinbata had no proverbs or wise sayings that I could discover. The hierophants of the rites, the wise men, the spirit-finders and the reputed warlocks seemed to have only trivial secrets. There were no philosophers to stand aside and make life an object of contemplation. But in the senses that they had an outlook on life and the world and that the outlook had categories they could be said to have had a 'philosophy.' I tried to understand it as far as I could.

The myths and their comments on them might be generalised in the following way.

Things began. How or whence, no one knows. But there was a state of life that, though differently, contained all that now exists. Strife divided it into the present parts. The parts remained connected by common source (The Dreaming) but were made distinct, separate and in some cases opposed. That mysterious transformation (*demŋinoi*) led to the fact, constitution and appearances of all the entities now recognised as totems (*miṙ, ŋakumal*). They are distinct from men, but as brothers (fathers, sisters, friends) to them because of connections through places of marvel (*ŋoigumiŋgi* and *dimbitj*). Powers immanent in those places are still available to men. The Dreaming that was, still is: *demŋinoi* still happens. Because of that many remarkable events now occur. Child-spirits enter the corporeal world and survive it. Pure spirits and creature-spirits that 'did not start anywhere' but 'found themselves' persist and may intervene in men's lives. Men of mystical ability draw special powers from the existent Dreaming. They do so not by thought (*bemkanin*), which is 'like a dream in the head,' but by dream (*nin*) itself. Theirs is an omnipotence of dream, not of thought. It lets them cross all the divisions of time, space and category that *demŋinoi* put into the radical unity of the beginning. Ordinary people cannot do so: they are separate, limited existents, distinct and sometimes opposed. Even people who are in some sense the same (e.g. siblings and clans of the same moiety) are distinct in other senses. They can cohere, or lose identity, only for purposes for which they are the same, which are the purposes settled on their clans as sacred corporations. In other matters they are distinct identities so that there must be restraint or tension between them. People who are distinct and opposed (e.g. spouses and clans of the other moiety) cannot cohere or lose identity at all. But they depend on each other for many things and must therefore associate. But they can do so only with symbolised or actual hostility.

That measures, in an impressionistic and approximate way, the struggle between circumstance and principle, identity and relation, independence and interdependence, which seemed to me to characterise Murinbata society. It disallows any hypothesis or postulate that the society or culture was a 'unified system' or an 'organic' or 'integrated whole.' In couple with the empirical facts, it may lend some force to my contention that in Murinbata life there were only workings towards system and transient captures of unity. I would contend that nothing more was possible in a somewhat anarchic society which, while being caught up in change and development, was segmented into like (but not identical) and unlike (but not independent) parts that had to compete for many of the scarce goods of life, and to do so under conjugate principles, i.e. a set of principles no one of which covered all real-life situations.

Why then religious unity? Two facts in correlation have to be noted. Murinbata religion had as its focus the inexorable limits on all men's lives: the only occasions on which all Murinbata appeared to feel a moral duty to help one person was when he was afflicted by the inexorable. One can perhaps catch a glimpse of the middle term by reference to the religious developments already mentioned, which I will now summarise and connect with religious practice.

7. The Dynamics of a Developing Religion

I. The religion was one of those constructed, as someone has said, in the third person. But there was a propensity to religion in the first person. That propensity was exemplified in three things—the invocation of Nogämain, the direct addresses to clan-spirits, and the blooded oblation and symbolical destruction of initiates at the highest rite. The forms of prayer and sacrifice were latent, but the practices had not actualised. In terms of Hume's principle—that one cannot think of things that one has not antecedently felt—the Murinbata may be said to have developed a 'feeling' for prayer and sacrifice but to have stopped short of the 'thought.'

II. The religion had been in the course of development for at least the better part of a century, probably longer, before European influence made itself felt directly. The religious emphases had changed several times over that period. But only those changes were accepted that would fit in with the established ritual forms, which thus became perpetuated. There was a distinct tension between the attractions of change and the forms of permanence.

III. In the recent past the religion centred on inexorable events of human life-puberty, maturity and death—but, strangely, not upon conception and birth. A woman's discovery that she was pregnant was regarded as a sign that a child-spirit had made a prestation of itself by its own volition, and at a place and time of its own choice. Nevertheless, the inexorables were thought of as being in sequence along a stretch of a cycle with two parts, one corporeal and determinate, one spiritual and less determinate. The spiritual part of man had by necessity to move through that cycle even as fleshly man. The principle of the religion was to make fleshly, determinate and social life correlative with the spiritual cycle. But life in human, worldly society was at all times a function of that cycle, and subservient to it.

IV. The 'definition' of the life-situations in which the cosmic sequence was 'recognised' had changed over the last century, particularly in respect of puberty and maturity. There were gaps between the physiological stages and the social recognitions of them as religious occasions. The last change before European influence set in was to desacralise physiological puberty and to sacralise the rift between growing boys and females. Evidently, the connections between religious recognition and particular physical stages were not rigid or intrinsic. In the last change the growth of 'understanding' became more important than the attainment of physical puberty and manhood.

V. Neither the impregnation of a woman by a child-spirit nor the birth of a child was ritualised, and a 'father' and 'mother' were thought to have no causative part in either event. A pregnancy could be aborted and a new child abandoned or killed, without moral fault or mystical risk. That is, a new life could be treated as an unsolicited and unwanted prestation without value in itself. But if it were kept, that is, accepted into the society of the living, then value was imposed on it. That changed its status from prestation to treasure. It became a named identity. An accepted life, growing in human society, was then subject to two necessities: as a spirit, it had to move along an inexorable course and, as a human person, it had to be given value and status appropriate to progressively developing functions of its worldly life. The religion divided the spiritual course into arbitrary (and changing) segments and made correlative with them changes of social function, value and status.

VI. Human and social necessity was thus 'defined' in terms of a cosmic and spiritual necessity. The person himself was treated as helpless. He had to surrender to imperatives. He could neither create new values and status for himself, so that other people must confer them on him, nor could he by himself vacate the values and status conferred on him in the past, so that that too must be done by others for him. The two tasks—to obliterate the old and to confer the new—were made moral duties for the class of men most opposed to him in organised social life. His own people—the clan which had given him his first place and value in social life—could not be asked to destroy what they had conferred, and could not alone command what had to replace it.

VII. There were thus two data for religious practice, a cosmic datum and a social datum, both imperative. The rites that developed the data were compound and complex. In respect of the cosmic datum, they were rites of assent, and implicitly of reverence, towards a spiritual imperative and, in respect of the second, fiduciary rites towards an imperative of men. They were unrepeated and progressive because the spirit's course was irreversible and because its life-functions were developmental. Their dynamism was therefore integrative. In the compound-complex aspect they coupled two dominant types of symbolism: (*a*) the forcing of a person outside human fellowship and, after transformation, his restoration to fellowship; and (*b*) the removal from him of all social value, status and functions and, after their destruction, the conferring on him of enhanced value, status and functions. What I have called the enthusiasm for 'ever-new values of actuality' (p. 266) evidently had its dynamic in the discrepancy between 'restoration' and 'enhancement.'

VIII. Nothing could be discovered about the aetiology of the symbolisms. But in several respects they constituted a work of artless genius. They bracketed, as having in common something dismaying and relevant to men, several distinct structures of existence, including the cosmological, social and probably ecological structures, as well as the structures of functions, values and status within the total process of life.

IX. There were distinct correspondences of form and symbolism between the rites and myths. And both rites and myths had a structure or design-plan of a dialectical or progressively integrative character.

X. The myths seemed the first springs of contemplative religion, using allegorical idioms. In several important myths the dominant theme was an irreparable injury to man at the beginning of life under instituted forms. The sense of injury—whether a needless or a necessary injury was hard to make out—was expressed in several metaphors, but the common signification seemed to be a paradox, antinomy or dualism common to all the structures of existence. Thus, it did not appear that Murinbata society could be regarded as the religion's source and object. Rather, the religion appeared as the society's completion, within the ambit left by the injury.

With relation to (III) it is consistent that a people in a hard environment, with a poor material culture and little detached knowledge, should develop a religion around the inexorable. But anthropology does not seem to have made any postulate about primitive man, or primitive religion, under which two things are 'consistent': an effort to transcend the inexorable and to transform cosmic strokes against the individual into group celebrations at which everyone, however opposed, should be under duty to help, honour and gratify the afflicted and, by so doing, bring about a unity that, however transient, was higher than any other occasion of social life made possible. Murinbata religion was clearly more than a religion of activists who, assenting to the limits of life, pursued the values of actuality. No social imperative made them celebrate joyously what could not be changed.

It is impossible to say positively that European influence may not have had something to do with the developmental aspect (II) of the cults. It is my firm opinion that there was no incorporation of Christian elements, and I hope that the facts presented will silence gratuitous doubts based on feelings that Aborigines, being 'primitive,' could not possibly have had serious thoughts about life. But the period of European influence in Australia, even in the Northern Territory, is longer than the period which anthropological inquiry can touch. The external structure of Aboriginal life was very sensitive to influences from a distance. Faraway changes may have precipitated cults, or enabled cults to develop, that affected the Murinbata long before they had even heard of Europeans. Against that possibility one must set the strong architecture of the facts in (III)–(X).

Their construction seems to me intrinsically Aboriginal, and thoroughly consistent with the whole tenor of that culture. But, in particular, the involution of development mentioned in (II) argues very strongly for endogenous as against exogenous influence. Elements of foreign Aboriginal culture certainly reached the Murinbata, but were not all equally assimilable. The test was the extent to which they could be made conformous with existing structures. One might say that development took a spiral course and that the spiral turned inward, not outward. It intensified rather than weakened Murinbata culture. The means of that involution can be seen in the devolution of sacred custom. When the greater attractions of Punj could not be resisted, the Murinbata did not discredit Manggawila: they gave it lower place and lesser sacredness of the same orders. They also kept the later Punj in continuity with the earlier form of the rite. The same principle probably led to the persistence of form throughout the other rites.

8. The Religious Economy

I would depict the Murinbata as valuing continuity both for its own sake and for the sake of the aesthetic appeal of its symbolisms, but also as making it a rational principle. Their mentality had what might be called an Adrasteian mould in that it imposed on time and change an image of persistence as the main character of reality. It could not deny Chronos but gave Adrasteia the triumph. In religious mood, they were enthusiastic but not ecstatic; they venerated but did not worship their sacra; they welcomed change insofar as it would fit the forms of permanence. In that way they attained stability but avoided inertia.

Obviously, a religion like theirs, that did not look back to a golden age or forward to an after-life that would resolve the dubieties of history, did not thereby escape any of the problems of this life. In some sense it may even have exacerbated them. One of them was the problem of variable value. It is characteristic of value that not even sacred values stay stable. They rise or fall unless they are *kept* stable since stability is not the same as inertia. Too great or too rapid a swing of sacred values is likely to bring down the whole structure of religion, by tainting the new with the discovered defects of the old. A collapse of Murinbata religion would have broken up their society—and later did—because of the intimacy of the connection. The problems were handled by these people very well. They cited The Dream Time as if it were an absolute although, as I have pointed out, it was but the moving shadow of their changing life. They held that it had left them with a stock or capital of things, good or bad, with a place in life and that there would be a continuous flow from the stock if they conserved the sources by honouring a received tradition. In point of fact, 'the tradition' was constantly adapted to new sacra and a new distribution of values, and political force was used to impose and maintain such assimilations. In that situation the appeal to an authoritative ground had its conveniences for those who guarded and interpreted the tradition and, as I have shown, the custodians used their positions repressively, on occasions abusively. But a cynical evaluation of those facts would not be warranted. This was not a society in which political institutions had separated; there was no intellectual detachment from beliefs; 'believing' was not itself a test of religiosity; and fanaticism had not developed concerning particular formulations of belief—indeed, there could be no fanaticism since apparently dispute about the mysteries did not occur. If one can speak of an 'innocent' authoritarianism, this was it. The Murinbata had not yet discovered that men could dispute the truth or falsity of the great events from which men themselves had issued. *There* was authority, not divine, but the consequence of things happening to, or done by, beings greater than ordinary men. What issued was *murin ḍaitpiṙ*, 'true words.' Truth, once exhibited, remained a datum.

To what extent they 'believed' their beliefs, or 'really' saw the world from such viewpoints, would be hard to say. They could not adduce a principle for every situation. Probably only a handful of men and women at any time had a compendious knowledge of the culture. Fewer still can have had a detached knowledge. General statements which they made to me about tendency in belief and conduct were often disputed and, I thought, best taken as norms idealised by the few, even when followed by the many. But it seemed to me that those idealisations, that is, rationalisations about structures of fact and value that may or may not have been the case, were of particular interest in themselves; and, in matters of religion, intrinsically more interesting than anything I might learn from disciplining study to the level of statistical tendency. When I speak of a religious economy in an Adrasteian mould I am well aware that I am dealing in impressionism. But, then, the Aborigines were themselves impressionist. It is worthwhile to set out the prudential way in which, under their larger art of life, they disposed a limited estate between ends which had appeal. The facts of (I)–(X) may then seem facts of good reason.

Souls were conserved by being put into cycle between the corporeal and incorporeal domains. The mortal part of men was buried in their clan-estates, which were kept in the perpetual possession of the clans as sacred corporations. The mystical property of each estate—the ability to fructify the totem species, to control vital phenomena such as rain, disease and wind, and to dream of song- and dance-giving spirits—were guarded as jealously as the products of the abilities and the outward emblems of the clan's identity and rights. No one could cast off his clan or partition the estate. Malpractice was suspected if the flow of life-benefits from the estate weakened, for example by the disappearance or scarcity of a totem species and, as pointed out earlier, clans raided each other, not to capture land, which would not have been thought a rational act, but to steal the animating principle from totem-places. Why more was not made of *talu* or *intichiuma* rites to regenerate natural species remains unexplained: the region was rich in foodstuffs but not so rich that no shortages occurred. The emphases were rather on guarding the sacred places and their mystical powers. The succession of cults could have had something to do with the comparative diffuseness of the 'increase' customs. But even so that characteristically Australian complex—the notion of an original endowment of each clan with the means of life, a corporate plan of entitlement to the flow, and a conservational usage—was very patent. The cults exercised their appeal within the larger society made up of many clans of similar outlook. It was in part because of the similarity that the association between clans in the religious rites could only be an association of support, not of competition. Nothing was being allocated at such times. There could be no struggle for a division of what had already been divided.

In the social aspect, the purpose of the rites was to combine, for practical ends of life, including the interest of someone particularly afflicted by a limit on life, what had originally been disbursed. Inexorable changes, forced on men by the cosmic structure of life, could not be denied: all that could be done was to quarrel with them or to make them correlative with living. As I have remarked elsewhere, the Murinbata, like all the Aborigines, gave the impression of having stopped short of, or gone beyond, a quarrel with the terms of life. The myths are evidence that they reflected and felt a fatal impairment, but the rites are evidence that they met the issue in a positive way. They brought the inexorable within the total economy of living and put positive values upon it, so as to integrate it with social actuality and actuality's values.

But what then of the diffuse syndrome which I described as a propensity to religion in the first person? And, in particular, the 'sorrow for Mutjingga'?—an emotional disposition present, as far as I could ascertain, for the first time. They are puzzling questions to which I have not found answers. With a further observation, I will leave the account as one of a *dynamic* religion in which *successive* cults had celebrated a *continuous* significance that in the last cult appeared to have been *enhanced.*

The Murinbata, like many other Aborigines, postulated that the birth of a child was not caused by human intercourse. But I heard or saw sexual symbolisms which made the acceptance—I do not doubt that fact—of the postulate seem very nearly incredible. At the same time the schema of mystical impregnation by child-spirits was plainly another exemplification, though a shadowy one, of the structural schema of the rites and myths: death put a soul outside human society; it went away, came back transformed, and entered life again in a new state and locus. On the facts, the Murinbata were but one or two steps away from a discovery that the birth and/or social acceptance of a new life could be made a cosmically-defined occasion for a religious rite. One or two steps in the devolution of an extant rite—as from Manggawila to Djaban—would have sufficed had the discovery been made. Would it have brought them an equivalent step nearer the discovery of human agency in procreation? I saw here an analogue of the 'feeling' and the 'thought' in relation to prayer and sacrifice. In the mystery of agency in birth, the Murinbata had a 'feeling' for human causation but had not attained the 'thought.' It is an interesting speculation what might have followed from the positive discovery. A mystery dissolved would have desacralised a cardinal datum. The social imperative of 'initiation' could no longer have rested on a religious necessity. The religion could no longer have been merely correlative with a cosmic plan.

The first paper in the series (I) 'The Lineaments of Sacrifice' was written in the field. At that stage I had in mind to write a set of perhaps three. So many distinct problems had to be noticed that I could not manage them in less than six. Even so I have had to leave the subject far from exhausted. I see now that (I) would perhaps have been placed better as (VI) and (VI) as (I).

While I was writing (II) in early 1960 Professor J. A. Barnes drew my attention to the fact that Professor Lévi-Strauss had already published a brilliant paper on the morphological analysis of myth. I had been unaware of that fact. Rather than consciously straddle two approaches which, though obviously convergent, depended on distinct sets of concepts, I thought it the proper course to continue with the approach stated in (I), which I had believed peculiar to myself. I had developed it in response to three connected matters: a certain disagreement with 'structuralist' anthropology, which seemed to me to have become an unclear mixture of false statics and covert dynamics around discrete topics, without any true central or branch-theory; a loss of faith in Durkheim's dual categories, which had had a stultifying effect on the study of Aboriginal religion; and my inability to 'make sense' of the theoretical problems of religious and quasi-religious cults, notably the Melanesian cargo-cults, but including the absence of that type of cult from Aboriginal Australia.

In respect of the first matter, I developed the perceptual model of 'social transaction' from Radcliffe Brown's paradigm of convergent interest and social value and, connected with it as indispensable logical tools, the concepts of 'transitive operations,' operations that 'symbolised transitivity,' and 'signed conduct.' The set made a dynamic schema which promised an escape from the 'double-headed penny' which Professor Raymond Firth, in my opinion rightly, identified as a central weakness of structuralism.

My interest therefore lay in the operational structure of transactional life, not in the functional structure of 'relations' between 'points' in a 'network.' In other words, in the composition and structure of observable processes—such as initiation—sufficiently distinct to be identified and followed through from start to finish. The stable character of Aboriginal initiations made them suitable; almost, so to speak, a ready-made statics, because of their 'denial' of time or, what is very much the same thing, their compounding of change. Having rejected Durkheim's dual categories as logically defective (a point that van Gennep saw clearly in requiring an 'intermediate' ground between 'the profane' and 'the sacred'), and also as empirically inadequate (Tjirmumuk seemed neither sacred nor profane), I could find the real point of difference from conventional structuralism: that a *datum* had been made from what seemed to me the essential *problem* of study. That is, the stability and constancy of social and religious institutions.

To postulate that 'institutions *must* exist if people are to live together' is to assume everything that historiography takes for granted while investigating nothing that it studies, and to take for granted precisely what anthropology should investigate if it is to illumine historiography at the same time as its own problems.

www.ingramcontent.com/pod-product-compliance
Lightning Source LLC
La Vergne TN
LVHW010601100826
845148LV00014B/2797
* 9 7 8 1 7 4 3 3 2 3 8 8 5 *